Praise for Barry Forshaw

CRITICAL ACCLAIM FOR *EURO NOIR*

'An informative, interesting, accessible and enjoyable guide as Forshaw guides us through the crime output of a dozen nations' – *The Times*

'An exhilarating tour of Europe viewed through its crime fiction' – *Guardian*

'Exemplary tour of the European crime landscape... supremely readable' – *The Independent*

'This is a book for everyone and will help and expand your reading and viewing' – *We Love This Book*

'Like all the best reference books, it made me want to read virtually every writer mentioned. And, on another note, I love the cover' – *crimepieces.com*

'If I did want to read something so drastically new, I now know where I would begin. With this book' – *Bookwitch*

'Barry Forshaw is the master of the essential guide' – *Shots Mag*

'This enjoyable and authoritative guide provides an invaluable comprehensive resource for anyone wishing to learn more about European Noir, to anticipate the next big success and to explore new avenues of blood-curdling entertainment' – *Good Book Guide*

'Fascinating and well researched... refreshing and accessible' – *The Herald*

'An entertaining guide by a real expert, with a lot of ideas for writers and film/TV to try' – *Promoting Crime Fiction*

'... a fabulous little book that is like a roadmap of Europe crime fiction' – *Crime Squad*

'Fascinated by Scandinavian crime dramas? Go to this handy little guide' – *News at Cinema Books*

Also by Barry Forshaw from Pocket Essentials

Nordic Noir
Euro Noir

and from Kamera Books

Italian Cinema

Brit Noir

The Pocket Essential Guide to the Crime Fiction, Film & TV of the British Isles

BARRY FORSHAW

POCKET ESSENTIALS

To all the authors, publishers and filmmakers who
have talked to me during the preparation of this book

First published in 2016 by Pocket Essentials,
an imprint of Oldcastle Books Ltd,
PO Box 394, Harpenden, Herts, AL5 1XJ
www.pocketessentials.com

Editor: Judith Forshaw

A CIP catalogue record for this book is available from the British Library.

ISBN
978-1-84344-640-8 (print)
978-1-84344-641-5 (epub
978-1-84344-642-2 (kindle)
978-1-84344-643-9 (pdf)

2 4 6 8 10 9 7 5 3 1

Typeset by Avocet Typeset, Somerton, Somerset TA11 6RT
in 9.25pt Univers Light with Minion Pro display
Printed and bound in Great Britain by Clays Ltd, St Ives plc

For more about Crime Fiction go to www.crimetime.co.uk / @crimetime.uk

Contents

Contents

Introduction

The current state of British crime writing

It might be argued that the low esteem in which British crime writing was held for so many years allowed it to slowly cultivate a dark, subversive charge only fitfully evident in more respectable literary fare. And precisely because genre fiction was generally accorded critical indifference (except by such astute highbrow commentators – and fans – as WH Auden), this critical dismissal was consolidated by the fact that readers – while relishing such compelling crime and murder narratives – looked upon the genre as nothing more than harmless entertainment. Since the status of crime writing was subsequently elevated by writers such as PD James, many modern writers now utilise the *lingua franca* of crime fiction in innovative fashion, with acute psychological insights freighted into the page-turning plots.

Similarly, informing much of the work of contemporary British crime writers – the subject of this study, as opposed to writers of the recent past or the Golden Age, or historical crime fiction – is a cool-eyed critique of modern society. But not all current practitioners are this ambitious in terms of giving texture to their work. For that matter – and let's be frank here – a great many modern writers are little more than competent journeymen (and women); the genre is still beset by much maladroit or threadbare writing, particularly in an age of self-publishing, where editorial input is painfully conspicuous by its absence.

Nevertheless, prejudices have been eroded (hallelujah!), and crime fiction on the printed page is now frequently reviewed in the broadsheets by writers such as myself alongside more 'literary' genres, but often in crime column ghettos (although solus reviews are not unknown). However, literary editors – in my experience – still favour overly serious writers above those they perceive as 'entertainers'. So, what's the state of modern crime writing in the UK today? I've attempted to tackle that question in the following pages.

This is not a social history of the British crime novel, though it touches on the more radical notions of the genre; however, the 'readers' guide' format I've used (with entries ranging from the expansive to the concise) hopefully allows for a comprehensive celebration of a lively genre – a genre, in fact, that continues to produce highly accomplished, powerfully written novels on an almost daily basis. What's more, despite the caveats above, Britain – including Scotland (not yet cut away from the rest of the UK, despite the wishes of Ms Sturgeon and Mr Salmond) – and Ireland are enjoying a cornucopia of crime writers who have the absolute measure of the four key elements of crime writing (social comment is a bonus). And those four key elements? They are:

1. strong plotting
2. literate, adroit writing
3. complex characterisation
4. vividly evoked locales.

Murderous secrets and professional problems

Readers have plenty of cause to be thankful, as these crowded pages will demonstrate. But this wasn't an easy book to write. The range of contemporary crime fiction (as opposed to the historical variety) in the UK is surprisingly broad, given that the geographical parameters of the British Isles and its Celtic neighbours are proscribed compared with the massive canvas of the United States. But the parochial nature of much British crime fiction might be precisely what imbues it with its customary sharpness – when murderous secrets confined in British suburban spaces are set free, the results are explosive. And then there is the perception of the British love of order (although such stereotypes are in flux at present); crime novels are particularly satisfying in that we are invited to relish the chaos unleashed by the crime and criminals before the status quo is re-established. This is a process that has a particular resonance for the British character – more so than for, say, Americans (the barely contained pandemonium of the large American city is never really tamed). Of course, when Charles Dickens and Wilkie Collins introduced several of the key tropes of crime fiction in such classics as *Bleak House* and *The Woman in White*, neither author had any thought of creating a genre. It is instructive to remember that their books, while massively popular, lacked the literary gravitas in their day that later scholarship dressed them with; this was the popular fare of the time, dealing in the suspense and delayed revelation that was later to become the *sine qua non* of the genre. In generic fiction, the inhabitants of 221b Baker Street and their celebrated creator are, of course, the most important factors in terms of generating an army of imitators – notably Agatha Christie's Hercule Poirot – and Holmes clones continue to surface to this day, dressed in contemporary garb rather than deerstalker and Inverness cape but still demonstrating impressive ratiocination.

In the twenty-first century, apart from the sheer pleasure of reading a meaty crime novel, the 'added value' in many of the best examples is the implicit (or sometimes explicit) element of social criticism incorporated by the more challenging writers. Among popular literary genres, only science fiction has rivalled the crime novel in 'holding the mirror up to nature' (or society). Best-selling modern writers have kept alive this rigorous tradition, although rarely at the expense of sheer storytelling skill, the area in which the crime field virtually demolishes all its rivals. When, in recent years, crime fiction became quantifiably the most popular of popular genres (comprehensively seeing off such rivals as romance fiction), it was only the inevitable coda to a process that had been long underway, and one that should be celebrated all the more for this added value of societal critique.

Given that the issue of class is still an important one in Britain, it is surprising how little the subject exercises current writers. From the Golden Age onwards, the ability of the detective figure to move unhampered (and in insolent fashion) across social divides has always accorded the genre a range not to be found elsewhere – while this is also reflected in American hard-boiled fiction, money rather than class is the signifier there. Similarly, detectives from a patrician background are rare indeed in contemporary crime; it has taken an American writer setting her books in Britain, Elizabeth George, to keep the Sayers/Wimsey blueblood tradition alive with her aristocratic sleuth Lynley. Most of the slew of coppers who populate the genre are middle- or lower middle-class but sport a bolshiness that suggests working-class resentment – think of Rankin's Rebus, Billingham's Thorne et al. The resentment of the (often) male policeman, however, is generally reserved for his superiors (who are constantly attempting to take him off sensitive cases) or the intransigence of the system he is obliged to deal with.

In terms of gender, while the middle-aged, dyspeptic (and frequently alcoholic) male copper still holds sway, eternally finding it difficult to relate to his alienated family, the female equivalent is the woman who has achieved a position of authority but who is constantly obliged to prove her worth – and not necessarily in terms of tackling male sexism, although that issue persists as a useful shorthand. The influential figure of Lynda La Plante's Jane Tennison has to some extent been replaced by women who simply get on with the job – and their professional problems are predicated by the fact that they are simply better at solving crime than their superiors: in other words, a mirror image of the male detective. This hard-to-avoid uniformity inevitably makes it difficult for writers to differentiate their bloody-minded female protagonists from the herd, but ingenuity is paramount here – one female detective in the current crop, for instance (MJ Arlidge's DI Helen Grace), differs from her fellow policewomen in having an inconvenient taste for rough sex and S&M.

About the book

Looking at mainstream crime fiction in the modern age (and leaving aside the legacy of the past), it is clear that the field is in ruder health than it has ever been. In fact, such is the range of trenchant and galvanic work today that an argument could be made that we are living in a second Golden Age.

The remit of this study has been as wide as possible: every genre that is subsumed under the heading of 'noir' crime fiction is here, from the novel of detection to the blockbuster thriller to the occasional novel of espionage (though they are the exception). But – please! – don't tell me that some of the authors here are not really 'noir'; let's not get locked into a discussion of nomenclature. 'Noir' here means 'crime' – the distinctly non-noir Alexander McCall Smith may not want to be included, but he is. My aim here was – simply – to maximise inclusivity regarding contemporary British crime writing (historical crime apart – that's another book), whether from bloody noir territory to the sunnier, less confrontational end of the spectrum.

I offer preliminary apologies to any writers from the Republic of Ireland, who may be fervent nationalists and object to appearing in a book called *Brit Noir*; their inclusion is all part of my agenda of celebrating as many interesting and talented writers as I can. Although it's not quite the same, sometime before the last Scottish referendum, I asked both Val McDermid and Ian Rankin if they would still want to be included in a study of British crime writers if the vote were 'yes' to cutting loose from the UK, or if they ought to be dropped as they were now foreigners. Both opted for the former option.

It should be noted that *Brit Noir* is principally designed to be used as a reference book to contemporary crime – i.e. (mostly) current writers – as opposed to a text to be read straight through. But if you want to do the latter, how can I stop you? And you'll note that I've erred on the side of generosity throughout, avoiding hatchet jobs; in a readers' guide such as this, I feel that should be the modus operandi.

A note on locating authors in *Brit Noir*

One problem presented itself to me when writing this study (well, a host of problems, but let's just stick with one). If the layout of the book were to be geographical – i.e. placing the work of the various

authors in the regions where they have their detectives operating –
that would be fine with, say, Ian Rankin, who largely keeps Rebus
in Edinburgh. But what about his fellow Scot Val McDermid? Her
Tony Hill/Carol Jordan books are set mostly in the North of England
– and, what's more, in the fictitious city of Bradfield. Should I have
a section for 'Bradfield' with just one author entry? And what about
those authors who set their work in unspecified towns? You see
my problem, I hope – but that wasn't all. What about the writers
with different series of books set in different places, such as Ann
Cleeves? Or Brits who place their coppers in foreign cities? I briefly
considered elaborate cross-referencing, but decided I'd rather use
my energies in other areas. So here's the solution: if you want to
find a particular author, don't bother trying to remember the setting
of their books and thumbing fruitlessly through the Midlands or the
North West. Simply turn to the index at the back of the book, which
will tell you precisely where to find everyone.

Section One:
The novels and the writers

England and Wales

London

Success was something of a double-edged sword for **MO HAYDER** with her début novel *Birdman*: the book enjoyed astonishing sales, but called down a fearsome wrath on the author for unflinchingly entering the blood-boltered territory of Thomas Harris's Hannibal Lecter books. Part of the fuss was clearly to do with the fact that a woman writer had handled scenes of horror and violence so authoritatively, and there was little surprise when the subsequent *The Treatment* provoked a similar furore. Actually, it's a remarkably vivid and meticulously detailed shocker: less grimly compelling than its predecessor, perhaps, but still a world away from the cosy reassurance of much current crime fiction. In a shady south London residential street, a husband and wife are found tied up, the man near death. Both have been beaten and are suffering from acute dehydration. DI Jack Caffery of the Met's murder squad AMIP is told to investigate the disappearance of the couple's son, and, as he uncovers a series of dark parallels with his own life, he finds it more and more difficult to make the tough decisions necessary to crack a scarifying case. As in *Birdman*, Caffery is characterised with particular skill, and Hayder is able (for the most part) to make us forget the very familiar cloth he's cut from. The personal involvement of a cop in a grim case is an over-familiar theme, but it's rarely been dispatched with the panache and vividness on display here.

Is there anyone else in the crime genre currently writing anything as quirky and idiosyncratic as **CHRISTOPHER FOWLER**'s Bryant and May series? (And let's disabuse readers of the mistaken notion that this is a historical series, as many seem to think – it wouldn't be in this book if it were.) Fowler eschews all recognisable genres, though the cases for his detective duo have resonances of the darker corners of British Golden Age fiction. In *Bryant & May and the Bleeding Heart*, the Peculiar Crimes Unit is handed a typically outlandish case in which two teenagers have seen a corpse apparently stepping out of its grave – with one of them subsequently dying in a hit-and-run accident. Arthur Bryant is stimulated by the bizarreness of the case but is tasked with finding out who has made away with the ravens from the Tower of London. (Not an insignificant crime, as it is well known that when the ravens leave the Tower, Britain itself will fall.) The usual smorgasbord of grotesque incident and stygian humour is on offer, and if you aren't already an aficionado, I suggest you find out what the fuss is about before the forthcoming television series clinically removes Fowler's individual tone of voice.

It is both a virtue and a curse when one doesn't require a great deal of sleep. Sometimes – when I'm wide awake in the wee small hours with only the sound of urban foxes outside my window suggesting something else is alive – I feel that I'd prefer to be like ordinary people who need eight hours' shuteye. But here's the virtue of this unusual state: it gives one ample time to catch up with all the writers one wants to read; sometimes they are old favourites, sometimes new discoveries. And – a real pleasure – sometimes in these nocturnal explorations I encounter the work of a writer who (while moving in familiar waters) demonstrates an innovative and quirky imagination, transforming narratives with whose accoutrements we're familiar. Debut writer **SARAH HILARY** was most decidedly in that category, and even though her character DI Marnie Rome may initially appear to owe something to other female coppers (Lynda La Plante's Tennison, for example), Marnie turns out to be very much her own woman – as is Hilary herself, with her crisp and direct style.

In *Someone Else's Skin*, DI Rome is dispatched to a woman's shelter with her partner DS Noah Jake. Lying stabbed on the floor is the husband of one of the women from the shelter. Rome finds herself opening the proverbial can of worms, and a slew of dark secrets will be exposed before a final violent confrontation in a kitchen. As well as functioning as a well-honed police procedural, this is very much a novel of character – DI Rome in particular is strikingly well realised, and even such issues as domestic abuse are responsibly incorporated into the fabric of the novel. *Someone Else's Skin* is a book that hits the ground running, and readers will be keen to see more of the tenacious Marnie Rome.

With **SJ WATSON**'s *Before I Go To Sleep*, British publishing saw something of a phenomenon. Watson may have borrowed the book's central premise from Christopher Nolan's film *Memento* (memory-deprived protagonist struggling to make sense of their life), but the assurance with which he finessed his narrative belied his inexperience and rivalled that of such old hands as Robert Harris. Watson's follow-up novel in 2015 was *Second Life*.

The refreshingly forthright **STELLA DUFFY** has made a success of several careers: in the theatre, in broadcasting and as the creator of a variety of books in different genres (including the historical field). As with the earlier work of Val McDermid, Duffy's protagonist is a lesbian, the private investigator Saz Martin, who has been put through her paces in such tautly written, quirky novels as *Fresh Flesh*. There is a social agenda behind the books, but never at the expense of the exigencies of strong, persuasive storytelling.

For some time now, **MARK BILLINGHAM**'s lean and gritty urban thrillers featuring DI Tom Thorne have been massive commercial successes. And such books as *In the Dark*, a standalone novel in which Thorne makes only a cameo appearance, demonstrate that Billingham can make trenchant comments about British society while never neglecting his ironclad narrative skills. Billingham, who has a background in stand-up comedy, has quoted some interesting statistical findings in his talks to book groups: many women would rather spend time reading a thriller than having sex. Billingham appears to be bemused by this statistic, but (if the truth were told) the author himself is part of the problem: his crime novels are undoubtedly a source of pure enjoyment (without the bother of having to take off one's clothes), although thrillers such as *Lifeless* are journeys into the most disturbing aspects of the human psyche. It's interesting that Billingham's books have a reputation for extreme violence, because they deal more in atmosphere – a real sense of dread is quietly conveyed to the reader.

In *Buried*, ex-DCI Mullen, a retired police officer, is distressed when his son disappears. Is he the victim of a kidnapping? Tom Thorne begins his inquiry by seeking everyone who might have a score to settle with the boy's father. And he discovers something intriguing: Mullen has not mentioned the person who would appear to be the prime suspect – a man who had once made threats against Mullen and his family and who, moreover, is under suspicion for another killing. Billingham always does considerable research for his books to ensure the authenticity of his police detail, but he was obliged to make up some of the procedural aspects here as the Met is particularly secretive on the issue of kidnapping. Billingham avoids the obvious set pieces that can instantly pique the reader's attention, and ensures that Thorne's encounter with evil is handled in a dispassionate fashion, even though Thorne himself is less strongly characterised than usual in this, his sixth outing. The recent *Time of Death* (the thirteenth Thorne) is Billingham on top form.

LAURA WILSON's work bristles with some of the best crime writing in the UK – she is one of the country's most searching psychological novelists working in the genre. There are also ghosts of one of Wilson's favourite novelists, Patrick Hamilton, in the luminous and richly detailed conjuring of the London of various eras in her books. Wilson has never been happy staying within the parameters of the conventional crime novel, and in *My Best Friend* she deploys a device whereby the novel is narrated by three strongly delineated protagonists. Her most recent work features her sympathetic copper Ted Stratton, while one of her most accomplished books is 2015's contemporary (non-Stratton) *The Wrong Girl*.

Many well-heeled TV presenters face a variety of pitfalls that could sabotage their comfortable lives: a messy divorce, inconvenient revelations about their private life. But Gaby Mortimer, heroine of **SABINE DURRANT**'s *Under Your Skin*, finds something more sinister to threaten her equilibrium. When running on the common near her London house, she discovers the body of a woman lying in the brambles, the victim of a savage strangling. But what Gaby is not expecting is the fact that she is to become the principal suspect for the crime. (The murder victim was wearing Gaby's T-shirt, and ever more damning evidence begins to point in her direction.) The police appear to be convinced of Gaby's guilt, but despite this, she tries to keep her life on track. But as many a TV personality (and politician) has found, it's virtually impossible to carry on with the day job when you are under scrutiny by reporters, and all around people regard you with suspicion. Things can only get worse – and they do, to the extent that Gaby begins to doubt her own sanity. But then an attractive journalist called Jack appears, apparently believing in Gaby's innocence and ready to help. Gaby's troubles, however, are only just beginning. Durrant has written for teenage girls, but there is absolutely nothing adolescent about this strikingly constructed and economically written thriller, a book that steadily draws the reader into the plight of its besieged heroine and springs a variety of surprises – surprises we are unable to second-guess. And both male and female readers find it easy to identify with Gaby, with the underpinnings of her life relentlessly pulled away. In fact, she is the kind of woman in extreme situations that Nicci French used to write about before turning to a series character, and *Under Your Skin* has all the authority of the best novels by French. Durrant's treatment of the characters' psychology is, admittedly, straightforward rather than nuanced, but that strategy ensures that the inexorable grip never slackens. Let's hope that she continues to spend her time writing for adults: we need thriller writers who can reinvigorate the genre – and it looks like Durrant may be able to do just that.

The amazing – and immediate – success of **MARTINA COLE**'s crime novels must be a source of despair to those writers who have struggled for years. Right from the start, she has enjoyed reader approval for her distinctive, gritty fiction. Even the workaday TV adaptations of *Dangerous Lady* and *The Jump* merely brought more kudos her way (she's been less lucky than Colin Dexter in her transfer to the screen – but with her sales, she should worry). In *Broken*, a child is abandoned in a deserted stretch of woodland and another on the top of a derelict building. DI Kate Burrows makes the inevitable connections, and when one child dies, she finds herself up against a killer utterly without scruples. Her lover Patrick offers support in this troubling case, but he is under pressure himself. A body is found in his Soho club, and Patrick is on the line as a suspect. And Kate begins to doubt him… In prose that is always trenchant, Cole delivers the goods throughout this lengthy and ambitious narrative. Kate is an exuberantly characterised heroine, and the sardonic Patrick enjoys equally persuasive handling from the author. *The Good Life* – which Cole has certainly earned the right to enjoy – continued her run of bestsellers (as did, most recently, *Get Even*).

Speaking to **MICK HERRON**, I learned about his adept use of London locations. 'I rarely choose locations: research averse, I've found that my novels tend to be set in the areas I frequently inhabit. Silicon Roundabout is a whirling dervish of a road junction that comes into its own on winter afternoons, when dark arrives early, and the advertising hoardings scream out their video messages above the red and white kaleidoscope made by furious traffic. Few things are as irresistibly noir as neon. It's like glitter laid on grime; a cheap makeover that only looks good as long as the light is bad. So it's round here that I have Tom Bettany wander in *Nobody Walks*: unkempt and haggard, carrying his dead son's ashes in a bag, he circles the streets looking for drug dealers among those who haunt the bars and bop the night away. What he finds isn't quite what he thought he was looking for, but that too is an aspect of noir – that you can't avoid the fate that awaits you, whichever streets you choose to wander down.' Herron's 2016 novel *Real Tigers* has received enthusiastic early notices.

Perhaps because of a reaction against what detractors called the laddish fiction of **TONY PARSONS** (although he clearly had complex strategies in play in his examination of sex and relationships), the writer has recently taken a new direction, reinventing himself in *The Murder Bag* as a pugnacious crime writer – although even in this new venture he has encountered resistance. If you are shell-shocked from the army of novels featuring tough maverick cops – and are convinced that nothing new can invigorate the genre – perhaps you should pick up *The Murder Bag*. Yes, we've met detectives at loggerheads with their daughters (as here) before, from Wallander to Rebus. But there are two things that instantly lift this one out of the rut: parenting is a speciality of the author's work and it's treated with a nuance largely absent elsewhere in crime fiction. And Parsons, a quintessential London writer, evokes his city with pungency. Bolshie DC Max Wolfe is investigating a homicide in which a banker's throat has been cut; a second victim is a homeless heroin addict. The connection: an upscale private school. This first crime novel was followed by *The Slaughter Man*.

LYNDA LA PLANTE – the creator of *Prime Suspect* – is a woman of conviction. Many things clearly make her blood boil – not least the way in which she perceives this country's justice system as being heavily weighted on the side of the criminal rather than the victim, and the ease with which violent sexual offenders can work the system and be back on the streets in a derisorily short time. Authors frequently remind us that the views of their characters are not necessarily their own, but after reading a typical La Plante novel there can be little doubt that it's the author's persuasive (and often incendiary) views that leap off the page – not least because they are espoused in the book not just by the unsympathetic misogynist coppers, but also by the driven DCI James Langton and even La Plante's vulnerable but tough heroine DI Anna Travis.

In *Clean Cut*, Langton is in pursuit of a truly nasty group of illegal immigrants who have murdered a young prostitute. Then Langton himself is viciously slashed in the chest and leg with a machete and hospitalised – with the prospect of his police career coming to an end. Langton is conducting a clandestine affair with another detective, DI Anna Travis, who has a similarly daunting load on her shoulders: a fierce commitment to the job, battles with boneheaded colleagues, and a readiness to place herself in highly dangerous situations. But her biggest problem is her fractious relationship with the withholding Langton – difficult enough in his selfishness and lack of commitment before he is brutally wounded, but almost insufferable as he concentrates his frustration on Anna whenever she visits his nursing home. She is working on another, related case in which the body of a woman has been found sexually assaulted and mutilated – and soon Travis and Langton are up against something far more sinister than squalid people trafficking (involving voodoo, torture and a truly monstrous villain).

There are various factors that ensure *Clean Cut* is a visceral read: the assured plotting, the pithy heroine (we're always on Anna's side, even though we are irritated by her desperate reliance on a man who treats her so badly), and the poisonous secret that the heroine is left with at the end of the book. But it's La Plante's passionate conviction (burnt into the pages) that society has become the hostage of criminals that really gives the book its charge. In 2015, we were given a glimpse into the early professional life of La Plante's signature character with *Tennison*, tied into a new TV adaptation.

The inaugural novel in a new series of London-set thrillers by a then-new (now established) British writer had all the hallmarks of staying power. **SIMON KERNICK**'s *The Business of Dying* showed that the author meant business; and the plotting is as cogent as you'll find this side of the Atlantic. DS Dennis Milne is a maverick copper with a speciality sideline in killing drug-dealing criminals. But everything goes wrong for him when (acting on some bad advice) he kills two straight customs officers and an accountant. At the same time, he is investigating the brutal murder of an 18-year-old working girl, found with her throat ripped open by Regent's Canal, and his probing leads him towards other police officers. Soon, it's up for grabs as to whether Milne will go down for his own illegal dealings before he cracks a case that is steeped in blood and corruption. Since this debut, Kernick has rarely failed to deliver tough and authentic storytelling in book after book. Another theme of that first novel was the transitoriness of so much that we hold dear in life (ironically, even before the novel was published, two of the three Kings Cross gas rings that adorned the hardback jacket were swept away by Eurostar... nothing is permanent, as Kernick's rugged novel argued).

The unvarnished writing of **DAVID LAWRENCE** gleaned much praise; both *The Dead Sit Round in a Ring* and *Nothing Like the*

Night demonstrated that a gritty talent had appeared on the crime genre. Initial success, of course, can be a double-edged sword, but Lawrence showed no sign of faltering, and *Cold Kill* had the same steely assurance as its predecessors. When a woman's body is found in a London park, DS Stella Mooney finds herself involved. Robert Kimber confesses to the murder; his flat appears to reveal all the apparatus of a killer, with its photos of young women and grim text written about each of them. Other murders, equally savage, seem to be down to him, but Stella is not convinced. Is someone else manipulating the disturbed Kimber? All of this is handled with the forcefulness we have come to expect from Lawrence, with Stella Mooney as fully rounded a protagonist as ever. And if revelations in the plotting owe something to Thomas Harris, Lawrence is hardly alone in drawing water from that particular much-visited well. Nevertheless, he remains his own man, and *Cold Kill* is authoritatively gripping. Early success, however, was not followed up.

ANDREW MARTIN (a man who does not hesitate to say exactly what he means on any occasion) may be well known for his award-winning historical crime series featuring railway detective Jim Stringer, but he had hankered to write a novel about the super-rich, partly in the hope (he noted) that it might make him at least slightly rich. And while people are fascinated by the moneyed, he hadn't noticed many crime novels on the subject. It might be asked: why would the super-rich resort to crime? They would need a very good reason. And Martin set himself other challenges. The super-rich of London are mainly foreign, and he has succeeded in getting those voices – specifically Russian ones – right. Martin's approach to multiculturalism, which he decided to take on after spending many years imaginatively inhabiting the mono-cultural world of Edwardian Britain, is provocative. *The Yellow Diamond* concerns an imaginary unit of the Metropolitan Police set up to monitor the super-rich of London. It's based in dowdy Down Street, at the 'wrong' end of Mayfair. A principal character is a woman in her fifties, Victoria Clifford, who was the waspish personal assistant to the senior detective who set up the unit. However, he was rendered comatose by a bullet soon afterwards, and Clifford must find out why he was attacked.

Many of us have had friends who seem relentlessly bound on self-destruction – and not just by the time-honoured route of drink or drug abuse. The loss of their job is the inevitable corollary – but how do we save those friends, when anything we say sounds hollow or sanctimonious? The trick of **NICCI FRENCH**'s highly persuasive *Catch Me When I Fall* is to embody such notions in the reckless protagonist, Holly, who risks her happy marriage and successful career by venturing into dangerous terra incognita: alcohol-fuelled semi-orgies, where she risks brutal beatings, and wakes up from her stupor to find she's been having sex with some highly unsuitable partners – one of whom breaks out of the confines of her alternative existence and threatens her fragile everyday life. But there's an intriguing sleight of hand at work here: while the reader might be tempted to metaphorically shake Holly by the shoulders and suggest she gets her act together, French makes such a comfortable distancing impossible by involving us in Holly's increasingly nightmarish life. We're forced to lose our objectivity, and we find ourselves taking on Holly's guilty actions as part of our own response to the book. The 'transference of guilt' theme was a speciality of Alfred Hitchcock, but nothing that the director made could match the positive riot of guilt transference that decorates the pages of *Catch Me When I Fall*: Holly's best friend/business partner Meg is ineluctably drawn into the chaos of her life, as are Holly's husband and various other characters in the novel, including a sympathetic male, Stuart, who unwisely confides to her his problems with premature ejaculation. And, finally, there's the guilt dumped on the reader, obliged to take on the consequences of Holly's actions, whether we want to or not. The novel, like so much of French's work, hardly makes for a comfortable read. 'Nicci French' is, of course, the personally engaging husband-and-wife team of Nicci Gerrard and Sean French, and this book, more than most of their work, poses some intriguing gender-related questions about the duo's division of labour: a female protagonist, as ever, but initially the lack of balanced male figures is worrying. In fact, the preponderance of brutal, weak or drippily complaisant males suggests another author named French – Marilyn – and *The Women's Room* (with its simple antithesis of female=good, male=bad), but Nicci French is much too sophisticated a writer for that, and some of the men – even those with less-than-honourable motives – are shown to be victims as much as Holly. Is this Sean French putting in tuppence for the male sex? We'll never know, as the couple rigorously avoid telling who does what. And who cares when the results are as dexterous and edgy as this?

More recent work involves a series protagonist, therapist Dr Frieda Klein, who first appeared in *Blue Monday*. In *Tuesday's Gone*, a social worker, Maggie, calls on the disturbed Michelle Doyce, a 'care in the community' patient. Maggie is struck by the smell and the squalor – hardly new experiences for her – but she is not prepared for the man sitting in a back room, whose blue marbled appearance is that of a corpse. Frieda Klein is dragooned into the case by her colleague DCI Karlsson, and the dead man is identified as confidence trickster Robert Poole. Klein and Karlsson soon encounter an army of the dead man's unlucky 'marks' – and Frieda discovers that whoever is responsible for the death of Poole has her in their sights. Solid, assured work, if less distinctive than their memorable standalones.

ALI KNIGHT's artfully constructed crime novels are set in London, with the recent *Until Death* a persuasive entry; it is a domestic noir thriller set mainly in the penthouse on top of St Pancras station. From every window of this gothic architectural masterpiece, the dynamism, bustle and freedom of London can always be seen, contrasting chillingly with the claustrophobia and secrets of the family who live there.

It took some time, but **FRANCES FYFIELD** has now acquired something close to the literary gravitas of the two late British Queens of Crime (and habitués of the House of Lords), Mesdames Ruth Rendell and PD James. Fyfield is now regularly identified as one of the heirs of a great tradition, and books such as *Staring at the Light* have mined the same vein of psychological acuity and dark menace as those of her fellow authors. Fyfield said to me that the ideal locale for a story is a small community where everyone thinks they know everything about one another, while really they miss the obvious. This is a key notion in all her books: nothing is quite what it seems. And – like all the best crime writers – her books aren't just about keeping us glued to the chair while our cocoa goes cold; they often have something pertinent to say about the human condition (though never in any po-faced fashion).

Fyfield's novels featuring Crown Prosecutor Helen West and DCS Geoffrey Bailey have built up a steady following, but more recent books take Fyfield's customary delving into the darker aspects of the human psyche to a new level of intensity – and that's very much the case with *The Art of Drowning*. Dedicated male readers of the author (and they are many – Fyfield's fiefdom is by no means an exclusively female one) have been a little unsettled by her recurring theme of male violence against women, and some of the men in *The Art of Drowning* are as distasteful a group of males as she has created. Such as Rachel Doe's lover, whom she discovers to be both a thief and a liar. Looking at her life (and not liking what she sees), Rachel tries a new tack: an art class, where she falls under the spell of ex-model Ivy Wiseman. Ivy is good company, having survived drug addiction, the death of her child and the loss of her home, and, like Rachel, she's a casualty of the sex war. When the women visit Ivy's parents, who have an idyllic, slightly rundown place near the sea, she begins to find true peace again with her new friends. Then she is told of the death of Ivy's daughter, who died by drowning. And she hears about the unpleasant Carl, Ivy's ex-husband (a lawyer), who her parents want to track down. Rachel decides to help them find him – but when she meets the sinister Carl, everything she had expected proves to be subtly off-kilter. She finds herself desperately out of her depth, and soon discovers that a savage internecine war within a family is not a good place to be. As ever with Fyfield, the characters here are indelibly etched – everyone from the vulnerable Rachel to the ambiguous people under whose spell she falls is drawn with tremendous vividness. And the plotting! If you feel that your unwritten novel will take the world by storm, don't pick up *The Art of Drowning*; you may be discouraged from setting fingers to keyboard.

In *Hunted*, **EMLYN REES** has produced a novel that will have you holding your breath throughout – possibly to the detriment of your health. Danny Shanklin comes to consciousness in a London hotel room he's unfamiliar with. He's dressed in a balaclava and a red tracksuit. On the floor is a faceless corpse – and Shanklin has a high-powered rifle strapped to his hands. Hearing the sound of sirens, he looks out of the window and sees a burning car and more bodies littering the street. This is the powerful opening to a truly kinetic piece of crime/thriller fiction, in which the stakes are always set at the highest level.

You're a highly successful writer of children's books featuring a kind of junior James Bond. Does this have you chafing at the bit, keen to cram an adult book with all the sex and violence you can't put into your books for a youthful audience? **ANTHONY HOROWITZ**'s first novel for adults, *The Killing Joke*, gave older readers a chance to see whether the author had less sanitised entertainment up his sleeve.

Horowitz grew up tended by servants in his family's London mansion, the scion of a well-heeled Jewish family. As he has remarked, his childhood was deeply unhappy – and it's an upbringing he brought to scarifying life in such autobiographical books as *Granny*. He made a mark as a children's author with his Alex Rider novels; the adventures of Horowitz's youthful spy have sold over a million copies in this country alone. But this is only one string to his bow: his screenplay *The Gathering* has been filmed, and his TV scriptwriting includes the BAFTA-winning *Foyle's War*.

The auguries were good for *The Killing Joke*, his first un-child-friendly novel. This is a scorchingly funny black comedy thriller in which none-too-successful actor Guy Fletcher overhears a sick joke about his estranged mother, a well-known actress, in a Finsbury Park pub. He ill-advisedly objects to the joke-teller – a brutal cockney builder – and is floored by a headbutt for his objections. This starts Guy on a bizarre odyssey to discover where all jokes originate – and, yes, there is one source, which Guy discovers – while putting his life in considerable danger. There is a real sense here of an author stretching his wings after the constraints of writing for children – the humour is very dark. Not that such territory is off limits for kids these days; a sex scene in a fairground, however, is another matter. Guy and his companion Sally force their way into a closed funhouse and enjoy each other on a carpet of plastic balls, while distorting mirrors reflect a grotesque (and very funny) version of the erotic cavortings. The humour in *The Killing Joke* is laugh-out-loud stuff, and Guy is a sympathetic hero; if what he finds at the end of his quest for the source of jokes is something of a let-down after the brilliantly sustained, tortuous plotting that precedes it, most readers will feel they've had more than their money's worth. Moving away from humour, recent work has been in the area of Conan Doyle and Ian Fleming pastiches.

ERIN KELLY has written a variety of novels of psychological suspense, of which *The Burning Air* is perhaps the most disturbing – and also the one that lays out most clearly the corrosive areas she moves in. Her first two books, *The Sick Rose* and *The Poison Tree*, borrowed titles from William Blake, but *The Burning Air* takes on most tellingly Blake's line about a destructive and dark secret love.

It is a family tradition for the MacBrides to visit Devon each Bonfire Night, but there is a pall over the latest gathering. The matriarch of the family, Lydia, is dead. Her husband, the customarily sober Rowan (a retired headmaster), is drinking himself into a stupor. The family is in meltdown, with the eldest daughter Sophie watching her marriage crumble, while grandson Jake (who is mixed race) has the police breathing down his neck. But there is one ray of optimism: Felix, Sophie's brother, has brought along his beautiful new girlfriend Kerry, who charms the unhappy family. She appears to be a natural babysitter, and Sophie leaves her baby daughter in her care. But both Kerry and the baby disappear. Has she abducted the baby? Or have both of them been taken? The distraught Sophie turns on her brother, claiming that the missing girl could – for all they know – be some kind of psychopathic monster. And the truth, when it arrives, is shocking.

When even the best writers of standalone novels of suspense are obliged to observe commercial imperatives and adopt continuing characters (most recently, for instance, Nicci French), one can only hope that the talented Kelly is not persuaded by her publisher to write about a series protagonist, be they damaged male detective or alcoholic female forensics specialist. Not that there isn't plenty of damage at the heart of this book – Blake's 'invisible worm' has been doing his worst in the MacBride family – but the balancing of the very different characters has an intensity similar to that of chamber music, with each player proving as crucial as the last the author has presented for our attention. If Erin Kelly has not quite attained the rarefied psychological astuteness of a Barbara Vine (and if the final revelation is a touch underwhelming), she has proved herself to be among the most accomplished and pin-sharp of writers at work in the crime genre, with family dysfunction a speciality. And William Blake can continue to be a source of appropriate future titles: 'Cruelty has a human heart'? 'Hire a villain'?

When the anodyne TV presenters Richard Madeley and Judy Finnigan announced some time ago that they were to emulate Oprah Winfrey's book club on their TV show, ironic noises were heard from the publishing trade – how could the British duo have the same seismic 'Oprah effect' on book sales? **WILLIAM BRODRICK** is a man who knows how wrong the naysayers were. The sales of his *The Sixth Lamentation* leapt through the roof and highlighted a mystery writer of panache. But without an R&J plug, how would Brodrick's subsequent books fare? Were enough people seduced by that debut novel to make *The Gardens of the Dead* another success? As with the first book, Brodrick is primarily concerned with plotting. And his second concern after plotting is… more plotting. This isn't to say that the characters here are not fully rounded; it's just that Brodrick is clearly persuaded that we all want to be transfixed by storytelling expertise.

Elizabeth Glendinning is a QC who knows that her death is imminent. But she has a pressing agenda – she will bring a guilty man, now free, back into the law courts. The plan that will take effect after her death involves six individuals, all of whose lives were changed by a significant trial. Elizabeth's posthumous plan is that Graham Riley will be arraigned by this group, led by the monk Father Anselm. Anselm receives the key to a security box that will bring back memories for him of his days as a barrister when a witness destroyed the case against Riley and it collapsed. This witness, George Bradshaw, found his life ruined after these events, and wanders London as Blind George, his short-term memory in pieces after an assault. However, Elizabeth's carefully oiled planning begins to break down, and Anselm finds himself unwillingly taking on her mantle, investigating Elizabeth's life (and that of her son, Nick). And there's an urgency to these investigations: lives are at stake...

Any fears that Brodrick's earlier book was a lucky accident were quickly allayed with *The Gardens of the Dead*. Certainly, the complexity of the narrative here is a little wearying at times. But as this labyrinthine tale unfolds, Brodrick is able to bring off a truly impressive feat: while we read on, agog for the next revelation, it becomes apparent that we're being treated to character studies quite as rich as those in many a more ostensibly 'literary' novel.

Are novels supposed to make us feel elated? Or is it acceptable to feel guilty and soiled, identifying with a character who colludes in the murder of a woman after some sordid group sex? If you feel the second option is one you'd rather avoid, you'd better steer clear of **NEIL CROSS**'s *Burial*. Such is the author's insidious skill (he is the creator of TV's *Luther*) that we are ineluctably involved in the messy private life of Nathan, a rather sad loser, whether we like it or not. The experience may make us feel a bit queasy, but it's possible to argue (as Cross might in defence of his scarifying, deeply disturbing novel) that the reader might experience a scrubbed-with-a-brush scouring after reading *Burial* – not necessarily a pleasant sensation, but certainly energising. As in such previous books as *Holloway Falls*, Cross marries literary values to the exigencies of a page-turning crime narrative – but that's 'literary' with a small 'l'. No flourishes here: everything is pared to the bone. Nathan, stifled in a radio journalism job and in the last phases of a disintegrating relationship, attends a party given by his right-wing radio host boss, and meets the slightly deranged Bob. After some ill-advised, cocaine-fuelled (and deeply squalid) three-way sex with Bob and a stoned young girl in a car, the girl – Elise – ends up dead. An accident? Bob was the last person in the car with her. The traumatised Nathan is persuaded to bury the body, enduring agonies of guilt as a result. But then Bob reappears in his life and tells him that the woods in which they buried Elise are about to be dug up for a housing estate. Nathan is soon making one catastrophic decision after another, with (inevitably) a macabre outcome.

It's easier for an author to invite identification when a protagonist has certain attractive moral or physical qualities – we can all happily imagine we're 'featur'd like him, like him with friends possess'd', but it's a more complex achievement to put us inside the skin of a no-hoper like Nathan. That's just what Cross does. When Nathan initiates a relationship with the unknowing, damaged sister of the girl in whose death he is implicated, the reader is squirming – both at his colossal misjudgement, and in fervent hope that he won't be found out. There are those who won't thank Neil Cross for taking us into such morally ambivalent territory, but even those feeling a little grubby won't be able to deny the author's sheer mastery of his unsettling task.

The divisions between the tough, streetwise British thrillers and the so-called Home Counties 'cosies' are much talked about, but certain books refuse to fit comfortably into either category. There is no denying, however, that Cross's earlier *Holloway Falls* is very scabrous stuff indeed: hard-edged and sardonically funny, this is not for those who like their thrillers to be a tad more relaxing. At the centre of Cross's uncompromising narrative is dysfunctional copper Bill Holloway, who fills his loneliness by having sex with prostitute Joanne Chapman (and asking her to dress up as his divorced wife). Then two postal deliveries shock him out of his lethargy: a video recording of his wife and her lover engaged in sex, then one of Joanne tied up and terrified, a gag over her mouth...

Many people (to their regret) have incautiously said yes to a friend's invitation to a stag or hen night. They can be pretty grisly occasions, but thankfully few of them have the grim consequences of the gathering in **RUTH WARE**'s *In a Dark, Dark Wood*. Ware's central character Leonora (who narrates the novel) finds that there is a price to be paid for deviating from her generally antisocial behaviour when she accepts such an invitation. The event brings up betrayals and guilt from the past, which, in a Frank Lloyd Wright-style house in an isolated forest, prove to be a recipe for catastrophe. While functioning as an exemplary crime novel, there is much keenly observed social comedy here (not a million miles from the acerbic work of William Trevor), and spiky characterisation is a particularly strong suit for Ware. Crime readers may have more than enough on their plates, but there is no ignoring this provocative writer.

Having established itself as boasting one of the most striking and provocative translated crime lists in the UK, the publisher Quercus felt obliged to keep up the momentum it had created, adding British writers to its impressive geographical spread. Which it certainly did with Brit writer **ELENA FORBES'** strong and assured debut *Die With Me*. The hallmark of this one is psychological acuity, as persuasive here as in such experienced names as Ruth Rendell and Sophie Hannah. It's assumed that the young girl found dead in a London church has committed suicide – but DI Mark Tartaglia isn't convinced. He finds that other suicides had presented the same features, but the inevitable clashes with authority and colleagues interpose themselves between Tartaglia and the grim truth. Forbes' novel provided the auguries of a long and successful crime-writing career to come. Her later *Evil in Return* touched on the well-worn theme of the past erupting into the present – a notion to which she brought something fresh.

Why did **MICHAEL DOBBS** waste his time as Deputy Chairman of both the Conservative Party and Saatchi and Saatchi? Or the myriad other jobs he's taken up over the years? He was clearly put on this earth to write thrillers of the most shamelessly page-turning quality – such as *The Lords' Day*, in which Dobbs addresses himself to the classic 'ticking clock' narrative, and screws the accelerating tension so tight that most readers will be consuming this one in just two or three sittings.

It's a year or so in the future: the State Opening of Parliament, with the Queen, her Cabinet and visitors gathering in the House of Lords. Suddenly, all is panic and confusion – the violent intervention of fundamentalist terrorists will make this day one to be remembered, for all the wrong reasons. In the best cinematic fashion, Dobbs cuts between a large cast of characters, marshalling the tension with a canny touch. There is ex-soldier Harry Jones, trying to persuade his estranged wife not to have an abortion and struggling with a failing career; there are the sons of the British Prime Minister and the (female) President of the United States (who could Dobbs have based his American head of state upon?); there are the squabbling politicians (some nicely acid *roman-à-clef* portraits here); and there are the terrorists, masquerading as cleaners to bring carnage into the heart of government. Here, Dobbs is particularly adroit at conveying the mindset of young men psyching themselves into theocratic fervour. And apart from the beleaguered Harry Jones, struggling with a grim hostage situation, some of Dobbs' most successful characterisations are those of real-life characters, including, audaciously, the Queen and Prince Charles. As a Kalashnikov is discharged in the House of Lords, shattering the canopy above the throne and causing panic, Dobbs has his royals behaving in a very plausible way – the Queen grasps Charles' arm as he tries to put himself between her and the gunmen – she realises that if they had intended to kill her, they would have already done so. All of this is handled with the panache we expect from Dobbs (despite some careless passages), and he still allows himself some cogent observations on the British – such as the fact that we allow our culture, and with it our self-confidence, to slip through our fingers, leaving us little but empty air.

Now that the secret is out – and we know it is Harry Potter's creator JK Rowling behind the masculine sobriquet '**ROBERT GALBRAITH**' – we are all obliged to play catch-up with a book that created barely a ripple on its first pseudonymous appearance. So: was *The Cuckoo's Calling* any good? After all, Rowling's first adult novel, *The Casual Vacancy*, incurred a decidedly mixed critical response, despite its prodigious sales.

In fact, the first Galbraith book is an accomplished piece that thoroughly deserves its retrospective success, even were it not by a celebrity author. As the beleaguered military policeman-turned-private eye Cormoran Strike investigates the apparent suicide of a supermodel, we are granted a measured but subtly involving reworking of crime novel mechanisms as the detective moves across a variety of class divides, finding that the police have got things wrong. Strike himself is a distinctive addition to the overcrowded ranks of literary private eyes. Strike's second appearance in *The Silkworm* was not as impressive, but *Career of Evil* – while notably implausible with its multiple maniacs – recaptured the energy of the first book. Written in an unadorned, non-literary prose perfectly suited to the author's purposes, *Career of Evil* confirms that Rowling's post-Potter initiative is proving to be a very welcome one. Both Strike and Robin Ellacott (Strike's female assistant, stuck in a dying relationship) are multidimensional, conflicted characters, and there is no gainsaying the sheer relish with which the writer tackles the genre. There are many unusual elements, such as Strike's cross-country odyssey and the active sexual history of his rock groupie mother – rock music is significant: the title of the book is from a Patti Smith lyric.

CLAIRE McGOWAN became a familiar figure on the London crime fiction scene as a recent director of the Crime Writers' Association, but it was clear from her assured debut novel that her real métier is delivering criminous diversions such as may be found in *The Fall*. There are elements of the police procedural here, with a well-drawn copper in DC Matthew Hegarty – though it has to be said that his is a familiar figure. The real achievement of the book, however, is its strikingly variegated cast of protagonists, particularly some vividly realised female figures whose individual characters fairly leap off the page. No doubt McGowan felt that we needed a conventional copper to draw her narrative together, but it's the women here who count – such as the feckless mixed-race Keisha, in thrall to a pretty worthless male; she is someone we find ourselves wanting to spend time with, however annoyingly she behaves. (The males in the book are a pretty sorry bunch.) McGowan has a keen ear for class and social nuance, and readers of *The Fall* found themselves looking forward to her subsequent books with some anticipation; the recent *A Savage Hunger* is particularly satisfying.

When Clark Kent wants to shuck off his reporter persona, he takes off his glasses and opens his shirt to reveal a big red 'S'. But what is a mild-mannered literary writer to do when he feels the urge to pen gritty crime fiction, with such titles as *Putting the Boot In*? In the case of Julian Barnes (known for his subtle and nuanced 'serious' novels), he invents the alter ego '**DAN KAVANAGH**', giving him access to the kind of writing in which bloody murder is done. It's a strategy that has been employed in the past by Poet Laureate C Day-Lewis (who cracked skulls as Nicholas Blake) and more recently by John Banville as 'Benjamin Black'.

However, Barnes/Kavanagh's sardonic sleuth Duffy has been around for several decades. He first appeared in an eponymous novel in 1980; as well as functioning as both a parody and a celebration of the detective genre, it introduced a sexually ambivalent ex-copper in an era when bisexuality in the crime genre was hardly quotidian. Its pithy sense of British locale and zeitgeist was an instant hit with aficionados, whatever their sexuality. Sadly, there were to be only four Duffy books, with *Putting the Boot In* the third outing for the character (Duffy's polymorphous libido is not central here). It presents a cold-eyed image of 'the beautiful game' in which massively overpaid (and none too bright) sportsmen demonstrate distinctly thuggish tendencies – but this is football in the 1980s rather than the present, and the endemic corruption here is a reminder that in soccer *plus ça change*. Duffy is hired when the star player of a Third Division club is the victim of an apparent mugging in which his Achilles tendon is damaged, and the club's manager foresees a host of impending attacks. The ingredients here? Racism, über-nationalist politics and empty celebrity, all handled with the customary Kavanagh acerbic touch. This may be the best Duffy novel – what perhaps dates it is its central concern with AIDS, but much of its interest lies in its 1980s accoutrements.

One might wonder, though, why Kavanagh's publishers Orion downplayed the crime ethos when they reissued the book in 2014 – the design on the jacket showing table football figures conveys only one aspect of the narrative. Julian Barnes' name, too, is not to be found anywhere on the inner sleeve, though erstwhile friend Martin Amis provides an encomium. There is, however, a blurred photo of 'Dan Kavanagh' with a text detailing the author's adolescence of truancy, venery and petty theft along with his time as a bouncer in a gay bar in San Francisco. Kavanagh, it seems, 'now lives in North Islington', clearly having written *finis* to his unlikely rip-roaring past.

The strapline for **TIM WEAVER**'s *Chasing the Dead* is 'Death is not the end. But he'll make you wish it was.' And, for once, a publisher has summed up the essence of a taut thriller. Alex, the son of Mary Towne, disappeared some six years ago. He did reappear – but in gruesome fashion, as a body found in a car wreck. Mary sees a figure she believes is her son on the street some months later and tries to persuade missing persons investigator David Raker to help her. Raker is to find that Alex's life was a complex one – and one that was very different from what his mother believed it to be. This is strong writing that thoroughly involves the reader: the start of an impressive series, as was evidenced by the later *What Remains*. And if you're one of those readers unhappy with the new elephantiasis in crime fiction, when so many novels are obliged (as is *What Remains*) to be over 500 pages long, you might just have your mind changed by Weaver's impressive narrative. The author manages to justify the book's arm-straining length – not least with the layers of psychological penetration that he freights into his ambitious novel. Troubled detective Colm Healy is a man bereft; he has lost everything he enjoyed in his tenure as one of the Met's most efficient policemen. His failure to track down a merciless, motiveless killer has led to the destruction of both his career and his marriage. But Healy has one friend left: missing persons investigator David Raker (whom we have met in earlier Weaver novels). What follows is a lacerating joint investigation, taking the characters (and readers) into the furthest reaches of obsession – and a quest for redemption. It's a dark, complex and visceral read.

The pseudonymous **TOM CAIN** (actually David Thomas, no shrinking violet when it comes to assessing his own skills) has been refining his craft in the field of the blockbuster thriller for some time now, and he knows exactly how to make the reader's pulse increase its customary rate. In *Revenger*, the world is in meltdown, with Iran's nuclear facilities a radioactive rubble, the Euro having fallen apart and the wrecked economies of the world suffering daily unrest. Cain's protagonist Sam Carver is just seeking a quiet drink with an old friend, but quietness is something not to be found in London anymore, and Sam is caught up in a riot. Things get very violent, and, to his dismay, Sam finds himself blamed for the mayhem, with the police and an old enemy on his trail. This is characteristically visceral stuff from Cain. As David Thomas, the writer made a mark with *Blood Relative*. A bloodbath awaits Peter Crookham when he arrives home. His brother, Andy, a journalist, is lying dead, the victim of multiple stab wounds, and Peter's wife Mariana is covered in blood. Peter is convinced that his wife is innocent, but he discovers that the object of his brother's final investigation was, in fact, Mariana's complex past. Looming large in her life is a single man – a mysterious figure who had an affiliation with the East German security service, the Stasi. As well as being a compelling thriller, this is a novel about identity, delivered with professionalism.

In *Then We Die*, **JAMES CRAIG**'s Inspector John Carlyle is dismayed when he hears that his mother is getting a divorce after 50 years of marriage. But his professional life is also to be more testing than usual, when he comes across the execution of a rich businessman in an upscale London hotel. The murder victim appears to be the latest in a line of individuals targeted by a relentless Israeli hit squad, but Carlyle decides that tackling this murderous crew will at least distract him from the deeply destabilising events at home. As always with James Craig, the ever-accelerating pace here is handled with the authority of a master. While James Craig's sequence of Inspector Carlyle novels (numbering such gritty and impressive entries as *Never Apologise Never Explain*, *Buckingham Palace Blues* and *London Calling*) has long been marked by its cool authority, *Then We Die* is one of the best.

The notable success of the TV adaptation of *The Long Firm*, starring Mark Strong (some time before his current level of film celebrity), consolidated the reputation of the uncompromising **JAKE ARNOTT**, whose trilogy of books set in London established a new high watermark for caustic, powerfully drawn crime fiction. But what makes Arnott's sequence different from most of the competition is the realisation of the antihero, Harry Starks, an East End gangster who also happens to be gay. Starks debuted in Arnott's first novel, *The Long Firm*, which also boasts a vividly delineated 1960s setting and mixes in elements of the Kray twins, whose violent reign included flirtations with both politicians and visiting celebrities. The first book's successor, *He Kills Coppers* (also adapted for TV), moved the sequence from the 1960s to the Thatcher era, echoing the social criticism of rapacious acquisitiveness also to be found in

John Mackenzie's film *The Long Good Friday*. The third part of the Arnott sequence is *Truecrime*, which is set in the 1980s and 1990s.

Tyro novelist **ADAM HAMDY** spent eight years working in the glitzy Neverland of the movie business (following a career as a management consultant) before plucking up the courage to write a novel. As a screenwriter, he continues to work with producers and studios on both sides of the Atlantic, developing original material and adapting novels such as David Mitchell's *Number9Dream*. Hamdy's novel *Out of Reach*, set in London, has been described as a short sharp shock with a twist ending that leaves readers reeling. The book charts the story of Thomas Schaefer, an unconventional private investigator, who is drawn into a dark, warped world while searching for his lost daughter. Hamdy's next novel, *The Pendulum Effect*, has a New York setting and tells the tale of John Wallace, a Londoner who is framed for his own attempted suicide. Hamdy has a passion for research that borders on the obsessive: not satisfied with simply taking up shooting to provide authentic descriptions of gunfire, he has earned a marksmanship certificate and has even undertaken basic gunsmith training. Hamdy has a degree in law and a second in philosophy; as he says, as a philosopher he can explain why something is morally wrong; as a lawyer he can advise how to get away with it.

In *The Gilded Edge*, Detective Vince Treadwell is investigating the case of two apparently unrelated murders: a young black woman from an unprivileged background and the well-heeled Belgravia resident Johnny Beresford. As Treadwell's investigations take him from the illegal drinking holes of Notting Hill to the upscale gambling haunts of Berkeley Square, the reader is given a rich and atmospheric picture of every aspect of London, from the highest to the lowest. **DANNY MILLER** showed in the earlier *Kiss Me Quick* that his is a characterful voice, and his abilities are once again demonstrated at full stretch in this novel.

Modern black British crime writing has an unarguable signature book: *Yardie* by **VICTOR HEADLEY**. This gritty gangster saga, accused by some of being crassly written, focuses on a youthful

Jamaican immigrant's battle on the streets of London to lead the drug-dealing underworld. Headley's book, the first in a series, stirred up controversy, with some black readers criticising an appeal to the lowest common denominator and an exploitative presentation of criminal black stereotypes. A riff on *Scarface*, Headley's persuasive vision of this milieu, with an examination of music and food in the immigrant community, enjoyed massive sales – particularly among young black readers who often admitted that this was the first book they'd read. The unforgiving utilisation of Jamaican patois was a problem for some readers, but was worth the effort.

In **JANE CASEY**'s *The Kill*, the streets of London are awash with fear, but a ruthless killer is not targeting ordinary citizens – the target is policemen. Reassigned as a matter of urgency to investigate a series of savage attacks on her fellow officers, Maeve Kerrigan and her boss Josh Derwent have a troubling double problem: find out (very quickly) what is the motive behind these acts of brutality – and stop them. Meanwhile, the killer strikes again. More impressively kinetic thriller writing from the talented Jane Casey, who is proving to be an able practitioner of the genre.

The formidable **BEN AARONOVITCH** has an eccentric writing style – and literary preoccupations – that is very different from that of most of his colleagues. His speciality in his 'Rivers of London' sequence is a marked infusion of fantasy elements, and the London that his copper Peter Grant negotiates is a phantasmagorical location, appropriate for a protagonist whose other profession is that of wizard. Aaronovitch uses cleverly placed London-centric elements in such books as *Whispers Under Ground*, which makes the London Underground a strange and menacing place.

MAGGIE HAMAND's debut novel in 1995, *The Resurrection of the Body*, was an assured piece of work, with ambitions beyond the customary remit of the crime novel. In the past, it was possible to believe in miracles and to lead a life of faith, but for Richard Page, vicar of a poor East End community in a more confused, cynical time, faith is not quite so straightforward, and the experience he endures during the celebration of Easter proves how fragile his devotion really is. The Good Friday service is shockingly interrupted when a man staggers in, bleeding from wounds inflicted during a vicious knife attack. There is no identification on him, and when he dies no one comes forward to claim the body. Then, on Easter Sunday, even more bizarrely, the corpse disappears from the morgue, leaving the police baffled but suspicious. The events that follow are even more disturbing, and draw the vicar into a bruising quest to uncover the man's identity and explain the unexplainable. His obsession will bring him into conflict with the police, with his superiors, his congregation and even his wife. As reality slips beyond his control, Page's faith is battered almost beyond endurance. *The Resurrection of the Body* provocatively addresses notions of love, religion and madness within the context of the mystery novel. *The Rocket Man*, which appeared in the same year (1995), was a change of pace for Hamand, but equally striking. More recently, she has published *Doctor Gavrilov*; this was hailed by Julian Rathbone as 'like the very best le Carré', and is a thriller concerning attempts by a Middle Eastern country to procure nuclear knowhow in the immediate aftermath of the collapse of the Soviet Union.

One of the quirkiest and most individual literary talents in the UK, **KIM NEWMAN** could hardly be described as conforming to any tenets of the crime genre (or, for that matter, any other genre) in his body of work, but his often surrealistic multiverse synthesises a dizzying variety of elements from many aspects of the crime field. There is a particular stress on lovingly rendered vintage elements, referenced in a massively ingenious series of genre pastiches. However, the term 'pastiche' does not do justice to Newman's achievement – implying (as it does to many readers) an element of parody. Newman's encyclopaedic knowledge of everything concerning British fictional crime protagonists in their literary, cinematic and televisual incarnations always celebrates as opposed to guying his subjects (Newman is as celebrated a film and TV critic as he is a novelist). The list of subjects in Newman's oeuvre is ambitious: *The Night Mayor* is a film noir/science fiction hybrid, set in a computer-generated world derived from 1940s thrillers; *Anno Dracula* – perhaps his most accomplished novel (though not relevant to this study) – evokes the Jack the Ripper murders; *The Quorum* boasts as heroine a female private detective (Sally Rhodes, who has featured in Newman's short stories). And writing as Jack Yeovil, Newman produced *Beasts in Velvet*, which riffs on notions of Dirty Harry versus a serial killer in a fantasy setting. Some of his other Yeovil stories also have crime/detective elements, notably 'No Gold in the Grey Mountains'.

MIKE PHILLIPS, aka 'Joe Canzius', is a one-off. Black writers have tackled the urban crime scene before – and often with conspicuous success. But this Guyana-born practitioner of the thriller, while au fait with most aspects of black culture in both the US and the UK, is quintessentially British, and the author's own clear-eyed vision is refracted through this heady mix to create a remarkable series of books. Phillips' principal character, the crime-involved journalist Sam Dean, is a conduit for the reader to venture into a world rich and strange for many a white crime aficionado. And Phillips' invigorating, often brutal prose never attitudinises – we are allowed to make up our own minds about the characters (black or white, honourable or callous) we encounter. There is a sharp social intelligence and analysis at work in Mike Phillips' novels, but never at the expense of a cracking crime plot. As a journalist, he stored up the savvy that would be so crucial to his tough-but-honest journo hero, and with the first Sam Dean novel, *Blood Rights* in 1989, it was immediately clear that a striking new voice had arrived on the British crime-writing scene. A less-than-successful BBC TV adaptation of the novel did not lessen the steadily growing impact that successive Sam Dean novels, such as *Point of Darkness*, began to make.

As Joe Canzius, Phillips writes even tougher urban thrillers; these include *Fast Road to Nowhere*, in which the reader is forced to root for an amoral petty thief hero in a dangerous city landscape. It has often been pointed out that Phillips' writing has more in common with American urban crime writers than with most British middle-class authors – despite the fact that his main protagonist, Dean, is very English. In terms of plotting, Phillips has no interest whatsoever in the Christie-style classic mystery plot in which various elements of puzzle are slotted into place; his is a messy, chaotic universe, with the author only just managing to pull everything together, creating a rough kind of closure. Phillips is aware of the perception that his Joe Canzius books are more squarely aimed at a black readership, but (he has said) this is not really the case. His first published work – a collection of short stories – was aimed at a black readership, but after that he decided that he wanted to write for whoever chose to pick up his books. Certainly, Sam Dean is a relatively easy character for white readers to identify with – while he is scathing about racism, he is often in as much danger from black villains as from prejudiced whites. And, of course, he is the ideologically firm centre of the books – tough, but very moral.

Without attempting any radical surgery on the police procedural format, **PAUL CHARLES** has demonstrated a proficiency in the genre that has proved to be very durable. Such books as *The Justice Factory* (featuring Charles's resilient protagonist DI Christy Kennedy) have all the requisite ingredients, including a striking opening: a living body staring from the pit of a rain-drenched grave. Utilising pithily described locales – Camden and Primrose Hill – Charles places his various plot points with authority, allowing Kennedy to work uneasily alongside WDC Anne Coles as murder continues to be the fulcrum through which the characters are delineated.

The refreshingly unsparing style (in her life and her writing) of the writer **RUTH DUDLEY EDWARDS** has meant that she is noted as much for her uncompromising analysis of political and societal issues as she is for her wickedly sardonic crime writing in which a variety of self-important establishment figures and shibboleths are ruthlessly punctured. *Killing the Emperors* is a typically lacerating Edwards piece in which the mechanics of the crime novel are balanced with a cutting satirical edge – it is a take on the crazy, corrupt world of conceptual art. Edwards has frequently demonstrated that, for her, nothing is sacred, and it is this quality that makes her books so mischievously diverting.

One of the best-known and affectionately regarded figures on the British crime scene is the witty writer **SIMON BRETT**, who, as well as being a toastmaster par excellence, is the creator of the wonderfully diverting, lightly comic Charles Paris novels, successfully adapted for radio. This is a medium in which Brett has enjoyed considerable success; the misconceived film of his non-Paris novel *A Shock to the System*, however, has drawn some of his most hilariously cutting comments. His inclusion in a study such as this – with the word 'noir' in the title – shows how loosely that appellation is being applied; 'noir' is something these books certainly aren't. But, ah, the civilised entertainments of Simon Brett! It's a breath of fresh air to pick up one of his witty and sardonic essays – perhaps the books sit neatly in the cosy genre, but this is the finest writing in the field. An example is *The Shooting in the Shop*, with a plot involving a store that is mysteriously burnt down, thus involving heroine Carole Seddon. Several suspicious characters are in the frame – including a comedy writer who isn't very funny. Unlike Brett. To say that Brett has been turning out books like this for years sounds like faint praise; in fact, readers are in awe of his consistency.

The leading female black British crime writer is unarguably **DREDA SAY MITCHELL**, although she refreshingly resists ethnic identifications in her writing. Born in London to Grenadian parents and growing up on an estate in the East End, Mitchell is a ubiquitous broadcaster and also specialises in literacy programmes for underachieving black boys. Her first novel, the gritty *Running Hot*, won the Crime Writers' Association's award for best first novel in 2005, an achievement that was consolidated by her later *Killer Tune*. Her success is due to the fact that she writes about the streets where she grew up in sharp and idiomatic prose, and her recent *Death Trap* is a typically powerful novel.

With her distinctive retro mode of dress, **CATHI UNSWORTH** is – as she would probably be the first to admit – a woman born out of her time, pleasurably in thrall to an earlier era in terms of the music, fashion and rebellious attitudes. She first made her mark as a writer on popular music, but one of her principal skills is her evocation of her beloved London, which has a thoroughly individual and idiosyncratic timbre. Her books customarily receive excellent reviews, but particular approbation was enjoyed by *Bad Penny Blues*, which begins with the savage killing of a prostitute. *Weirdo*, however, is the book that has enjoyed perhaps the greatest acclaim. A young girl is convicted of killing one of her classmates one summer in 1984. Two decades later, new forensic evidence suggests that Corinne didn't act alone... More recent work, such as the quirky, atmospheric *Without the Moon*, demonstrates that Unsworth has her formidable gifts still firmly in place.

Pungent, edgy, visceral (and told from beginning to end in an unchanging present tense), **ADAM CREED**'s *Suffer the Children* is as good a snapshot of the state of the modern British (urban) crime novel as you're likely to encounter. In a London where everyone feels at risk from street crime, and knife-wielding drug dealers jostle with predatory child molesters for tabloid headlines, DI Will 'Staffe' Wagstaffe has all the necessary accoutrements for his thankless job: brusque manner, damaged love life, aggro from both his boss and the press. When a convicted paedophile is killed in his own home, Staffe is obliged to put the families of abused children under intense scrutiny; whatever Staffe and his colleagues think of the murder victim and his ilk, they are obliged to protect other known offenders. As the beleaguered Staffe struggles with press hostility and the less-than-benign influence of his ex-partner Jessop, he is forced to confront a very uncomfortable issue: how far should parents go to protect their children? This moral dilemma – the police's duty to protect those they despise – is a theme treated even-handedly by Creed; the reader is allowed to balance their responses to the incendiary issues at the heart of the narrative. This makes for a distinctly trenchant read, although the present-tense device won't please everyone.

Creed's writing gods, self-evidently, are the tough Americans George Pelecanos and James Ellroy. The bleak vision of British society laid out for us here is minatory and unsettling; not perhaps the one we all live in, but certainly a world that anyone living in a major city intersects with at one time or another. Another presiding influence is *The Wire*'s David Simon; the banal, quotidian activities of low-level drug dealers are evoked with skill and economy, very much in the manner of the cult show. On the strength of *Suffer the*

Children, it was clear that Creed had the smarts to make a mark in an overcrowded field.

Best known for his gritty, abrasive novels featuring the London private eye Nick Sharman, **MARK TIMLIN** (no stranger to unvarnished abrasiveness himself) imported the ethos of the American hard-boiled novel into a vividly realised south London setting, with crackling dialogue a speciality. Sharman was filmed for television with Clive Owen, but fell foul of one of the recurrent bouts of hysteria concerning screen violence and was not renewed. The books (including *All the Empty Places*) have recently been reissued.

Long a valued stalwart of the magazine and website *Crime Time*, **RUSSELL JAMES** – a man who doesn't pull his punches – is a crime writer (and a historian of the genre) who absolutely refuses to be categorised. He is as adept at a kind of unsparing British hard-boiled writing as he is at black comedy – and entries in that genre rarely come blacker than *The Newly Discovered Diaries of Doctor Kristal*. James has set his quirky and beguiling comedy in the Swinging Sixties, and the format consists of the diaries of a doctor, a virginal 35-year-old with a predilection for homicide (the wordy subtitle is 'whose strange obsessions cause him to murder some annoying patients'). The eponymous Dr Kristal is a really unusual creation in a genre that has had its fair share of eccentric murderers, and one of the particular pleasures of the book is seeing how the old Adam – sexual desire – can upset the best laid plans of even those who regard themselves as safely above such things. Dubbed 'the Godfather of British Noir' by Ian Rankin, James is also seen at his best in the much-praised *Painting in the Dark*, a novel split between two timelines. In the late twentieth century, a compelling new political leader, Tony Blair, sweeps to power. An art crime from the contemporary era is contrasted with the 1930s, when upper-class British toffs found themselves mesmerised by the new politics of Nazi Germany, and when the book's heroines, Sidonie and Naomi Keene, were house guests of Adolf Hitler and Hermann Goering. In 1997 London, that hidden past comes crashing back, bringing darkness in its wake.

The energetic **HELEN SMITH** is the author of several acclaimed novels, including the dystopian *The Miracle Inspector*, but her signature series may be the lively 'Emily Castles Mysteries'. She is also the author of children's books, poetry and plays. In 2015, she set up BritCrime, a free online crime fiction festival involving more than 40 British crime writers, which has proved to be a clever initiative.

Socially committed writing was on offer when **COURTTIA NEWLAND** published his first novel, *The Scholar*, at the age of 23, immediately making a mark as one of the few British writers who accurately – and non-exploitatively – portray teenage life in London's inner cities. *The Scholar* enjoyed bestseller status, and the writer's second novel, *Society Within*, located on the same fictional Greenside Estate in West London, enjoyed good reviews. Newland's third book, *Snakeskin*, inhabited the same locales, but was more avowedly a detective novel, dealing with an investigation into the murder of a Labour MP's daughter.

Experienced crime fiction journalists (which is what this writer is supposed to be) theoretically possess a radar that spots highly successful books before the general public picks up on them. Well, I can modestly mention that this was the case with the early work of Thomas Harris, but I certainly didn't predict that *The Girl on the Train* by **PAULA HAWKINS** was to become such a phenomenal, record-breaking success. It struck me on first reading as a perfectly efficient Hitchcockian thriller, but I wouldn't have bet on it accruing the kind of success it has. Hawkins, however, clearly has her finger on the pulse of what the reading public likes. The relatively unsympathetic Rachel is an alcoholic who suffers from losses of memory, and is smarting from the pain of her husband abandoning her for a younger woman. When she notices some suspicious happenings from a train window, the police pay no attention. Needless to say – they should. The basic premise may owe something to Hitchcock's *Rear Window* (or Cornell Woolrich's original novella – not to mention Agatha Christie's *4.50 from Paddington*), but Hawkins handles it with aplomb.

Where the Devil Can't Go marked **ANYA LIPSKA** out as a crime writer of bravura skills, and her pungent novel *Death Can't Take a Joke* continued her upward trajectory. Presenting an edgy, visceral vision of modern London at the mercy of ambitious Eastern European criminals, *Death Can't Take a Joke* boasts complex protagonists, sharply realised locales and a keen social awareness. Lipska is at the forefront of a new wave of culture-clash crime writers.

SHEILA BUGLER's crime series featuring DI Ellen Kelly is located in Greenwich and Lewisham, south-east London. Until recently, Bugler lived in this area and it's the part of London she knew and loved best; the author has been successful in making this little pocket of the capital seem real and tangible, with landmarks such as a characterful local pub called the Dacre Arms featuring in all the novels. New readers should perhaps start with her first novel, *Hunting Shadows*.

ANDREW CARTMEL's *Written in Dead Wax* is the first in a series featuring a nameless, sardonic narrator and protagonist – somewhat in the manner of Dashiell Hammett's Continental Op or Len Deighton's anonymous secret agent. Somewhat more soft- than hard-boiled, the character begins as a crate-digging record collector who haunts charity shops and boot fairs looking for rare records, either to add to his own extensive collection or to sell so he can earn a marginal living. His business card describes him as the 'Vinyl Detective' and some people take this description more literally than others. Such as the enigmatic, seductive woman who offers him a huge sum of money to find a priceless lost jazz record on behalf of an obscenely wealthy, rather sinister Japanese client. The narrative voice and the menacing world of double-dealing and hired killers channels classic noir, but there are also contradictory elements of the cosy and puzzle crime fiction. Set largely in a vividly depicted London, the book also ranges abroad, to Los Angeles and Omura in Nagasaki Prefecture, Japan.

Other writers and key books
PETER ACKROYD: *Hawksmoor*
DS BUTLER: *Deadly Obsession*, *Deadly Justice*

WILL CARVER: *Girl 4, The Two*
KIMBERLEY CHAMBERS: *The Betrayer, The Victim*
LIZA CODY: *Head Case, Backhand*
TAMMY COHEN: *Dying for Christmas, First One Missing*
JJ CONNOLLY: *Layer Cake, Viva La Madness*
MAT COWARD: *Over and Under, Open and Closed*
DENISE DANKS: *Phreak, Better Off Dead*
STEPHEN DAVISON: *Dead Innocent, Kill & Cure*
LUKE DELANEY: *The Toy Taker, Cold Killing*
MICHAEL DONOVAN: *Behind Closed Doors*
LOUISE DOUGHTY: *Apple Tree Yard*
PENNY HANCOCK: *Tideline, The Darkening Hour*
LAUREN HENDERSON: *Pretty Boy*
GRAHAM ISON: *A Damned Serious Business, All Quiet on Arrival*
JESSIE KEANE: *Dirty Game*
ROBERTA KRAY: *Nothing but Trouble*
AVA MARSH: *Untouchable*
ALEX MARWOOD: *The Killer Next Door*
GF NEWMAN: *Sir, You Bastard, You Flash Bastard*
KATE RHODES: *A Killing of Angels, Crossbones Yard*
JACQUI ROSE: *Trapped, Taken*
SIMON SPURRIER: *A Serpent Uncoiled, Contract*
JERRY SYKES: *Lose This Skin*
PETER TURNBULL: *Deep Cover*
SUSAN WILKINS: *The Mourner*

The South and South East

All popular entertainment fields end up chasing their tails, so why should crime fiction be any different? Most of the time, it isn't. A book or an author makes a mark with a new idea, and publishers scramble over themselves to get their authors writing similar books, staying just the right side of plagiarism. There are, however, some talented writers who are either so quirkily idiosyncratic – or just plain bloody-minded – that their books resolutely resist conforming to whatever the latest modishness is. Foremost among this admirable company is the award-winning **BELINDA BAUER**, who – in the space of half a dozen books – has become one of the most individual of crime writers. Her first novel was the very distinctive *Blacklands*, shortlisted for the Crime Writers' Association Debut Dagger and, a year later, winning the CWA Gold Dagger. Her most recent book was *Rubbernecker*, which had her admirers claiming that this was her best work, and so expectations were high for *The Shut Eye* when it appeared in 2015.

Anna Buck's son Daniel has gone missing, leaving behind only five footprints in cement as a sign that he ever existed. But this memento becomes immensely important to his devastated mother, who polishes the footprints daily as if they were religious relics. The suicidal Anna is a woman clearly hovering near the fringes of insanity, and it is hardly surprising when she turns to a TV psychic, Latham, for clues as to what happened to her son. Readers are inevitably sceptical of this man, but one beacon of hope may be on offer for Anna, if she can but take advantage of it: DCI John Marvel, who, despite a cold, withholding personality, is clearly a man who will leave no stone unturned in a search for the truth.

The Shut Eye (the expression means a genuine psychic) is very satisfying, even though in terms of inventiveness it is a notch below the impeccable form of *Blacklands* and *Rubbernecker*. But, having said that, even lesser work from Bauer is streets ahead of most of her rivals. Her secrets are easy to discern: mastery of characterisation that makes most writing in the genre seem undernourished – both the tragic Anna and the curmudgeonly copper Marvel are fully fleshed-out three-dimensional figures, the contrast between her gullibility and his cynicism piquant and sharp. And, as so often with Bauer's work, along with the quirkiness mentioned above, a growing sense of malign horror lurks at the edge of the narrative that ensures an intensity of reading experience. By the time of the climax, in which the footprints in the cement acquire a bizarre new significance, readers will find themselves rushing to the final pages.

A relatively recent trend in crime writing has been the appearance of socially committed novels set in cloistered immigrant communities in the UK. Anya Lipska tackles it with Poles in London, and **EVA**

DOLAN's ambitious *Long Way Home* focuses on Peterborough's immigrant workers, menaced by ruthless gangmasters. With two quirky coppers from non-English backgrounds and a vivid panoply of a Peterborough that is some distance from customary perceptions of the historic cathedral town, this is crime fiction of authority, making some cogent points amidst the pulse-racing stuff.

In *No Mark Upon Her* by the reliable **DEBORAH CROMBIE**, DCI Rebecca Meredith is also an Olympic rowing hopeful, but when she sets out to train on the river in Henley in late October, she disappears. The search by the police suggests that she may have been the victim of murder. Scotland Yard commissions Detective Superintendent Duncan Kincaid to investigate, and he soon discovers that the missing woman's ex-husband had a reason for wanting her dead – and he was not alone. A complex and dangerous investigation ensues. Deborah Crombie has a highly impressive list of crime novels to her name, and *No Mark Upon Her* may comfortably be regarded as a signature book.

She may be best known for her adroit historical crime fiction, but *Dying to Know*, by ex-Crime Writers' Association Chair **ALISON JOSEPH**, is a vauntingly ambitious crime novel about particle physics: contemporary fare that balances ideas and storytelling nous. *Dying to Know* is set around a (fictional) particle collider in Kent. An apparent serial killer is targeting physicists working there, and DI Berenice Killick, herself an outsider, has to investigate. A smart and thoughtful novel that circles ideas of faith and science, *Dying to Know* asks a lot of the reader but still delivers a page-turning story. Joseph has contributed to the essays in *Detective: Crime Uncovered*, a collection put together by this writer that covers both British and international crime writing.

The time may come when we grow tired of feisty female pathologists in books and on TV, but that time is not yet; this sub-genre remains as popular as ever, with new additions appearing at a rate of knots. And there will undoubtedly be a ready audience for the fifth in **NIGEL McCRERY**'s *Silent Witness* murder mystery series, in which pathologist Professor Sam Ryan (as incarnated on TV by Amanda Burton) roots among the dead flesh for clues to crack an imponderable mystery – dealing (as usual) with sceptical colleagues and contradictory evidence. While many readers would assume that Patricia Cornwell gave birth to this particular genre, she was, in fact, only the midwife, and Ed McBain was the first to bring the world of pathology into the mainstream with his *87th Precinct* thrillers. And Nigel McCrery's prose suggests that he might have gone further back for inspiration than Ms Cornwell – to the source, in fact. In the efficient *Tooth and Claw*, DCI Mark Lapslie is the victim of a rare and troubling neurological condition that cross-wires his senses. This debilitating condition has effectively ruined his marriage and put his career into a backwater. His colleagues now routinely regard him as a drunk or, worse, unbalanced. Isolating himself in an Essex coast cottage, Mark tries to attain some kind of equilibrium. At the same time, 22-year-old Carl Whittley is similarly confined to his house, caring for his crippled father. But there is a signal difference between the two men: Carl is a monster who has just tortured a minor TV celebrity to death and blown to pieces an anonymous commuter. Inevitably, these two damaged individuals are to meet in a lethal game which will have a terrifying – and very final – outcome.

COLIN DEXTER's Oxford Detective Inspector Morse is one of the key protagonists in British detective fiction – a surly, complex and brilliant character who Dexter has guided through a series of elegantly written novels. Channelling Arthur Conan Doyle's Sherlock Holmes (both the intellect and sharp temper), Inspector Morse is a figure who has triumphed on both page and screen. Morse's creator Colin Dexter shares with his sleuth a certain erudition (with a strong affection for AE Housman – Dexter is fond of quoting the poet's *A Shropshire Lad*). The highly successful TV series featuring persuasive performances by the late John Thaw as Morse made no easy bids for sympathy, and increased the popularity of the character, both cementing the sales of the books and expanding the number of Morse admirers across the globe (notably in the US). Intriguingly, the TV series actually had an impact on the books, with Dexter effecting changes in the characters. Dexter's first detective novel, *Last Bus to*

Woodstock (published in 1975), established the author as a master of the crime genre. In the book, we encounter an Inspector Morse – and his sidekick, DS Lewis – who are not the characters with whom we are now conversant. Several of the familiar notions are here (Morse's penchant for crossword puzzles, classical music and real ale), but Lewis is, in fact, the older copper, becoming younger only in the later books. We have for the first time the wonderfully drawn milieu and landscape of Oxford, in both its academic and non-academic aspects. The book was followed by such excellent entries as *Last Seen Wearing*, *The Silent World of Nicholas Quinn*, the distinctive *Service of All the Dead* in 1979 and *The Dead of Jericho* two years later, along with many others. Dexter wrote *finis* to the series with *The Remorseful Day* in 1999, which featured both Morse's death and the revelation of his first name, Endeavour.

A few pages into **HILARY BONNER**'s *No Reason to Die*, it's clear that the engine for her plot is the controversial deaths of several young soldiers at Deepcut barracks (here rendered as the isolated Hangridge army training base in the heart of Dartmoor). No doubt, a dozen other crime authors are kicking themselves that they didn't see the literary possibilities in this story with quite the alacrity of the canny Bonner (once a journalist before turning to crime), but there's an obvious danger here in trivialising a serious issue – one that's still the source of bitter dispute between the parents of the soldiers and the army authorities – for what is essentially a diverting entertainment. However, Bonner is a responsible writer, and plays fair by the source of her inspiration.

Perhaps this might be down to her years as one of Fleet Street's finest. Unhappy with the way things were going at the *Mirror*, she decided to work on some chapters that had been in her bottom drawer and turn them into a novel. And that book, *The Cruelty of Morning*, was her first success. She never looked back, and a series of unfussy, tautly paced thrillers have followed, while the indefatigable Bonner has tried her hand at several other pursuits, including being a very active chair of the Crime Writers' Association. But Bonner's métier lies in writing books such as *No Reason to Die*. Ex-reporter John Kelly has appeared before in her work; here, he's at his lowest ebb, contemplating the uninspiring spectacle of his life and finding it hard to cope with the slow, painful death of a lover. While out drinking, Kelly takes under his wing a drunken young squaddie, until the latter is spirited away by two men – fellow soldiers (Kelly assumes) at the young man's base. But then Kelly learns that he has died – and that his death is not an isolated one: several young soldiers (both men and women) have perished at the headquarters of the Devonshire Fusiliers, principally from gunshot wounds. If the final revelations don't quite have the moral force that Bonner seems to have been preparing us for, the steady stripping down of layers of misdirection shows real storytelling skill – while this book isn't likely to be on the bedside tables of many army personnel, it's a gripping read for the rest of us. After something of a hiatus in her writing career, Bonner came storming back with such books as 2015's *Death Comes First*.

Those who have followed the protean writing career of **NJ COOPER** over the years have learned to expect the unexpected – it's certainly been an unpredictable journey for the Cooper aficionado. There is no denying that the author has transmogrified into a very different entity from the writer who used the name 'Natasha', but – whatever the name – in an assured and compelling series of novels, Cooper has established a reputation as one of the most reliable of current crime fiction practitioners. In *Vengeance in Mind*, the businessman and philanthropist Dan Blackwater is discovered murdered in his house on the Isle of Wight. He is lying on the kitchen table, his body mutilated and knives transfixing his wrists and ankles. Also in the house is his personal assistant, Sheena Greeves. What is her connection with the murder? She appears to have no memory of the event, but she remains DCI Charlie Trench's prime suspect. However, Charlie is aware that things are not as they seem, and calls upon forensic psychologist Karen Taylor to help probe the distraught woman's clouded memory. But what the duo brings to light is far more than they expected. *Vengeance in Mind* is one of Cooper's most trenchant novels, bristling with her usual authoritative plotting but also taking on board the unvarnished picture of British society that has become her signature.

Cooper's Trish Maguire series (written as Natasha Cooper) was much admired; Laura Lippman wrote of *A Poisoned Mind*: 'A smart, complex, grown-up entertainment that rewards the reader on every page.' That book is a fine example of this writer's legal series about barrister Maguire, whose prime motivation is a hatred of injustice and all forms of cruelty. Here, Cooper offers a two-stranded narrative about toxic damage: one layer deals with an explosion in waste-chemical tanks on a farm in Northumberland; the other with the effects of childhood trauma and poor parenting.

While once comfortably established as a newspaper literary editor, **HENRY SUTTON**'s real vocation is as an unorthodox and provocative novelist, and *My Criminal World* is a persuasive example of his work. The book functions on a variety of levels: both as a mesmerising piece of crime fiction and as a subtle detonation of the genre. Sutton is interested in the way in which the tropes of the field work, and uses such things very much to his own ends. *My Criminal World* is proof of both his skill and the unending flexibility of the crime genre.

JUDITH CUTLER has chiselled away at the rock face of British crime writing for some considerable time, and while she might not have enjoyed the financial success of some of the more stellar names in the genre, she has quietly established a reputation for herself as a professional and reliable crime writer. The series of books featuring DS Kate Power (such us *Staying Power*, *Power Games* and *Will Power*) is so good that one can forgive Cutler the groan-inducing, punning titles that she (or her publisher) favours. *Hidden Power* is one of the most solid outings for Kate. Promotion is on the cards, and (for once) her personal life is on a roll: she's happy with lover Rod Neville, and has even won a holiday in a prize draw. Inevitably, she can hardly relax and enjoy her vacation at the South Coast holiday complex, where some very strange things are happening. Investigating what begins to look like a sinister conspiracy by working undercover as a cleaner at another venue in the same chain, she is soon in danger, barely aided by her partner Craig, an unpleasant misogynist. All the usual Cutler fingerprints are here: smooth, involving plotting and characterisation that sustains its effects through nicely drawn conflicts (this time a clash with her unlikeable colleague, who is more dangerous than the villains).

In *The Doll's House*, by hotshot **MJ ARLIDGE**, a young woman wakes in a cold dark cellar, totally disoriented – she has no idea how she arrived there or who kidnapped her. And nearby, the body of another young woman is found buried on a remote beach, but she was not considered to be missing – her family have been getting regular texts from her for years. DI Helen Grace is soon on the track of a particularly unpleasant monster. With a manipulation of tension that is always fluid and cinematic, MJ Arlidge's novel grabs the reader by the throat – as does his single-minded, unconventional policewoman Helen Grace, with her unorthodox S&M sexual tastes. More recently, the taut *Liar Liar* continued Arlidge's upwards trajectory.

Nobody – least of all the cast and crew – take the self-parodying TV series *Midsomer Murders* seriously, not least because of its ludicrous methods of dispatching the various victims. But for anyone familiar with the original novels of **CAROLINE GRAHAM** (and dismissive of the TV adaptations), one word will spring to mind again and again: plotting. This is what Graham does – impeccably. In such books as *Death in Disguise* and *A Place of Safety*, Graham has conjoined persuasive characterisation with narrative assurance of an impressive order. In *A Ghost in the Machine*, we're given a comfortable, in-each-other's-pockets community that is party to a dark secret. Kate and Mallory Lawson take possession of a relative's well-appointed house in the village of Forbes Abbot, and pleasurably anticipate the destressing that the move from metropolitan life will hopefully bring. But they're in for a disappointment: the village's internecine feuds seem to have a lethal edge. When violent death ensues, the doughty DCI Barnaby finds himself with a very tangled web – quite as baffling as the Midsomer Murders that usually keep him occupied.

In a series of elegantly written crime novels set in the past (including *The Savage Garden* and *The Information Officer*), **MARK MILLS** has demonstrated that he is a novelist of real psychological acuity, as interested in the bruising interaction of his characters as in the mechanics of the crime plot; the best writers in the genre have, of course, long practised such tactics. But there is one area that Mills has made very much his own: the untrustworthiness of appearances, and the pitfalls for those who make no attempts to look beneath seductive, attractive surfaces.

It is this notion that informs *The Long Shadow*, Mills' first book set in the modern period. And if the book does not initially exert the grip of his earlier work, this is actually part of the slow-burning strategy that – by the final chapter – renders this the most richly textured book Mills has yet written. His protagonist, Ben, has entered his forties with a faltering screenwriting career. What's more, his wife has fallen in love with a well-heeled business type, and Ben finds himself in an insalubrious flat, his life clearly in a downward spiral (another source of worry being his fractious interaction with his teenage son). But his luck suddenly appears to change: a wealthy investor is prepared to back his latest screenplay. However, all is not what it seems. Ben's generous backer is someone he knew at school, Victor Sheldon, now a hedge fund millionaire. Ben drives out to Sheldon's Oxfordshire estate to rewrite his screenplay. While there, he immerses himself in a sybaritic lifestyle, agreeing to be a business go-between and even undertaking an affair with another recipient of Sheldon's largesse, a young sculptress. But things are to turn very nasty.

The Long Shadow of the title is a Proustian one – the shadow cast by the events of childhood. The rivalry between the two schoolmates initially seems to be a thing of the past, but Ben is insufficiently rigorous in examining quite what the relationship really consisted of, and he pays a heavy price for his self-deceit. There is an echo of a literary model in the mix here: JG Farrell's *Troubles*, in which a hapless central character is slow to identify just who his enemies are. Beneath its glittering carapace, this is a rather bitter narrative, but *The Long Shadow*'s meticulousness and intelligence pay dividends.

It seems a million years ago that **PETER GUTTRIDGE** was one of the sharpest and wittiest writers of comic crime that this country has produced. He's still an excellent writer, but his territory has shifted

– not that his new sequence of Brighton-set crime novels dispenses with humour, but the tone is decidedly darker, and the world presented to the reader a much more dangerous one than any of the author's lighter novels featuring beleaguered detective Nick Madrid. This new series began as a trilogy but has now extended to five volumes – Guttridge is nothing if not unorthodox. As in the acclaimed first volume in the sequence, *City of Dreadful Night*, in *The Last King of Brighton* the benighted seaside town is every bit as menacing as that conjured by Graham Greene as a location for the murderous Pinkie to ply his trade. Criminal kingpin Dennis Hathaway maintains a successful criminal empire by a combination of ruthlessness and greasing of police palms. His son John has no idea how his father makes his money, and pursues the customary teenage enterprises of the 1960s: playing in a group and seeking sexually available girls. But as he reaches 17, John is made aware of the corruption on which his legacy is built. In the present day, John is now in charge of his father's empire, and has learned just how the world works. But then a man is found brutally murdered on the South Downs, having been tortured to death – and this act of monstrous violence is to have a seismic effect on John's life. Guttridge combines pithy and evocative scene-setting with dialogue that has the ring of authenticity, and he successfully banished the recurrent problem of the second novel in a sequence (when a lowering of temperature is almost inevitable) – this book is every bit as visceral as its predecessor. It had readers impatient for succeeding volumes – including the fifth, 2014's *Those Who Feel Nothing*.

The industrious **PETER JAMES** has always enjoyed success – in whatever genre he has tackled, from horror to the supernatural to crime (the latter his current fiefdom, though he hasn't entirely cut his earlier genres adrift). *Dead Like You* is a typical example of his increasingly popular series featuring Brighton detective Roy Grace. This one sold even more spectacularly than its predecessors, keeping crime heavyweights James Patterson and John Grisham from the number one slot in the UK bestseller lists. And after lengthy delays, Grace has made his debut on stage – in Malvern, in fact, where Shaw premiered some of his plays. So what is the secret of the James/Grace success? It's simple: over many years and many books, James has refined his storytelling skills and has the measure of the police procedural narrative. In *Dead Like You*, Brighton's Metropole Hotel is the venue for a grim crime: a woman is brutally raped when she enters a room. Subsequently, another woman is similarly assaulted – both have their shoes taken by the rapist. Working on the case, Detective Superintendent Grace realises that these two incidents have disturbing echoes of a sequence of crimes that shocked Brighton in 1997. The rapist (who earned the nickname 'The Shoe Man') notched up five victims, the last of which he had murdered before vanishing. Grace is confronted with two unpleasant possibilities: that the original Shoe Man who evaded justice ten years ago has reappeared, or – equally disturbing – there is a copycat at work.

A clever ploy that has tantalised readers of James's Grace books has been the mystery surrounding the disappearance of the detective's wife, Sandy – a disappearance that James has allowed to remain unsolved. The writer's best work, however, may be a standalone with an SF flavour, *Perfect People*.

Winner of a much-desired Crime Writers' Association Dagger, *Half Broken Things* is one of the most impressive novels from **MORAG JOSS**, a writer who has balanced total narrative authority with keen psychological underpinnings in such books as *Funeral Music* and *Fearful Symmetry*. There are two central concepts in *Half Broken Things*: the impermanence of the crust of reality that conceals uncomfortable truths, and the ineluctable hold of the past over the present. Jean Wade earns her living housesitting, but in her sixties loses her job. However, coming across the keys to the locked cupboards and secrets of the final home she is housesitting, the upscale Walden Manor, she is able to assume ownership. What follows is a strange transformation: Jean begins to change things in the house, while forging a surrogate family. This family includes Michael and Steph, who have, like Jean, not made a success of their lives, and the bolthole the trio fashion is predicated upon an extrapolated – and illusory – past. But the happiness they enjoy proves to be fragile, when hidden things from years ago begin to impinge upon their day-to-day existence. And the results for their liaison are catastrophic. The degree of insight into the subterranean aspects of the human mind are laid bare as unerringly here as in any avowedly 'literary' novel, and such specialists in this kind of narrative (in the non-crime field) as William Trevor are pleasingly echoed.

LC TYLER, as well as doing duty as chair of the Crime Writers' Association, is one of the UK's most civilised and inventive writers in comic crime territory. *The Herring in the Library*, with its Christie-esque title, might be said to be a signature book; this is very much a traditional country house mystery with a limited number of suspects, all of whom were present at the time of the murder. It also has elements of the 'locked room' mystery, and Cluedo is another theme that runs through the book – Colonel Mustard and Miss Scarlet are mentioned in the opening and many of the rooms in the house have the same names as rooms on the Cluedo board. The assembled guests at Muntham Court become aware over dinner that there are tensions in the room. In the middle of the meal, Sir Robert stands and makes a short speech – each of the guests, he says, occupies a special place in his life and he intends that the evening will be a very special one for them. He then leaves the room. There is some speculation as to what he is planning, but, shortly afterwards, he is discovered in his locked library – strangled. A deliciously witty parody (as are all Len Tyler's books) that still functions on its own terms.

Slowly but surely, **LEIGH RUSSELL** has been building a reputation as a solid practitioner of the modern crime genre, and *Dead End* is a worthy addition to her CV. The body of headmistress Abigail Kirby is found by the police; her tongue has been cut out as she lay dying. Russell's copper, DI Geraldine Steel, realises she is up against an unpleasant nemesis when a witness is blinded and then killed. But Geraldine has other problems on her plate apart from the violence erupting around her: her daughter has left home to meet a girl she made friends with online – and this action may well have grim consequences. At the same time, DS Ian Peterson is drawing closer to the serial killer, and both police officers are in for an encounter that will take them into the darkest recesses of the human psyche.

Steel and Peterson are a strikingly realised duo in a field that is overcrowded with such teams, but Russell has the smarts to render her protagonists in such a way that we're not reminded of her many rivals. At nearly 400 pages, this is one of the longest of the author's books, but crime fiction admirers will find that those pages turn very swiftly.

SIMON SHAW fashioned a line in Shakespearean titles with such novels as *Bloody Instructions* and *Dead for a Ducat*. Synthesising the cold-eyed psychological intensity of Ruth Rendell with a laser-sharp observation of the social scene, Shaw's speciality has been a series of carefully arranged *danses macabres* between his characters. In *Killing Grace*, he incorporates a destabilising element: the motivations of his three protagonists unfold in a continually disorientating fashion, constantly inviting the reader to think they have the necessary bearings, only to abandon the compass.

The charismatic Lewis is irresistible to women, and his work as a builder allows him to avail himself of the houses, beds and sexual charms of his clients' wives. But his dalliances are beginning to lose their charm: he is broke, and he's finding it harder to stick to his motto – don't get involved. The seductive Julie has made him break his code, and his relationship with her lasts long after he finishes the job on her house. Peter McGovern is a very different kettle of fish: wealthy, but as unappealing as Lewis is attractive. But Julie is his wife, and when the two men meet by accident over a game of pool, all three lives will be changed irrevocably. Mixed into this dangerous brew is the deceptively angelic Grace, whose fragile good looks conceal a ruthless sensibility and an acerbic tongue. When she becomes involved with both men, the outcome for one or more of the characters is bound to be bloody. Shaw's smoothly amoral tale is notable for its dispassionate telling: the author never nudges his readers but guides them inexorably through a narrative that becomes ever more sinister.

Lindy and her teenage daughter Izzy move to Stagcote Manor in the Cotswolds in what they hope will be a much-needed new start for them. They leave behind an unhappy life in London, but the alienated daughter is almost immediately unhappy, feeling trapped in a new existence that was supposed to be the answer to their problems. There is something about their new house that subtly disturbs her, and as she explores it (and the village in which it is located) she comes to believe that a host of local superstitions held by the villagers all relate to the manor. As she begins to investigate, it appears that these superstitions have a rational – and dangerous – basis. **RS PATEMAN**'s *The Prophecy of Bees* is psychological suspense delivered with great skill by an author much acclaimed for his debut, *The Second Life of Amy Archer*.

In a very short time, the writing reputation of **ISABELLE GREY** has achieved the kind of status that other writers take years to attain, and her considerable experience working in television has given her work a strong visual component. And her Colchester-set *Good Girls Don't Die* provides a clear demonstration of her skills. Accused of grassing up a fellow officer and driven out of home and job, DS Grace Fisher is licking her wounds while working in the Major Crimes Investigation Team in Essex. A female student goes missing, last seen at a popular bar in Colchester. Then a second student is murdered and left in a grotesquely posed position…

FELIX FRANCIS novels bear the strapline 'A Dick Francis Novel' – as Hemingway didn't quite say, 'The Son Also Rises'. In *Damage*, Jeff Hinkley is a resourceful undercover investigator for the British Horseracing Authority. He is used to double-dealing and crooked behaviour in the equestrian fraternity, but, while looking into the unorthodox activities of a racehorse trainer at the Cheltenham Racing Festival, he finds himself investigating a brutal murder. Is the death related to the initial reason why the trainer was banned – the administering of illegal drugs to horses? As earlier Felix Francis outings such as *Silks* have demonstrated, the Dick Francis franchise is ticking over in the hands of his son and heir. Francis *fils* had been involved with his father's novels in various capacities for over 40 years, and he is adept at forging a simulacrum of the familiar style. The original flavour is here, and Dick Francis fans probably won't complain.

VERONICA STALLWOOD has made a speciality of the Oxford-set crime novel, often matching (and at times surpassing) that other purveyor of crime under the Dreaming Spires, Colin Dexter. Her prose has a brisk, no-nonsense efficiency, and her sense of locale is always sure-footed – she has lived in Oxford for many years, and knows well both the city and its university. Yet she views Oxford with the sharp eye of an outsider and brings it to life in an unsentimental way, far removed from the chocolate-box images usually shown on television. She flings open the oaken doors of venerable colleges and shows what's really happening inside, based on her own experience of working at the Bodleian, Oxford's library, as well as in various colleges. And her sleuth, Kate Ivory, a 30-something romantic novelist, is also less than perfect – 'a flesh-and-brains heroine', as one critic put it, who enjoys white wine, chocolate biscuits and the company of unsuitable men. An ever-expanding circle of friends and lovers, not to mention her mother and her literary agent, has joined Kate over the years, developing strong characters and stories of their own. Stallwood's 'Oxford' novels, published from 1993 onwards, include *Oxford Exit*, *Oxford Knot* and *Oxford Letters*, with the fourteenth – and final – title being *Oxford Ransom*. These ingenious novels (all of which feature the resourceful Kate) have a devoted following. And Stallwood's finely tuned standalone suspense novel *The Rainbow Sign*, based on her experience in the Lebanon, demonstrated that her adroit plotting matched that of any of her contemporaries.

Experienced TV writer **SIMON BOOKER**'s Morgan Vine in *Without Trace* is an ace investigative journalist. At least, that was the plan. But at 36 her career is in the doldrums and her love life's a joke. She's living in a converted railway carriage on the beach at Dungeness and still carrying a torch for her old flame, Danny Kilcannon. He's in prison, convicted of murdering his stepdaughter. But Morgan knows he's innocent, so she helps him to win his appeal and regain his freedom. But when her own daughter goes missing, Morgan is forced to confront the possibility that she might have been wrong – and that the love of her life might be a ruthless killer after all… *Without Trace* is set to be the first in the series of psychological thrillers featuring Vine, and Booker's hard-won expertise is evident on every page.

His face is familiar from many television appearances, and his voice from lengthy radio duty. **MARK LAWSON** may be best known as a formidably well-read cultural commentator and interviewer, but a particular speciality is crime fiction, and his insights into the genre are nonpareil – for several years, he has been a key figure at the Harrogate crime writing festival. Although he had been a novelist in the past, 2013 marked his return to fiction with the distinctive *The Depths*. The book is set in Buckinghamshire and deals with a dramatis personae who enjoy a sheltered lifestyle while the rest of the UK suffers from cuts and austerity. An act of violence upsets this ordered pattern, and Lawson's delineation of its grim consequences demonstrates the hand of a master.

WILLIAM SHAW's *A Song from Dead Lips* was a novel that arrived with considerable fanfare from its publisher and an encomium from the celebrated historical crime writer CJ Sansom. It is, in fact, a period piece itself, set in the Swinging Sixties but concerned with exploring the darker undercurrents of the summer of peace and love – and thus not up for consideration in a study devoted to contemporary-set crime fiction. Shaw, however, produced (in 2016) a novel set in the present day that is quite as adroitly written as his earlier work. *The Birdwatcher* is a stygian and intelligent crime novel that takes in both the Troubles in Northern Ireland and a contemporary murder investigation, dealing with the Ulster Volunteer Force, migrants in Kent and modern-day policing. In Dungeness, Police Sergeant William South has a keen reason for not wanting to be on a murder investigation: he is himself a murderer (the victim was his only friend). A quiet, reticent birdwatcher, South finds himself paired with the strong-willed DS Alexandra Cupidi, newly recruited to the Kent coast from London. Together they find a body, violently beaten, inside a wooden chest. But – too precipitately – they light upon a suspect: Donnie Fraser, a drifter from Northern Ireland. His presence in Kent disturbs South because he knows him. As a boy, South and his mother fled their home in County Armagh, and, for many reasons, he has never looked back. If the past is catching up with him, South wants to meet it head-on. *The Birdwatcher* is a pungent, powerful tale that takes on the apprehension of a life lived in fear of retribution. Shaw's Breen & Tozer series is splendid, but let's hope he tackles the present again – albeit with the past looming in Damoclean fashion.

Is this a recipe for success? Take one long-established literary copper (such as RD Wingfield's misanthropic DS Frost), in cold storage since the death of his creator, and hand him to two younger writers to reinvigorate the character... two writers, what's more, who clearly haven't got much sympathy for the miserable old bugger. Somebody at the publisher deserved a pat on the back for the notion, however, as – against all the odds – the success of *First Frost* (first fruit of the duo's collaboration) was incontestable: this became a palpable hit, and proved that there was plenty of life in the terminally un-PC Jack Frost. Which may or may not have been good news for the writers James Gurbutt and Henry Sutton (then working together as 'JAMES HENRY'), who were obliged to continue chronicling Frost's investigations: their Frankenstein monster had them by the scruff of the neck. Actually, there are precedents for not liking one's characters: the best film featuring Mickey Spillane's thick-ear detective Mike Hammer, *Kiss Me Deadly*, is a dark surrealistic gem made by a director (Robert Aldrich) who loathed the brutal gumshoe.

Ironically, *First Frost* received an imprimatur from the actor David Jason, who incarnated the character on TV for so many years (and, it has to be said, softened the rough-tongued copper into someone more lovable); his words of praise for the novel have one wondering how closely he read it.

One of the many clever touches here is the strategy of taking the reader back to the detective's early years. In recession-hit 1981 Britain, as the IRA plans its mainland campaign, workaholic DS Jack Frost (even at this younger age not noted for sartorial elegance or liberal opinions) is already an irritant for his superior, Superintendent Mullet. The alcoholic head of the CID has disappeared, but his booze-fuelled absences are habitual; a second disappearance, that of the second-in-command DI Allen, is perhaps more significant. Frost has his hands full with the chaotic state of the vermin-infested police station, missing colleagues and a 12-year-old girl who has been abducted from a department store. While the exact location of the fictional town of Denton is never established, the authors (in an interview on the *Shots* website) have stated that it is somewhere in the vicinity of Slough or Reading.

To those who study the entrails of such things, it's no surprise that *First Frost* is so bitterly diverting. James Gurbutt is a publisher who worked for the late Wingfield's original publishing house, and Henry Sutton, ex-literary editor of the *Daily Mirror*, has written several acerbically entertaining novels under his own name. The duo (now separated) show an effortless command of the idiom here, but perhaps their dislike of the protagonist, once described as 'the most unattractive cop in mainstream crime fiction', was the sand in the oyster that has produced this dark pearl.

The 15 books in **DOROTHY SIMPSON**'s eminently consistent Inspector Thanet series are set in Kent, and it is difficult to choose which one is the most representative. Perhaps a bid may be made for two titles: *Puppet for a Corpse* and *Last Seen Alive* – the latter, in fact, bagged the Crime Writers' Association Silver Dagger, a notable bauble.

Other writers and key books

CATHERINE AIRD: *Little Knell, The Complete Steel*
JO BANNISTER: *Breaking Faith*
VICTORIA BLAKE: *Cutting Blades, Skin and Blister*
GLENN CHANDLER: *Dead Sight, Savage Tide*
ELIZABETH CORLEY: *Requiem Mass*
LIZ EVANS: *Who Killed Marilyn Monroe?, Sick As a Parrot*
ELIZABETH HAYNES: *Revenge of the Tide*
DERYN LAKE: *Dead on Cue, The Mills of God*
AMY MYERS: *Murder in Hell's Corner, Classic in the Barn*
MARK PETERSON: *Flesh and Blood*
PAULINE ROWSON: *Undercurrent, Footsteps on the Shore*
REBECCA WHITNEY: *The Liar's Chair*

The Midlands

Is the following a Britain that you recognise? Violent confrontations between young black males in urban areas, which end up with somebody bleeding from a stab wound or a bullet? Or Eastern European pimps, trafficking vulnerable young women into this country for enforced sexual slavery? Or a police force hamstrung by constant accusations that they are not respecting the human rights of the criminals?

A *Daily Mail* editorial? No, this is the world we are taken into by one of the most respected writers in this country, whose record as poet and publisher consolidates his credentials as an unimpeachable part of the literary establishment. So when **JOHN HARVEY** presents this scarifying picture of Britain in his Nottingham- and London-set novel *Cold in Hand*, attention must be paid – in fact, reading this worrying but utterly trenchant book will be a more disquieting experience for readers of the *Guardian* than the *Mail*, as liberal shibboleths are toppled. With utterly unflinching rigour, Harvey strip-mines this dystopian society and renders the contemporary horrors with customary skill. Policewoman Lynn Kellogg is caught between brawling street gangs, and unwisely attempts to defuse the situation. The result is bloody mayhem: one young girl is mutilated, another lies dead, shot by a young man wearing a bandanna wrapped tightly round his head. The policewoman herself is shot and hospitalised. She is visited by her anxious lover, another copper – whose name happens to be Charlie Resnick. Now (Harvey fans may feel), we can relax. Good old Charlie, mainstay of the Nottingham police force, jazz lover, a man whose very presence reassures us that some kind of order can be brought out of the chaos. Such consolations, however, are not what John Harvey is dispensing in this book: at every opportunity, he snatches away from us the feeling that all could be made right in this worst of all possible worlds. The problems Charlie runs up against while investigating the death of the girl are only the tip of the iceberg, and some very nasty people traffickers are stirred into the lethal brew. As in so much of the best crime fiction, what we have here is basically a state of the nation novel, and Harvey repeatedly suggests that his own vision may have become as nihilistic as that of the sociopathic characters that populate *Cold in Hand*. But this is no hand-wringing tract – the book is quite possibly Harvey's most authoritative in years: visceral, engaged and, yes, unputdownable. One hopes that Harvey's announced retirement from the crime genre is temporary – readers would be sure to welcome more outings for Resnick, and for retired copper Frank Elder, who features in a more recent series.

Like Dickens' fat boy, **SJ BOLTON** (aka Sharon Bolton) is in the business of making our flesh creep, and such books as *Sacrifice* demonstrated how comfortable she is with the orchestration of tension. Does your repertoire of quotes from Friedrich Nietzsche consist only of the shop-worn 'that which does not kill us makes us stronger'? If so, it's time to add a second quote that's rapidly moving up the Nietzschean hit parade: the one about avoiding battling monsters for fear of becoming a monster yourself (and its chaser: if you gaze into the abyss, it will also gaze into you). The latter makes an appearance in Bolton's frisson-generating *Blood Harvest*, and it's hardly surprising that this particular aphorism is so popular with crime writers: after all, it's basically a paradigm for 99 per cent of the genre in the twenty-first century. What makes *Blood Harvest* such a satisfyingly atmospheric 400-odd pages, however, is its clever synthesis of two sure-fire strategies: the slow-burning supernatural mystery in which the dark secret of a town or community is gradually uncovered by a vulnerable protagonist; and the dark psychological crime narrative.

The later *Dead Scared* is constructed in prismatic fashion, with each brief segment creating a chilling totality, and if the theme here is familiar – the mysterious suicides of undergraduate students – the treatment is decidedly original. The unfortunately named Detective Lacey Flint is handed a tough assignment. After a gruesome series of suicides at Cambridge University, involving immolation and decapitation, Flint is persuaded by her boss, DI Mark Joesbury, to go undercover and assume the role of a psychology undergraduate, working with the one person who will know her real identity: the psychologist Evi Oliver. Adopting a nervous, vulnerable persona, Flint is able to discover just what has driven so many female undergraduates to take their own lives. With the psychologist and her distant boss her only contact with the outside world, Flint's initial confidence that she can deal with the situation is eroded when a truly terrifying onslaught of mass bullying comes her way. More than in previous books, Bolton utilises extremely brief chapters in the fashion of James Patterson, but (unlike Patterson) she never forgets that characterisation is equally important in a novel such as *Dead Scared*. She even freights in the device of unresolved sexual attraction; Flint and her boss Joesbury clearly belong in bed together, but frustratingly – both for them and for the reader – that consummation does not happen. But, as in the best work of Stephen King (a writer Bolton clearly admires), the balance of human sympathy and ever-accelerating disquiet is handled with real authority, building to a truly vertiginous climax.

STEPHEN BOOTH is a reliable, if unspectacular, author, and such books as *Lost River* suggest a writer of skill. The book begins with the tragic drowning of a young girl in the idyllic setting of Dovedale. Detective Ben Cooper witnesses the event but is unable to help – and as he gets to know the dead girl's family, he discovers a well-hidden dark secret. Booth enjoys walking the hills of the Peak District, and the sense of place here is palpable. Such psychological thrillers as *Blind to the Bones* and *Black Dog* were already strong work from Booth, but *Lost River* is one of his most accomplished.

Set in a fictitious town (but probably in Derbyshire), **SARAH WARD**'s *In Bitter Chill* arrived with encomiums from a respected trio of writers: Yrsa Sigurdardóttir, William Ryan and Chris Ewan. This impressive crime debut is the work of a writer best known for the website *Crime Pieces* and as one of the Petrona Award judges for translated Scandinavian crime fiction. It's a debut that hits the ground running, showing that the author has the measure of the exigencies of the police procedural and – more importantly – the conflicted psychology of her characters. The novel begins in 1978 with the disappearance of two young girls. One of them, Rachel Jones, returns, her memory of events fogged, and lives on to become a central character in the narrative. Her companion Sophie Jenkins is never found. Thirty years pass, and the suicide of the missing girl's mother sets in train a sequence of new events that will have significant consequences for the damaged Rachel. While it is true to say that Sarah Ward does nothing radical with the apparatus of the crime novel, she proves to be highly adept at characterisation – notably of the unhappy Rachel – and passes with flying colours the test of making her team of coppers distinctive and vividly characterised. The dénouement, too, is unlikely to be guessed even by diehard aficionados of the genre.

The amiable **MEL SHERRATT** made something of a mark with *Taunting the Dead*, set in her native Stoke-on-Trent, and followed this up with a genuinely unsettling tale of a child's game being given a sinister grown-up twist. The second book in the DS Allie Shenton sequence, *Follow the Leader*, begins with a man's body being discovered on a canal tow path. In his pocket is a magnetic letter of the alphabet. Some days later, a second victim is discovered with the letter 'D' tucked into her clothing. It becomes clear to Allie and her team that, in order to track down a ruthless killer, they must play the eponymous children's game. Sherratt's work is direct, unfussy and involving.

For some considerable time, the hardworking **ANN GRANGER** has been consolidating her reputation as one of the most reliable practitioners of the crime fiction genre, a process continued with *A Better Quality of Murder* (though that book – and the others in her sequence featuring Lizzie Martin – has a Victorian setting, so is not for this study). She is content to work within the parameters of the field in her more contemporary series (of which she has three: Fran Varady, Campbell & Carter and Mitchell & Markby), but there is plenty of room for an author who consistently manages to ring the changes as satisfyingly as Granger does.

Other writers and key books
HELEN BLACK: *Blood Rush, A Place of Safety*
JENNY BLACKHURST: *How I Lost You*
MAUREEN CARTER: *A Question of Despair, Dead Old*
JEAN CHAPMAN: *Deadly Serious, A Watery Grave*

AJ CROSS: *Art of Deception, Gone in Seconds*
ROD DUNCAN: *Backlash, Burnout*
STEVEN DUNNE: *The Unquiet Grave, The Reaper*
PRISCILLA MASTERS: *Smoke Alarm, A Fatal Cut*
ANN PURSER: *Sorrow on Sunday*
CHARLIE WILLIAMS: *One Dead Hen, King of the Road*

The North West

New entries in the thriller field now have to be tougher than the rest in order to make their mark. This is something that the clubbable Liverpool-born **ED CHATTERTON** accomplishes effortlessly in *A Dark Place to Die*. Ed was educated at the same primary school as this writer, but that buys him no favours here (he doesn't need them, anyway!). This key novel, vividly written, begins on a cold winter's morning. DI Frank Keane is summoned to the scene of a crime on the shoreline of Liverpool. The body appears to be that of a man, but it has been systematically tortured and burned, and is now tied to a pole on the beach. With comparatively little evidence, Keane and his partner DS Emily Harris have a hunch that the killing is gang-related, and they begin an investigation that takes them into the dark world of organised crime. Chatterton is a notable and distinctive practitioner in the crime fiction field, and also works profitably in other genres.

The socially committed **NICHOLAS BLINCOE** made a considerable mark with the unorthodox *Acid Casuals*, taking the reader into a variety of threatening criminal milieus in the city of Manchester, a key stamping ground for the author. Blincoe has an intimate acquaintance with the trendy, sometimes minatory world of the Manchester club scene, awash with drugs and various unsavoury criminal types who control the nominal managers. The antihero of *Acid Casuals* is not your typical crime novel protagonist; he is a young man who samples this scene while concealing a secret identity: that of a Brazilian transsexual. She returns to Manchester for revenge on her old boss, and what follows is dark and quirky fare indeed. Blincoe is a notably political writer – less so here than usual, but his genre filigrees are welcome and unusual.

Merseyside is the customary haunt of **RON ELLIS**, with such efficient if unspectacular books as *Grave Mistake*; while staying in the business for years, Ellis has never made the breakthrough that many of his contemporaries have enjoyed. Heiress Joanna Smithson is abducted from a Liverpool car park, and her father, fearing the kidnappers' actions if he involves the police, calls in DJ-cum-private eye Johnny Ace, counting on his celebrated problem-solving skills. But as soon as Johnny gets involved, Joanna kills one of her captors in self-defence, and she finds herself in court with the prosecution forging a case that presents her as a murderer. Johnny has his work cut out attempting to prove her innocence, and he has another case to tax him: he has been requested by a writer on the Wavertree Corinthians football team to find goalkeeper David Blease, who disappeared from Liverpool 20 years ago. Anybody who knows their Raymond Chandler know that any investigator simultaneously engaged on two cases is in for big trouble, and that's certainly the case here. Ace, frankly, is an unlikely character, but he is markedly different from most bruisers in an overcrowded field. Ellis draws on his own DJ background to infuse his books with an authenticity that makes his frequently outrageous plotting plausible.

Still on Merseyside, **KEVIN SAMPSON**'s distinctive *Clubland* is set in a Liverpool every bit as dangerous as any American city: we are plunged into a sleazy ghetto of sex tourists, strippers and drug addicts, where life is every bit as cheap as on Elmore Leonard's Delta. Sampson's north of England setting in *Clubland* is marked by its narrow horizons constrained by placing the action between Runcorn and Birkenhead, via the mean streets of Liverpool. But the language here has all the demented idiosyncrasy of American writers, with violent criminal Ged Brennan's first-person narration voicing his irritation with the young thugs stealing his thunder in a form of often impenetrable dialect that resembles nothing so much as a Scouse version of Anthony Burgess's Nadsat in *A Clockwork Orange* (although viewers of the TV drama show *Brookside* may know that 'keks' are trousers). Sampson allows us little respite from his relentlessly unpleasant dramatis personae – even the progressive-minded Margo, with her visions of urban regeneration, is an unsympathetic character. *Clubland* is a deeply amoral immersion in a mean-spirited world, where the interlacing of cut-throat humour barely undercuts the omnipresent menace. Things have changed since Raymond Chandler's day – now it would appear that British crime writers are quite as tough as the Yanks.

Killing the Beasts was a disturbing psychological thriller that dealt with ideas that also appeared in **CHRIS SIMMS'** first two novels – compulsion and mental instability. The idea for his debut novel, 2003's *Outside the White Lines*, came to him one night when broken down on the hard shoulder of a motorway. Staccato chapters alternate between the viewpoints of The Searcher, The Hunter and The Killer, each character roaming the roads of Britain in pursuit of his own obsessive agenda. Simms followed this up with another standalone, *Pecking Order*. Largely set on a battery farm, the plot follows the naïve but cruel Rubble who is duped into believing that he's been enrolled as an agent on a sinister government project. Partly inspired by the 1960s experiments of Stanley Milgram into man's obedience to authority, the novel also touches on such diverse issues as euthanasia and the ethics of factory farming. Simms then changed publishers with *Killing the Beasts*, which inaugurated the series featuring Manchester policeman DI Jon Spicer. Descended from the Irish immigrants who helped build the world's first industrial city, Spicer never shies away from Manchester's violent and lawless corners in his investigations. The novel is set during 2002, with the city's hosting of that year's Commonwealth Games providing a spectacular backdrop to the action. The plot revolves around a killer who, apart from sealing his victims' airways with a viscous gel, leaves them totally unscathed.

The follow-up novel in the series, *Shifting Skin*, deals with an equally macabre killer (one who uses surgical skills to remove large swathes of his victims' flesh), while *Savage Moon* contains multiple references to the horror classic *An American Werewolf in London* – the novel is concerned with a brutal killing that takes place on the notorious Saddleworth Moor, to the edge of the city. Simms attracts critical acclaim for the fashion in which he combines details of DI Spicer's domestic life with pithy descriptions of police procedure and convincing glimpses into the minds of his (rather unlikely) killers.

The fact that the hard-working **CATH STAINCLIFFE** is among the most productive of crime novelists (in a variety of areas) does not alter the fact that she is one of the most imaginative and consistent writers in the field. That's very much the case with her contributions – which she produces in tandem with her own dedicated work – to the novels based on the TV franchise Scott and Bailey. In titles such as *Ruthless*, Staincliffe develops Britain's answer to the female cop team Cagney and Lacey with impressive new levels of psychological depth, as the duo investigates the death of a man in an abandoned chapel that has been set on fire.

The industrious **BILL JAMES** has long enjoyed a reputation as one of the most authoritative crime writers in Britain today, and each new book adds lustre to this reputation – it's a mystery why (as yet) his sales don't match those of many a far less talented author. But is life (or publishing) ever fair? In *Girls*, Assistant Chief Constable Desmond Iles has been quietly tolerating the activities of drug lords Ralph Ember and Mansel Shale, as there are far more dangerous villains around. But when foreign dealers move on to the scene, the ante is upped for everyone – with spectacularly nasty results. This is another first-rate novel from the ever-reliable James, whose *Play Dead* appeared in 2013.

The very well-read **MARTIN EDWARDS** has enjoyed acclaim for a variety of endeavours, of which his day job (as a lawyer) is perhaps the least known. He is one of the UK's premier crime fiction anthologists, as well as being a noted expert on the Golden Age of crime fiction; his most recent book on the subject arrived with an encomium from no less than Len Deighton. *The Golden Age of Murder*, subtitled 'The mystery of the writers who invented the modern detective story', is the first book about the prestigious Detection Club, the celebrated social networking/dining club for crime writers; it also doubles as an examination of the great Golden Age writers who energised the form, such as Agatha Christie and Dorothy Sayers. And there are few writers better qualified than the knowledgeable Edwards to tell the story, which stretches from the now distant past to the edgy present. It's a picture of a little-known aspect of the cultural history of Great Britain.

Edwards' own two crime fiction series, set in different locales, have proved to be both critically and commercially successful, notably the Harry Devlin novels set in Liverpool. Devlin, like his creator, is in the legal profession, and such books as *Yesterday's Papers* offer both the diversions of crime fiction and vivid scene-setting of a high order. His second series is set in the Lake District and features a female and a male protagonist, policewoman Hannah Scarlett and historian Daniel Kind; the first book of the sequence was *The Coffin Trail*. *The Dungeon House*, the most recent in the series at the time of writing, sports Edwards' usual expertise.

NEIL WHITE's series of five books featuring crime reporter Jack Garrett and detective Laura McGanity enjoyed considerable acclaim. However, his fifth book in the series, *Cold Kill*, was followed by a standalone book, *Beyond Evil*, before a move to a new publisher saw him launch his new series with *Next to Die*. Once again, it featured two principal characters whose jobs put them in conflict, this time two brothers: Sam and Joe Parker, one a detective, the other a defence lawyer. The third book, *The Domino Killer*, begins with a man found beaten to death in a Manchester park. Then Detective Sam Parker discovers that the victim's fingerprints were found at another crime scene. This is more authentic, gritty crime writing from Neil White, who still works as a criminal lawyer as well as being a bestselling writer of crime fiction. His work has a real sense of palpable threat, something that is all too lacking in many contemporary crime novels.

LUCA VESTE enjoys an unusual heritage for a crime writer, an intriguing combination of Italy and Liverpool. The companionable writer studied psychology and criminology at the University of Liverpool and has edited the anthologies *Off the Record* and *True Brit Grit*. The caustic *Dead Gone* was a strikingly original debut, with a particular gift for characterisation and, perhaps unsurprisingly, a notable skill at evoking his native city (into which he freights some cogent social commentary). Veste also sports a pronounced taste for the macabre, which is given full rein in such books as *The Dying Place* and *Bloodstream*. Part psychological thrillers, part police procedurals, the Murphy and Rossi novels take in both sides of a contrasting city, exploring the changing landscape of Liverpool. In *Bloodstream*, mavens of social media Chloe Morrison and Joe Hooper are enjoying their celebrity when it is cruelly snatched away from them, along with their lives. Hard-bitten coppers DI David Murphy and DS Laura Rossi are to find that there is something rotten not just in the world of social media but in the police force itself. Astringent and artfully constructed crime writing that reinvigorates the shop-worn police procedural format.

CONRAD WILLIAMS – whose fiction leans towards the darker end of the spectrum – wrote *Dust and Desire* as an homage to Derek Raymond, whose Factory series left a deep impression upon him. The book deals with the dedication of youth versus the dogged determination of middle age, all underpinned by various familial tragedies. *Dust and Desire* attempts to limn the ugly urban jungles of the city with profane humour and a poetic style. The action takes place primarily in London, and is delivered from the driven protagonist Joel Sorrell's point of view, but episodes from the antagonist's past in Liverpool take up part of the novel, with the climactic scene acted out on the shed roof of St Pancras station.

Other writers and key books
TOM BENN: *Chamber Music, The Doll Princess*
PAULA DALY: *The Mistake I Made*
JM GREGSON: *A Little Learning, Least of Evils*
MANDASUE HELLER: *Lost Angel, The Game*
PHIL LOVESEY: *The Screaming Tree*
SARAH RAYNE: *The Death Chamber, Tower of Silence*

The North East

Not many writers have done it, but **DAVID PEACE** single-handedly forged a new crime genre: Yorkshire Noir. In 1999, the bitter *Nineteen Seventy Four* inaugurated his *Red Riding Quartet*, with the pungent *Nineteen Seventy Seven* the second book in the series. Like the first novel, the book vividly evokes the period and the corruption that was endemic in the police force during that time. Peace's troubled protagonists, policeman Bob Fraser and cynical reporter Jack Whitehead, are the reader's guides through a society where justice is always hard to find. Peace's youth in Ossett during the hunt for the Yorkshire Ripper imbued him with memories that continued to haunt him and supplied the basis and inspiration for the quartet. *Nineteen Eighty* (2001) and *Nineteen Eighty Three* (2002) were equally provocative and disturbing, showing that invention was still possible in an exhausted genre.

Surprisingly, Peace demonstrated that he could create another sequence of breadth and ambition – and *Occupied City*, the second part of his *Tokyo* trilogy continues the momentum of the first book, *Tokyo Year Zero*. The contrast with the earlier Yorkshire-set sequence could not be more extreme – except for a similarly dark and merciless view of humanity. The book marries a sweeping historical canvas with a tough crime narrative.

Many crime scribes lie awake at night, casting around for an innovation – any innovation – that will reinvigorate the genre. After all, hasn't everything been done? Alcoholic copper struggling with messy private life? Police superiors who try to bury inconvenient cases? And – most egregious cliché of all – the conflict between a cynical male copper and his put-upon female colleague (who always, of course, shows that she is no pushover)? **PETER ROBINSON** has discovered the perfect solution to this irksome problem for crime writers: he takes the clashing male/female copper motif and shoots it full of adrenaline, always finding some new wrinkle to convince us that we are encountering this scenario for the very first time. *All the Colours of Darkness*, one of the most distinctive books in his sequence featuring DCI Alan Banks and his associate DI Annie

Cabbot, is a salutary reminder why readers are so comfortable with the series: it's an old friend, but a friend that can still come up with the odd provocative remark to pique our attention. A body is discovered, and the copper in charge (this time, Annie Cabbot) is forced to call in her reluctant superior (a notably pissed-off Alan Banks) when it becomes apparent that the killing is something very unusual: it appears to be a double death involving gay partners. Mark Hardcastle, a popular set designer for a Yorkshire theatre, is found hanging near a river. When Annie calls upon his partner, Laurence Silbert, at the couple's expensive house, she finds him lying among the Chagalls and Kandinskys, his head beaten to a pulp. Is it a murder followed by a suicide? Both Banks and Cabbot are too wily to accept such an easy solution, and they begin digging into some very clandestine areas where all moral parameters are nebulous, and everyone involved – both police and suspects – appears to be in danger.

Is it a compliment to say that reading a Peter Robinson novel is like slipping into a well-worn pair of slippers? Certainly, the reader can relax in the knowledge that all the buttons we expect to be pressed when savouring a police procedural will be satisfyingly pushed, and the comforting rituals of the experience all duly namechecked by a consummate professional. But Robinson also has a way of undercutting the quotidian familiarity of the genre, and, with a deceptively unspectacular use of language, he sets about the process of thoroughly unsettling the reader. Robinson is also, of course, a man who does plotting with assurance – the kind of plotting, in fact, that exerts a considerable grip.

Slowly but surely, **JOHN BAKER**'s series featuring the tenacious Sam Turner acquired much favourable word-of-mouth, with *Poet in the Gutter* and *Death Minus Zero* nosing ahead in the popularity stakes (though we haven't heard much from him lately – he appears to have forsaken the genre). Baker struck out at a tangent in the Hull-set *The Chinese Girl*, with a narrative so rich with menace that readers didn't miss the absent Turner. Released from jail, Stone Lewis is trying to change his wasted life into something positive. Ill-advised tattoos on his face have people shying away from him as he wanders the outside world, and when he finds a battered Asian girl in the doorway of his insalubrious basement room, it isn't long before he's firmly back in the dangerous morass that he had tried to escape. We've read a million versions of the ex-con pulled back unwillingly into the criminal world before, but rarely delivered with the exuberance that Baker demonstrates here. He's also particularly skilful at marrying the disparate worlds of the American tough-guy thriller with the English novel of cold-eyed social observation. The cleverest trick here is making the non-tattooed reader identify so closely with the hapless Lewis, and we follow his dangerous odyssey with total attention. The danger is offset by Baker's trademark wit, and the novel was a welcome break from the Sam Turner series.

On Dangerous Ground? Well, one can forgive **LESLEY HORTON** cheekily re-using a title that firmly belongs to a famous noir movie. This book is very different from the earlier *Snares of Guilt*; it is a socially engaged piece in which all the minute observation is quite as important as the steadily accelerating thriller plot. The city of Bradford has a stated policy: there is no child prostitution crisis to deal with, as the problem doesn't exist. But DI John Handford and Sergeant Khalid Ali know that things are not quite that simple. A young girl and young boy are savagely murdered, and the two detectives find themselves in the middle of a truly disturbing criminal web in which children are becoming inextricably enmeshed in the city's lower depths, while the establishment attempts to draw a veil over the unacceptable facts. Horton herself has long experience of the issues she deals with here, and they are handled responsibly and intelligently but never at the expense of compelling writing. She is good on the racial clashes of the city, and while the ending may be discernible early on to the alert reader, the marriage of sociological observation and good thriller writing is accomplished.

Many of the best crime fiction novelists – from Elmore Leonard to Donald Westlake (when writing as Richard Stark) – are well aware that the withholding of moral judgements on their violent characters is a risky endeavour. It's undoubtedly true that stripped-down prose about totally amoral characters performing lethal actions can have an exhilarating effect, but those readers who are not criminals themselves (the majority, one would have thought) might be likely to find themselves alienated from such protagonists. But when the trick can be pulled off, the result can be writing that leaps off the page in its lacerating forcefulness. This is very much the case with **HOWARD LINSKEY**'s *The Drop*, a classic British gangster novel that evokes and matches some of the best writing in the genre, notably the iconic *Jack's Return Home* (*Get Carter*) by the late Ted Lewis, in its use of an unromanticised Newcastle setting. In fact, it's a measure of Linskey's audacity to go up against Lewis in using a milieu that was so thoroughly colonised by the earlier novel, but such is Linskey's authority that we admire both his chutzpah and his ability to stand comparison with any of his predecessors. White-collar criminal David Blake works for the gangster Bobby Mahoney, relishing his comfortable lifestyle. But then a lot of money – the eponymous 'drop' – goes astray, and Blake finds himself in the frame, with potentially extremely dangerous results. All of this is handled with great panache, and it's clear that Linskey is a writer worthy of attention. Simon Kernick – no slouch himself in this area – has said: '*The Drop* is a brutal, hard-hitting debut which opens up Newcastle's dark, violent underbelly like a freshly-sharpened stiletto.'

There were those who feared that Linskey's move to another publisher might draw his sting, with journos and policemen rather than criminals now at the centre of the narrative. Did it? Thankfully, not an iota; *No Name Lane* is lacerating fare that begins with a killer at his gruesome work and makes most current crime fiction look like thin gruel. Disgraced reporter Tom Carney returns to the North East, encountering Helen Norton, who is holding down his old job on the local paper. The duo investigate the disappearances of young girls, together with beleaguered policeman Ian Bradshaw. However, the first body to be found is not one of the girls, but a decades-old corpse. Does a murder from the past have a connection with an implacable monster of the present day? *No Name Lane* clocks in at a weighty 500 pages, but never falters in its grip.

Men fear death as children fear the dark, said Francis Bacon. In **SIMON LELIC**'s provocative (and contentious) *The Child Who*, children and death are chillingly combined in a juvenile dispenser of murder. Actually, there is a lengthy lineage of British writers specialising in malevolent children: John Wyndham's *The Midwich Cuckoos*, for instance, renders the prepubescent killers alien and 'other' – and to some degree (without relying on supernatural or science-fiction trappings) that is precisely what Lelic does here. The eponymous child is a mystery – but more tellingly so is the instinct that drives a provincial solicitor to risk the destruction of his own family in defence of the boy. The author's earlier books, *Rupture* and *The Facility*, showed a readiness to tackle deeply uncomfortable issues; the former dealt with a teacher murdering his pupils and a colleague in a school shooting, and questioned whether apparently psychopathic behaviour might have a more nuanced explanation than tabloid newspapers are wont to accept. But Lelic's unconventional take on such issues as bullying and alienated children in *Rupture* now appears to be a dry run for *The Child Who*, in which the reader's capacity for either outrage or sympathy is uneasily manipulated by the author. Is Lelic's child here 'evil'? Or is that word a useful catch-all term for the inexplicable?

Daniel is an unassuming 12-year-old boy who has committed a terrible crime: he has savagely killed a schoolmate, a young girl – and the reader is not spared a grim violation. Solicitor Leo Curtice is assigned the job of defending him, but his task is to have a seismic effect on his own life. Leo is under no illusions about the horror of the crime here, but shows an intuitive sympathy for the boy, perceiving that Daniel is a damaged, vulnerable victim himself, quite as much as the classmate he murdered. But extending sympathy to a perpetrator of abuse is dangerous territory, and, in a parallel with a real-life case, the reader is reminded of the hate-filled public perceptions of the murderers of James Bulger when attempts were made to present them as victims of abuse themselves. Is Leo right to risk the love and respect of his own family working out a personal agenda, however laudable? The answer to that is not to be vouchsafed in *The Child Who*; Lelic places such conclusions within the individual conscience of the reader. And it is that as much as anything else which shows that Lelic is a writer of note.

If you're looking for cosy, comforting crime fiction, it may be best if you stay away from **DAVID MARK**. Cosy he isn't. Mark's approach to the police procedural thriller is uncompromising – as *Dark Winter* and *Original Skin* resoundingly proved – and *Sorrow Bound*, a solid outing for DS Aector McAvoy is more of the same. The three individuals at the heart of the plot – McAvoy, his wife Roisin and Philippa Longman – have one thing in common: a mysterious enemy dedicated to their destruction. As the narrative moves inexorably towards its compelling climax, it's easy to see why such writers as Val McDermid and Steve Mosby are lining up to praise Mark.

Over the course of several novels, **MARI HANNAH** has proved herself to be an accomplished modern crime writer, and *Monument to Murder* is one of the most sheerly enjoyable of her books. A skeleton is discovered beneath the fortified walls of an old castle in Northumberland. In order to identify the body, DCI Kate Daniels enlists the aid of a forensic anthropologist. At the same time, prison psychologist Emily McCann (who has just lost her husband) finds herself dangerously inveigled into a convicted sex offender's fantasy, with disturbing mind games the unpleasant order of the day. Another resolute winner from the talented Hannah.

In *Black Flowers* by **STEVE MOSBY**, out of nowhere, a little girl appears on a seaside promenade holding a black flower. She has a frightening story to tell. But the story she relates will have dark consequences, and will claim a variety of victims. When Neil Dawson's father takes his own life, Neil is crushed by the event. But even as he comes to terms with his grief, he realises that there is a mystery he is obliged to solve. At the same time, Hannah Price is also mourning the death of her father – like him, she has joined the police force. For both protagonists, a journey into the past is to have the most grave and profound effects. Those who know their crime fiction have long been aware that Steve Mosby is one of the most interesting and ambitious of current practitioners, and this 2012 book is well up to his customary impressive standard. The book is not set in a specific real place, although the two main locations are roughly based on Leeds and Whitby. The more recent *I Know Who Did It* is equally accomplished. Charlie Matheson was killed two years ago in a car accident. So how can a woman who resembles Charlie – and who claims to be her – return from the dead? Detective Mark Nelson is called in to investigate and hears her terrifying account of what she has endured in the 'afterlife'.

Let's be frank, a great deal of work in the crime fiction field reads like a great deal of other work, so it is particularly refreshing when a very individual writer appears on the scene. Such as **NICK QUANTRILL**, whose prose is subtly unlike that of most of his contemporaries. His protagonist is doughty private investigator Joe Geraghty, whose area of operation is a pungently realised Hull in East Yorkshire. All of his work is worth investigating, but perhaps his signature book is *The Crooked Beat*, which frequently invokes the great private eye novels of the past.

Like the first two books in Liverpool-born **KATE ELLIS**'s Joe Plantagenet series, *Seeking the Dead* and *Playing with Bones*, *Kissing the Demons* is set in the ancient northern city of Eborby (a thinly disguised York). And as York is reputed to be the most haunted city in England, there is inevitably a supernatural element to her mysteries. Ellis's initial inspiration for *Kissing the Demons* arose from a conversation with her son's girlfriend, who had rented a rundown Victorian house with some friends. As the weeks went on, the house's occupants found that the place had a rather peculiar atmosphere. During her time there, formerly close friends would suddenly quarrel for no apparent reason and relationships broke down, so much so that it almost felt as if some hostile presence in the house were starting to control their lives. As well as all this, when a strip of wallpaper came away in the bathroom, the students found what looked like a bloodstain underneath. So, in *Kissing the Demons*, 13 Torland Place is a student house with a disturbing past. Not only was it the scene of five brutal murders back in the nineteenth century, but it was also linked to the disappearance of two teenage girls 12 years before the story begins. As with her earlier Plantagenet books, Ellis has been unable to resist mining York's rich seam of chilling ghost stories. But these elements aside, Kate Ellis's complete body of work is satisfyingly full of expertly turned, involving crime narratives. She's unquestionably the real deal.

DAVID STUART DAVIES is one of the world's leading experts on Sherlock Holmes (in fact, he and I recently co-edited *The Sherlock Holmes Book*). At university in the 1970s, he wanted to write his final dissertation on Arthur Conan Doyle but was told that the author was not important enough for such a project. As an antidote to this literary snobbery, Davies began writing an article on the films of Sherlock Holmes for his own pleasure. The article grew into a book and became *Holmes of the Movies*, published in 1976. He followed this with several ingenious examples of Sherlockian pastiche – not for discussion here, as the subject of *Brit Noir* is not historical crime fiction (although honourable mention should be made of *The Tangled Skein*) – and books featuring his own sleuth, Johnny One Eye, a young private detective operating in London during the Second World War. With *Innocent Blood*, we can forgive Davies borrowing a title from PD James: this second in a series of books based in 1980s Huddersfield is a gritty and involving crime thriller that explores a variety of themes, including stalking, murder and homophobia within the police force. Location is crucially important to the story and the book has a strong local connection; Davies has drawn on many Yorkshire landmarks that are still recognisable today. A child's body is found in woodland, but this is only the first victim in a series of apparently motiveless crimes. DI Paul Snow must discover the pattern among the victims and juggle his own hectic private life or face the terrifying consequences.

Early in his writing career *Crime Time* magazine described **STUART PAWSON** as 'Yorkshire's best-kept secret'. It was a description he was anxious to leave behind. His first full-length crime novel, 1995's *The Picasso Scam*, introduced Charlie Priest, the detective inspector who has featured in all Pawson's work so far. He is an art school graduate – and Pawson now does all his painting vicariously, via Priest. The intention was to make him a zany character who always did the right thing for the wrong reasons; however, it proved difficult to maintain this, and Charlie soon became his own man and developed his own unique personality. Priest is unusual among fictional detectives: he has a good relationship with his senior officers (he does the dirty work and gets results) and even believes in doing the paperwork ('Paperwork catches crooks,' he tells his troops), although he has been known to break this rule himself. Pawson enjoys relating the locker-room banter that leavens the grimness of the main storylines. *The Mushroom Man* overcame the 'difficult second book' hurdle and became a success in a very short time. And by the twelfth book in the series, *Grief Encounters*, reviewers held Pawson's work in high esteem. The author lives in Yorkshire, and although he tries to avoid the Professional Yorkshireman syndrome, he enjoys using the landscape as a background to his stories.

MARTYN WAITES is a brave man: he had the temerity to take on the UK's leading ghost story practitioner Susan Hill by writing a sequel to the latter's *The Woman in Black* – and turned in a very creditable job (Waites is something of a horror aficionado). He is also – in metrosexual fashion – 'Tania Carver', writing several books under this name in collaboration with his ex-wife Linda. In the Carver book *Heartbreaker*, after years of abuse, Gemma Adderley has finally plucked up the courage to leave her violent husband. She takes her seven-year-old daughter Carly and leaves the house, determined to salvage what she can of her life. But en route to Safe Harbour, a women's refuge, she disappears… However, Waites' work under his own name is his most impressive achievement: tough, authoritative novels that have a distinctive, gritty character. *Born Under Punches*, with its background of the Miners' Strike of 1984, is among his best work.

Real life has always heavily influenced the under-regarded **JOHN DEAN**'s writing. For him, stories come out of experience. A typical novel, *The Secrets Man*, was generated by a serious illness experienced by the writer's father; as Dean sat at his bedside day after day, he started to look around the hospital ward and to examine his surroundings. What he saw was five other beds, five other patients, each of them in a world of their own – and the idea for this novel germinated. What if one of the patients in a fictional hospital was an elderly villain who, in his heyday, had been the henchman of one of the city's gang leaders, who was still active in the criminal underworld? What if the elderly villain was known as 'The Secrets Man' because he was the only one entrusted with the confidences of the gang leader? What if, as illness unhinged his mind, his tongue was loosened and he started revealing those secrets? And what if everyone dismissed his ramblings as just that – except for the retired detective in the next bed who knew exactly what he was hearing? Dean's work is always full of invention, and that quality is fully in play in this key book. In *A Breach of Trust*, a crooked businessman suffers a fall at home and there is no reason to think it is anything other than an accident – until after he dies, when information emerges that points towards murder. DCI John Blizzard and his team are brought in to investigate and attention quickly focuses on the controversial closure of a local factory amid claims of widespread fraud and exploitation of the workforce. The detectives enter a world in which threats and intimidation are rife and hatred is never far from the surface. Dean sets his DCI John Blizzard books (such as this one) in the depressed fictional northern city of Hafton, while his Jack Harris novels are sited in the North Pennines.

Other writers and key books

PAULINE BELL: *Nothing but the Truth, Reasonable Death*
BEN CHEETHAM: *Justice for the Damned*
JOHN CONNOR: *The Playroom, Falling*
PATRICIA HALL: *Devil's Game*
BILL KITSON: *Minds that Hate, Altered Egos*
REBECCA MUDDIMAN: *Stolen*
SHEILA QUIGLEY: *Thorn in My Side, Every Breath You Take*
DANIELLE RAMSAY: *Blood Reckoning*
NICHOLAS RHEA: *The Sniper, Constable on View*

The West Country

Apart from recently reactivating Agatha Christie's Hercule Poirot franchise, **SOPHIE HANNAH** writes highly involving contemporary thrillers, set in a fictional UK town, that blend the psychological suspense genre with the police procedural. She has said: 'I wanted to combine the direct, visceral appeal of the first-person woman-in-peril narrative with recurring police characters whom readers would get to know better with each book.' Hannah's detectives are DC Simon Waterhouse, who has never, to his colleagues' knowledge, had a romantic or sexual relationship, and Sergeant Charlotte (Charlie) Zailer, who is mouthy, promiscuous, and in love with Waterhouse. Their relationship evolves over the course of the books. In *Little Face*, Hannah's first crime novel (a debut that effortlessly rose above the plethora of first crime books), a woman claims that her newborn has been swapped for another baby, and nobody believes her. Hannah's second thriller, *Hurting Distance* is the story of a woman who, in order to persuade the police to search for her missing lover with the urgency she feels is required, pretends he is a sadistic psychopath, thinking they will look for him more assiduously if they believe he is a danger to others. And in *The Other Half Lives*, the protagonist confesses to the murder of a woman who is still alive.

You're a woman with a happyish marriage, balancing a demanding job and an equally demanding young family, not greatly helped by your self-involved husband who routinely misreads your moods. You're watching television when a name in a news item leaps out at you: Mark Bretherick. You know this man – and details of the report confirm this. But you conceal this from your husband, for two very salient reasons: you had a brief, clandestine sexual relationship with Bretherick, and (more disturbingly) his wife and daughter are both dead, brutally murdered. Oh, and there's one more thing: the grieving widower on the screen is not the man you knew as Mark Bretherick... This is the premise of Hannah's *The Point of Rescue* – and when did you last encounter such an unusual situation? But the fresh and original have been Hannah's hallmarks from her debut novel onwards. Here, we are thoroughly involved in the chaotic life of the heroine, Sally Thorning. The novel starts with a bang (literally), as Sally is violently harangued by a childminder she has upset, then is pushed in front of a bus. Is the childminder responsible? Already, Sophie Hannah is scattering a host of clever and subtle touches such as Sally's response as she falls ('I am lying in between my handbag and the bus, and it occurs to me that this is good, that I am a barrier – my phone and diary would not get crushed...'). But it's not just the observation of small, absurd (but plausible) details such as this that grips. Sally, for obvious reasons, is unwilling to reveal her relationship with her erstwhile lover, and anonymously informs the police that something is very strange about this whole situation. And as the revelations about 'Mark Bretherick' tumble forth, the tension is screwed ever tighter.

Hannah is also a best-selling, prize-winning poet – her collection, *Pessimism for Beginners*, was shortlisted for the 2007 TS Eliot Award – although most crime readers would be happy if she never wooed that particular muse again.

The late Ed McBain semi-inaugurated the forensics genre in his *87th Precinct* novels, but two female American writers have parlayed his innovations into stratospheric sales: Patricia Cornwell and Kathy Reichs. But the field has not become an exclusively female sorority – or, for that matter, an American one. A highly talented male writer has offered a challenge to the female domination of the genre, albeit playing safe by using a woman protagonist. *The Coroner* by **MR HALL** was an instant hit when it appeared in 2009, with his vulnerable heroine Jenny Cooper (a divorcée who has suffered a nervous breakdown) struggling with a new job as coroner for the Severn Vale – with the aid of self-administered medication. In *The Flight*, the eponymous 'flight' is that of a plane that has crashed into the Severn estuary, wiping out its passengers – who, it transpires, are a particularly prestigious assembly. Another inadvertent casualty of the crash appears to be a solitary sailor whose boat was sunk. But when his body washes up, alongside it is that of a ten-year-old girl, Amy Patterson, who was listed as a passenger on the plane. Jenny Cooper finds that the girl appears to bear no injuries from the crash – in fact, she died separately several hours later. The crash investigation is carried out under conditions of the greatest secrecy, and Jenny's attempts to find out who is behind what appears to be a massive cover-up are further complicated by the demands of the dead girl's mother, insistent that Jenny finds out the truth. It appeared that MR Hall had decided to broaden his canvas with this fourth outing for his vulnerable protagonist, still dependent on prescription drugs. She is coming to terms with the nervous breakdown that we read about in the first book, *The Coroner*, but is still relatively fragile. Here, she is up against particularly dangerous and influential opponents, but the risky strategy of maximising the odds against her pays off. We are never given the dispiriting impression that the rules of blockbuster thrillers have been trotted out as a result of some editor's commercial suggestion; the book remains personal despite its larger, less focused concerns.

It is fortunate that most of us are not placed in the position of having to sacrifice our happiness in an ongoing battle with corruption. Hall's coroner heroine would clearly be sympathetic to Tolstoy's notion that his hero was truth – though the pursuit of truth has cost her dearly, and her delicate mental state has been stretched ever tighter over the course of an increasingly impressive series. *The Chosen Dead* is slightly different from its predecessors in that Hall places his stress on a particularly intricate narrative rather than on the travails of his beleaguered, substance-abusing protagonist; in fact, she has a slightly easier time of it in this book than her creator has previously allowed her. Cover-ups are often at the centre of Hall's work, but while, in real life, most of us roll our eyes at the various conspiracy theories trotted out by the paranoid, readers of crime fiction have to accept such things – a belief in the slew of nasty conspiracies at the heart of the genre is as essential as a temporary belief in the existence of the Greek gods when watching *Medea* or *Oedipus Rex*.

While **GRAHAM HURLEY** cannot be said to have done anything radical with the standard form of the police procedural during his long career, his level of consistency has remained remarkably high, with such books as *Touching Distance* laying out an involving narrative with maximum clarity and vividness. In *Sins of the Father*, a wealthy elderly man, Rupert Moncrieff, dies after a savage beating in his West Country waterside mansion. A hood has been placed over his head and his throat cut. His extended family – who were still living with him – have a variety of personal stories as well as their own motives for his death. In charge of the murder investigation is DS Jimmy Suttle, who, working with his estranged journalist wife Lizzie, is still coping with his own problems after the abduction and murder of the couple's young daughter Grace.

At one time, it looked as if **MINETTE WALTERS** would seize the crown of Britain's crime queen from the long-time joint holders Ruth Rendell and PD James, but her lengthy sabbatical (broken in 2015 with a short novel) rendered her essentially *hors de combat*. However, her impressive earlier work remains relevant. After the socially engaged *Acid Row*, her ninth novel, *Fox Evil*, had the kind of psychological acuity that readers had come to expect from her. An elderly woman is found dead in her garden, dressed only in a nightgown, with bloodstains on the ground nearby. In the frame for her death is her landowning husband, Colonel James Lockyer-Fox, and in the close-knit Dorset village in which the book is set, his guilt is a fait accompli. All of this is handled with maximum efficiency by Walters.

Walters has been building a total picture of modern Britain that cuts across all social strata, while still using the apparatus of the crime novel. Since pocketing the John Creasey Award for her debut novel, *The Ice House* in 1992, Walters' books have demonstrated her assurance in writing about a variety of groups (from the upper classes to council estate residents), while *Disordered Minds* reached into darker areas of the human psyche and *The Devil's Feather* tackled a more ambitious international panoply than before. In the latter book, five women have been savagely killed in Sierra Leone, and Connie Burns, who works as a correspondent for Reuters, expresses doubts when three youthful rebel soldiers are arraigned for the crimes. But her objections are disregarded – this is, after all, a murderous civil war in which the slaughter has been wholesale, and the fate of three brutalised children forced into phoney confessions is academic. Connie comes to believe that the killer is a foreigner with sadistic sexual predilections, cutting his own bloody swathe under the cover of a war-torn country. Burrowing into seclusion in Dorset, Connie knows all too well that her safety is fragile, and that a final, horrific confrontation is inevitable. Walters has a readiness to tackle larger themes than many of her more parochial English peers, and she is a writer who has always been read by men (some other female crime writers often tend to target a female readership), but with this book she resolutely joined such American specialists in the extreme as Tess Gerritsen, whose books feature female protagonists in scenarios that are perfectly tough enough for the most astringent male tastes.

But (as suggested above) mention of Walters' name always provokes a question: whatever happened to her? There was a time when her highly accomplished novels marked her out as the heir apparent to the two Baronesses, but then Walters seemed to vanish from the scene. By all accounts, she's been writing a *magnum opus*, but it certainly wasn't the book that appeared after her long literary hiatus: *The Cellar*. Not only is this a slim novella, it is only tangentially crime and arrives under the imprimatur of the Hammer imprint, specialists in the horrific. Is it substantial enough to end the Minette Walters drought? The theme here is domestic slavery. Muna lives in a dark cellar, exploited by the heartless Songoli family. But worms have a way of turning – particularly as Muna is not the illiterate drudge she appears to be. At just 200-odd pages, this is certainly a compulsive (and gruesome) read, but it also suggests that perhaps Walters has relinquished (if she ever harboured it) the notion of inheriting the James/Rendell crown.

Set on the North Devon coast, **CHRISTINE POULSON**'s *Invisible* features a protagonist, Lisa, who is in need of an escape from the demands of caring on her own for a son with cerebral palsy – and she has found this escape in a lover whose name is Jay. She meets him once a month and loses herself in a realm without responsibility – until one day when Jay does not appear, and Lisa discovers that the relationship is built on a lie. This is splendidly written fare from the reliable Poulson, written with keen psychological insight.

In **STUART PREBBLE**'s *The Insect Farm*, Jonathan and Roger Maguire are brothers, and each has an obsession. Jonathan is fixated on his seductive girlfriend Harriet, while Roger is constructing something very strange in a shed in their parents' garden: his own private universe, with a collection of millions of insects. But as this suggests, Roger is somewhat off the spectrum of normal behaviour, and after the death of their parents, his brother is obliged to give up his studies and look after him – forcing him to live apart from his beloved Harriet. This is a recipe for jealousy, and soon violent death is in the offing. Stuart Prebble is best known as a broadcast journalist, but has proved to be a protean and talented writer with this sturdy novel (reminiscent of Iain Banks' *The Wasp Factory*); it's a gripping read.

PETER LOVESEY's immensely enjoyable crime novels include Victorian period crime as well as contemporary police procedurals, all delivered in the author's quirky, engaging style. His novelist career began when he won a publisher's contest in 1970, granting him the chance to publish his first book, *Wobble to Death*, with his Victorian copper Sergeant Cribb. Subsequently, Lovesey produced another eight outings for Cribb, each one focusing on particular elements of Victorian society. In *Stagestruck*, over-the-hill pop star Clarion Calhoun is attempting to launch an acting career, but her debut at the Bath Theatre Royal gives her and the audience more than they bargained for. As she is rushed to hospital with third-degree burns, the theatrical community is thrown into uproar. It is up to the city's most intuitive detective, Peter Diamond, to look into the case, but there is a problem – his physical aversion to the theatre itself.

Who is the real **SUSAN HILL**? Is she Britain's best exponent of the classic ghost story? (An adaptation of her chilling novel *The Woman in Black* has been playing on the West End stage since 1989.) Or is she the heir apparent of Anthony Trollope? (Her *The Shadows in the Street* is crammed full of wonderful ecclesiastical squabbles, like *Barchester Towers*, with high and low church at each other's throats.) Or is Hill a practitioner of the police procedural novel, with a determined copper struggling to keep a difficult murder investigation on course? Actually, she is all three – and is equally adroit at whatever genre she turns her hand to. This is proved by *The Shadows in the Street*, an outing for her detective Simon Serrailler, which manages to steer a satisfying middle line between a series of brutal crimes (in which prostitutes have been targeted) and the Cathedral Close disagreements mentioned above. Whether Hill is dealing with the sex trade or church politics, we are never impatient to return to the other plot strand.

Serrailler is on holiday after some particularly bruising cases, but his attempt to recharge his batteries is abruptly cut short when two prostitutes are strangled in Lafferton (Serrailler's beat – though entirely fictional, Hill has compared it with Exeter or Salisbury). There is a host of suspects, including a variety of the women's punters and the college librarian, 'Loopy Les', who supplies the sex workers with sandwiches and tea at night. The punters are mostly regulars and are trusted by the working girls – but is one of them harbouring a secret psychopathic hatred of women?

As ever with Hill, the crime-solving aspects of the book are firmly under her belt, although it might be argued that Serrailler's team of detectives is sketched in more rudimentary fashion than usual. But the notable achievement of *The Shadows in the Street* can be found in the entertaining church-based squabbles involving the local Dean's wife Ruth (whose nickname, Mrs Proudie, is borrowed from Trollope) and the sympathetically detailed description of the lives of the prostitutes. The latter, with their forlorn dreams of a new life, are presented without any lofty moralising, but Hill never draws a veil over the more squalid aspects of their lives. If the book's denouement arrives rather out of left field, few will complain: Susan Hill's Serrailler novels, with their persuasive copper and his equally well-rounded family, are real treats.

All but one of the prolific **HAZEL HOLT**'s 20-odd Mrs Malory books maintain a commendable level of consistency. Her preferred setting is West Somerset, with locales based on Minehead (aka Taviscombe). A favourite of the author's own sizeable corpus of work is *A Necessary End*.

Other writers and key books
JANE ADAMS: *Blood Ties, The Power of One*
TOM BALE: *Blood Falls*
DAMIEN BOYD: *Kickback, As the Crow Flies*
CAROL ANNE DAVIS: *Kiss it Away*
MARGARET DUFFY: *Rat Poison, Prospect of Death*

DEBBY FOWLER: *Letting Go, Intensive Care*
LESLEY GRANT-ADAMSON: *Undertow, Patterns in the Dust*
SIMON HALL: *The TV Detective, The Death Pictures*
PETER HELTON: *Four Below, Falling More Slowly*
STAN HEY: *Sudden Unprovided Death*
DAVID HODGES: *Firetrap, Slice*
JANET LAURENCE: *Death and the Epicure, Recipe for Death*
JESSICA MANN: *The Voice from the Grave*
FERGUS McNEILL: *Knife Edge, Eye Contact*
ROBERT RICHARDSON: *The Dying of the Light*
BETTY ROWLANDS: *Smokescreen, Finishing Touch*
MARK SENNEN: *Touch, Bad Blood*
REBECCA TOPE: *The Sting of Death, A Cotswold Killing*

East Anglia

Since *Behind the Scenes at the Museum* (which deservedly won the
Whitbread Book of the Year award), **KATE ATKINSON** has acquired
a dedicated following of readers who wait for each new offering
with keen anticipation. And Atkinson – so far – hasn't disappointed,
delivering the same cool and effortless prose that distinguished
both that book and the equally beguiling *Human Croquet*. Part of the
pleasure with each new book is the anticipation in wondering: what
has she come up with this time? Surprisingly, *Case Histories* could
almost be seen as a crime novel (a genre one would hardly expect the
uncategorisable Atkinson to tackle), but the similarities are superficial
– principally, the resemblances are down to the fact that the central
character is a former police inspector who now earns his crust as
a private investigator. Jackson Brodie is struggling to deal with the
sultry heat of a Cambridge summer and his own unsatisfactory life,
with a dead marriage not the least of his problems. Thoughts of
mortality haunt him, and the one feeling that gives meaning to his
life is his belief that he can do some good for the people he deals
with in his professional role. As a brilliantly drawn cast of characters
intersect with the troubled protagonist, all the insight, humour and
sympathy that marked Atkinson's earlier work is brought into play.

The plotting here is deliberately discursive – Atkinson has other fish to fry than the standard concerns of the private eye novel. This is by no means her best book, but it's still a truly unusual and intriguing novel.

When creative writing courses focusing on crime fiction deal with locale, the approach suggested to students is usually along these lines: don't forget to establish a sense of place – but do it *economically*. Four or five pages of description of setting à la Thomas Hardy? Forget it. The orthodoxy in the twenty-first century has been to stress the primacy of arm-twisting narrative – but writers such as **ELLY GRIFFITHS** are having no truck with that. If Griffiths wants to spend her time placing us in a gloomily realised, almost tactile Norfolk, she won't be hurried – and her books are all the better for that. Not that she neglects the demands of satisfying plotting: while luxuriating in the texture of her books, the reader is always kept on tenterhooks as her plump, comfortable forensic archaeologist Ruth Galloway begins her customary examination of old bones and modern murder. *Dying Fall* sports a setting that is atypical for the series, but demonstrates that Galloway isn't always stuck in Norfolk. In the novel, Ruth is shocked to learn by phone that a college friend of hers, Dan Golding, has died in a fire in his Lancashire home. And when, two days later, she receives a letter from the dead man, she is distressed to read a frantic plea for help along with information about a discovery that will alter the field of archaeology irrevocably. And, as in earlier books, Galloway's relationship with DCI Harry Nelson proves fruitful as she begins her investigation. In the north on holiday, Nelson learns of the peculiar circumstances surrounding the death of the archaeologist – notably the fact that a neo-Nazi organisation at Golding's university has been making threats. Before too long, both Ruth and Nelson are in the kind of danger zone that Griffiths so cannily channelled in such books as *The Crossing Places* and *The Janus Stone*.

While even the most skilful of crime writers makes the occasional misstep, Griffiths has managed to sustain a remarkably high standard across her Ruth Galloway series, although the pawky mixture of ancient relics, Anglo-Saxon culture, a nostalgia for the trappings of Catholicism and bloodshed for the most contemporary of reasons may need some mixing up occasionally if it is not to slip into formula. But, as yet, there is no danger of that, and the pleasing mix of quirky characterisation (notably of the unheroic but tenacious Ruth) and the malign currents from the past that seep into modern life still delivers a considerable charge. The elements that Griffiths continues to draw on from her childhood walks along the Norfolk coast have plenty of mileage yet.

In thrillers such as **JAMES HUMPHREYS**' *Riptide*, the careful conjuring of atmosphere is absolutely crucial. Set in a secluded village, the various sights and sounds (misty beaches, sparsely populated streets, unfriendly taverns) are essential in locating the concealed deeds of mayhem and murder. Humphreys handles this aspect with the assurance of a master, but his real skill lies in the flinty-edged characterisation of his dramatis personae – not least his heroine, Sergeant Sarah Delaney. Against her will, Delaney is dispatched to the little-frequented village of Caxton on the Norfolk coast to look into a nasty incident. Two corpses have been sighted on the beach, but before she can investigate properly, the bodies have been claimed by the sea. And as Sarah slowly unearths the dark and dangerous secrets behind the deaths, she's also forced to confront troubling problems from her own past in the village: Caxton is the place where a man she loved once lived, before his sudden death. *Sleeping Partner* was an auspicious and impressive debut for James Humphreys, and *Riptide* displays the same casual assurance as the earlier book, notably in the area of its nimble plotting. The trick in novels such as this is to pay out just as many revelations as are necessary to keep the reader thirsting for more – and that's just what Humphreys does here. It's a real pleasure to be wrong-footed by the author as often as we are in this accomplished piece.

MIKE RIPLEY's brand of sardonic crime writing is genuinely unique: translating the American hard-boiled genre into a very English locale has caused many a writer to come adrift, but Ripley is fully in command of his quirky idiom, and his work is utterly different from that of other writers. Characteristic one-liners are prolific in *Angel Underground*, one of his best books. And Ripley's wry hero Angel has his hands full in a pleasingly crowded narrative. At the request of his eccentric mother, and against all his finer instincts, Angel is persuaded to join a shambolic archaeological dig in rural Suffolk, privately financed by the even more eccentric Arthur Ransome Swallow, a local landowner who is obsessed with finding the royal mint of Queen Boudica. Typically hard-headed, Angel is sceptical about finding any buried treasure, but he finds menace aplenty. Not only is there something fundamentally wrong with the way the dig is being conducted but everyone connected with it is being threatened or injured, including the detective, and it transpires that there is much more at stake than ancient history. Most worrying of all, Angel's partner Amy insists on joining the dig to keep an eye on him – but it appears that someone sinister is keeping an eye on her. The site descends into chaos. Ripley fans will need no recommendation here; newcomers will find this a very satisfying place to start. But – be warned – The Talented Mr Ripley is addictive.

Lancashire-born creative writing tutor **BENJAMIN WOOD** received an immense amount of attention for his first book, 2012's *The Bellwether Revivals*. But was it worthy of the hype it received? The novel begins with the discovery of bodies, one of which is on the manicured lawns near the river in Cambridge. Eden Bellwether is still breathing; he has (we are to learn) cast a hypnotic spell on a promising young working-class student, Oscar. The latter is in love with Eden's equally gilded, aristocratic sister, the beautiful Iris. Eden is a charismatic, eccentric figure who believes himself to be a healer, with the power of music the conduit for his skills. And while Oscar is mesmerised by the seductive Iris, the most crucial relationship he has is with her fascinating brother. If the basic premise here sounds familiar, that's because the 'appeal of beauty' that is built into the novel has as its lodestone *Brideshead Revisited* (not just Waugh's novel, but the celebrated television adaptation – we are reminded as much of Jeremy Irons and Anthony Andrews as reader-surrogate Charles in thrall to the upper-crust Sebastian). *The Bellwether Revivals* is, in fact, a cogent and timely examination of the conflict between religion and scepticism, a theme explored with more rigour than in the novel's template; we rarely doubt that

Waugh is on the side of grace and the supernatural. Donna Tartt's *The Secret History* is also in the DNA here, and there are echoes of another literary analysis of the unhealthy emotional bond between a brother and sister, LP Hartley's *Eustace and Hilda*. Does it matter that Benjamin Wood wears his influences so clearly on his sleeve? Some may find that the book reads like a contemporary filigree on its illustrious predecessors, but most readers will be as transfixed by this richly drawn cast of characters as Oscar is by his blue-blooded companions. The fact that Benjamin Wood can hold his own in such heavyweight company is a measure of his achievement.

NICCI GERRARD, the female half of the team who write as Nicci French, has long been a writer of immense skill in her own right, as her solus novels prove. *Missing Persons* describes an English family living in East Anglia. Primary school teacher Isabel is married to the academic Felix, who works at a university nearby. They have three children, only one of them unproblematic: Johnny, who is beginning his university degree course in Sheffield. But then suddenly (and without warning) Johnny appears to cut off all communication with his family. He has disappeared. The following seven years are the substance of this utterly involving novel.

JIM KELLY's chosen career was journalism, until he turned to full-time crime writing in 2003 after his first book, *The Water Clock*, was nominated for the Crime Writers' Association's John Creasey Award. All the popular and atmospheric Dryden books are set in 'The Black Fen', that area of misty marsh and isolated communities first used as a crime landscape by Dorothy L Sayers in her 1930s classic *The Nine Tailors*. *The Water Clock* introduced a trio of characters who have appeared throughout the series so far. Philip Dryden is the amateur sleuth who is reluctantly drawn into a series of mysteries as he goes about his trade as a journalist on *The Crow*, the newspaper Kelly has created for the tiny cathedral city of Ely. The author spent ten years in provincial journalism in Bedford and York before moving to Fleet Street and draws heavily on his experiences to produce a flavour of the inherently bizarre and lonely life of the local newspaper 'hack'. Dryden's sidekick is Humphrey H Holt, an overweight cab driver who fills his empty life by trundling around the Fens in a two-door Ford Capri looking for business. Humph, divorced, morose and taciturn, combats loneliness with incessant motion and finds in Dryden someone equally happy to avoid personal tragedy by immersing themselves in the lives of others. Dryden's promising career as a national journalist has been interrupted by a horrific car accident which has left his wife Laura in a coma: Laura is the silent partner in the central trio. She is a prisoner of 'locked-in syndrome' and is a patient at a private hospital in Ely, and Dryden's wanderings always end with a visit to her bedside, where he tells her of his day in the hope that somewhere, on some level, she is listening. (As the books progress, Laura emerges painfully from her coma and is able to participate more fully in her husband's investigations.)

The books in the series each have a distinct character, often determined by elemental forces. *The Water Clock*, in which a series of crimes are set in motion by the discovery of a rotting corpse on the roof of Ely cathedral, is told against the backdrop of Fen floods. *The Fire Baby*, the second in the series, takes place during a sweltering summer heatwave. All the books deal to some extent with crimes in the past as well as the present, and in the latter book, Dryden has to go back to the infamous drought of 1976 to find the clues he needs.

In **ALISON BRUCE**'s *The Calling*, a seductive young blonde woman is found gagged and trussed up, the victim of a sinister figure with a dark obsession. An anonymous caller contacts the police, informing them that she is not the first victim in a new wave of crimes – and that she will by no means be the last. DC Gary Goodhew quickly becomes aware that this caller may be the key to unlocking the mysteries; she is a neurotic, self-harming woman, and the youthful Goodhew is well aware that she will need careful handling if she is to help in tracking down a dangerous criminal. Bruce has already demonstrated her credentials in the field of crime with two striking non-fiction titles, *Cambridgeshire Murders* and *Billington: Victorian Executioner*. Her research has paid off, although this is a very modern piece of work with both a strong police protagonist and a dangerous, disturbing criminal.

EG RODFORD, influenced by Hammett and Chandler, writes noirish fiction set in contemporary Cambridge. Rodford's work features private investigator George Kocharyan, whose investigations take him beyond the Cambridge of spires, dons and punts beloved by tourists to the sordid underbelly, a world where town and gown coexist in mutual distrust. In Kocharyan's first outing, *The Bursar's Wife*, he gets drawn into the secrets of the university's elite as they struggle to maintain the cracking façade of their successful lives. Although dealing with dark subject matter, the book is written with a wry humour.

Wales and the Borders

The late crime writer David Williams (no relation to the Williams discussed below) initially found publishers highly resistant to the novels he set in his native country. He was told: 'Nobody commits crime in Wales!' While that may be a typically metropolitan attitude to somewhere far from London, it's true that the particular character of Wales fights against its use as a backdrop in the blood-boltered fashion of Edinburgh, the North of England and other more persuasively criminous settings. But there are two talented Welsh writers who tackle their Celtic locales head on – and although they do so in very different fashions, both bristle with sardonic humour. **MALCOLM PRYCE** delivers a hilariously surrealistic take on a Chandleresque private eye in a land of Druids and whelk stalls in novels such as *Last Tango in Aberystwyth*. This mines the same vein of black humour as its much-acclaimed predecessor, *Aberystwyth Mon Amour* – Pryce's invoking of art film directors in his titles (Resnais, Bertolucci) only adds to the number of bizarre juxtapositions that are his stock in trade. In this book, we meet again the wisecracking Louie Knight, whose trench-coated manner on the mean streets of Wales makes for a very funny book that also functions as an ingenious mystery. In *Last Tango*, we encounter another cast of off-the-wall characters (does Wales really have this many eccentrics?) as Louie becomes involved in Aberystwyth's 'What the Butler Saw' film industry. Academic Dean Morgan checks into a hotel and is mistaken for a sinister Druid killer – and his life takes an even more unfortunate turn when he falls for porn star Judy Juice. It's up to Louie, the town's only private eye, to uncover a highly unlikely cocktail of corruption and concupiscence. It's inevitable that this second book lacks the freshness of its predecessor, but all the off-kilter imagination that made *Aberystwyth Mon Amour* such fun is firing on all cylinders again here – and Pryce continued to maintain his surreal vision of Wales (and his film references) in further books in the series.

The second author referred to above is **JOHN WILLIAMS**, who goes for a synthesis of thriller and literary fiction, teeming with dangerous Cardiff lowlifes and some surprisingly complex riffs on notions of identity. The two earlier books in his Cardiff trilogy (*Five Pubs, Two Bars and a Nightclub* and *Cardiff Dead*) perhaps unearthed a seam of dark humour more aggressively than *The Prince of Wales*, but this is still a pungent trawl through a Cardiff underworld that most of us would do well to stay away from. Bobby Ranger is that rarity, a female pimp – and she's become keen to track down the father who abandoned her. At the same time, local hack Pete Duke is looking to dish the dirt on shady entrepreneur Leslie St Clair. All three characters are to have their lives changed irrevocably – and the venue for this event is an ex-cinema (now a theme pub), the eponymous Prince of Wales. It's no wonder that tough American writers line up to shower praise on Williams: his prose has the same no-mercy take on life at the extremes. But it's unlikely that Williams will end up on the Welsh Tourist Board's recommended reading list.

HARRY BINGHAM is a writer of real command. A typically well-turned narrative is *Talking to the Dead*, the book that introduced his series character DC Fiona Griffiths. In Cardiff, a woman and her young daughter are brutally murdered in a run-down flat. The officer investigating the killings is Griffiths, a woman who is comfortable dealing with death. She tries to put herself in the mindset of the victims and their killer, but her journey takes her to the darker recesses of her own past. The detective with a troubled past is a massively over-familiar motif in crime fiction, but it's to Harry Bingham's credit that he is able to re-energise the scenario here so that it seems as fresh as paint. The book gleaned a slew of admirers, no doubt because of the writing that lifts *Talking to the Dead* effortlessly out of the police procedural realms.

The Welsh Borders are a minatory place in the crime writing of **PHIL RICKMAN**, whose *Midwinter of the Spirit* was adapted in 2015 for television. *The Lamp of the Wicked* is the longest and darkest of the ongoing series of novels about Merrily Watkins, deliverance consultant – or diocesan exorcist – for Hereford, and it takes her into the residual fog still surrounding arguably the most sickening British murders of the twentieth century. Although most of them were committed in their now-demolished house in Cromwell Street, Gloucester, the killings of Fred and Rose West still cast their shadow over parts of Herefordshire, the county where West was born and grew up. Experts close to the case still believe that many of his victims have never been found. In this novel, DI Francis Bliss of Hereford CID is building a case against a man who seems to see himself as Fred West's successor. Merrily Watkins has already met this man. Now in police custody, he wants to talk to her. Rickman has noted that he approached this book with trepidation. The aim, he said, was to deal not so much with the graphic horror but with the emotional damage inflicted on whole families by a case that – mainly because of West's suicide while awaiting trial – has still never been fully investigated. Rickman says it was surprising how many people believed there were many more undiscovered victims... and possibly more people complicit in the murders.

With the success of the award-winning *The American Boy* (and subsequent Crime Writers' Association Dagger wins), **ANDREW TAYLOR** consolidated his following as an extremely distinguished writer of crime fiction. His prose is always elegantly turned and absolutely apposite in terms of the narrative he is addressing. In (for instance) *Naked to the Hangman*, the reader is taken to the last months of the Mandate in Palestine, and young police officer Richard Thornhill encounters sights that are emblazoned on his consciousness – and which, he fears, he will never shake. He is haunted by a thought that threatens his sanity – is he a killer? After the passage of years, a retired police officer is found dead in what is left of Lydmouth Castle, and DI Thornhill finds himself the suspect in a murder case. Taylor has few rivals when it comes to dispatching crime novels as deftly written as this. Also look out for Taylor's *The Roth Trilogy* (1997–2000), which triumphantly shows that crime fiction can deal with serious themes and use innovative literary techniques. In theology, the Four Last Things are Death, Judgement, Heaven and Hell, and Taylor cannily utilises this as the perfect foundation for a plot. Each book in the trilogy is self-contained and also works as part of the whole; this is not just a matter of an integrated storyline involving recurring characters and themes – each book modifies the other two, making the whole greater than the sum of the parts. Each of the novels uses the conventions of a different type of crime fiction – the first (*The Four Last Things*) is a psychological thriller, the second (*The Judgement of Strangers*) toys with the format of the cosy school of whodunits, and the third (*The Office of the Dead*) is about a woman in peril, though the perils are not of the conventional kind.

There are armies of fictional coppers vying for our attention, but with *A Fine and Private Place*, **FREDA DAVIES** made a plausible bid for her protagonist, DI Keith Tyrell, to take his place in the ranks. *Bound in Shallows* demonstrated that the earlier book was no one-off: this was another well-turned thriller, delivered with understated power. The body of a girl is found on the banks of the Severn after recent flooding, and Tyrell finds himself tracking a killer whose trail leads to the Forest of Dean. Soon the bodies are stacking up, and Tyrell begins to suspect that followers of the occult arts are somehow mixed up in the murders – which now appear to be the work of two killers. But Tyrell (like so many policemen in the world of crime fiction) has an unsympathetic superior officer balking him at every turn. He is taken off the case, but is soon ignoring such niceties. The unassuming manner of Davies' writing cleverly wrong-foots the reader, and ensures attention.

Other writers and key books
RHYS BOWEN: *Evan and Elle, Evan Only Knows*
CHRIS COLLETT: *Blood and Stone*

JM GREGSON: *An Academic Death, Murder at the Nineteenth*
KATE HAMER: *The Girl in the Red Coat*
ROBERT LEWIS: *Swansea Terminal, Bank of the Black Sheep*
STEPHEN LLOYD JONES: *The String Diaries, Written in the Blood*
HOWARD MARKS: *Sympathy for the Devil, The Score*
ALISON TAYLOR: *In Guilty Night, Child's Play*

Scotland

After the Scots voted in sufficient numbers not to break away from the United Kingdom in 2014, one corollary was that **IAN RANKIN** remained the bestselling British – as opposed to Scottish – male crime writer. Until the next referendum, that is. But what would British crime fiction do without Rankin? Apart from anything else, it would be somewhat lopsided in terms of the sexes, as there are markedly more queens of crime than kings. And, of the latter, Rankin is undoubtedly the ruling monarch, as such books as *The Naming of the Dead* have proved. Rankin was bemused by a host of media scare stories about the G8 meeting of world leaders in Scotland in 2005, and perceived that this would make an apposite background for one of his books. But (as he wisely realised) it would make more sense to have his tough detective Rebus on the borders of all the frenzied security arrangements, lost in the shuffle as his bosses are keen to keep this awkward policeman out of the public eye. Rebus is firmly on the periphery when the death of an MP (apparently a suicide) seems to tie in with hints that a serial killer may be at his gruesome work. Of course, the authorities want both situations to be very much minimised so that attention remains on this crucial world conference. But, inevitably, John Rebus jumps in with both feet, and encounters much resistance as his uncompromising methods bring him closer to the truth. Simultaneously, his colleague Siobhan Clarke is attempting to find the riot cop who assaulted her mother. So both of them have plenty on their plates.

Rankin's crime novels, initially inspired by the work of the late William McIlvanney, have been freighted with political issues, with their social commentary integrated into his forcefully entertaining narratives. After having created (in DI John Rebus) one of the most iconic of modern literary coppers, readers might have been tempted to wonder whether or not Rankin – despite his considerable success – has had a few anxious moments over a decision he made recently: he retired DI Rebus. Another remarkable Scottish crime writer – Arthur Conan Doyle – failed to slough off his famous detective and was obliged to bring him back from the dead. But Rankin wasn't killing off Rebus, just retiring him (and – surprise – he came back!).

After *Exit Music*, Rankin admirers were in some suspense – was there life after Rebus? A standalone heist novel, *Open Doors*, provided a reassuring answer – lightweight, but a delight. However, a big hurdle was ahead for Rankin: a new series character. And we were given the policeman Malcolm Fox in *The Complaints*. Had lightning struck twice? Fox is a very different kettle of fish. He shares Rebus's burliness and bolshiness (plus an old drink problem), but is more likely to prefer Sibelius to the Stones. He cares for a frail elderly father and has no female partner. But the main difference is his job: Fox works for Edinburgh's unpopular Complaints and Conduct Unit, rooting out corruption in the force. Fox is after a copper called Jamie Breck – and there's a personal element: Breck is involved in the inquiry into the death of the abusive partner of Fox's alcoholic sister. The changing relationship between Fox and Breck becomes a crucial plot element.

Some might have regretted that Rankin did not take the opportunity with this change of direction to choose a city to chronicle other than Edinburgh. Few have his skill at evoking the ancient town, but there's absolutely no doubt that Rankin could have matched other writers tackling something other than their own patch. But who cares? Let's face it, most Rankin admirers would be happy for him to take us down the mean streets of Auld Reekie for the rest of his career. And on the evidence of *The Complaints*, it looked as if Malcolm Fox would be just as sure-footed a guide to the city as his grizzled predecessor. Now, inevitably, Rankin has had his Batman versus Superman moment – pitting Fox against Rebus in later novels.

Just what kind of a novelist do you think **VAL McDERMID** is? If you're happy to regard her as the creator of the damaged criminal profiler Dr Tony Hill in a series of commanding and operatically violent thrillers – and you would be happy if she ploughed that particular furrow ad infinitum – then perhaps *A Darker Domain* is not for you. Yes, it's a crime thriller– but it's also a searing piece about society and wasted lives that crams more insight and anger into its 300-odd pages than many a non-crime novel. Actually, McDermid has been freighting in such things for years, but this is the book in which she (metaphorically) comes out of the closet as the serious novelist she's always been.

It's 1984. A crime involving an heiress and her son fills the Scottish newspapers; a kidnapping, a pay-off that goes wrong, leaving a woman dead and a child missing. The case is filed under 'unsolved' until ambitious newspaperwoman Bel Richmond, holidaying in Tuscany, investigates a crumbling old house. On the flagstones, she spots a rusty brown stain, and Bel realises she's stumbled on a crime scene. But she also discovers something else – a revelation concerning the decades-old kidnapping. Soon cold case expert DI Karen Pirie is involved, but Karen is already investigating another case from 1984. During the Miners' Strike, a miner from Fife, Mick Prentice, joined the so-called 'scab' strike breakers down south. But he has not been seen since. Mick's daughter, Misha, decides (despite the passing of years) to track down her disgraced father. But what really happened to him? The double mystery is a standard device of the crime novel, and McDermid orchestrates the tension with authority. She is performing, however, a canny balancing act here: crime narrative, yes, but she also paints a picture of a Britain riven by social and class divisions. We are forced to take sides in a 1980s dispute that seems as topical as ever – and if you think that McDermid will slip into standard left-of-centre platitudes, think again. In *A Darker Domain*, we begin to see Scargill and Thatcher as the twin villains of the piece: figures made for each other who between them left us a legacy of the Britain we live in today. After reading McDermid's novel, readers may wish that more crime fiction would have the guts to take on serious issues along with the puzzle solving.

The Scottish referendum mentioned above has engendered a discussion on the nature of Scottishness and nationalism. But how important are such things in the world of books? **LOUISE WELSH**'s *The Bullet Trick* may be published by the small Scottish publisher Canongate, but is the target market a Celtic one? Just a few paragraphs of the author's assured and highly imaginative novel make it clear that she would not be happy with just a local constituency – like many Scottish scribes (from Conan Doyle to Muriel Spark), Welsh is simply a writer, interested in the whole range of human experience and less concerned with the petty parochialism that both the English and the Scots have been displaying of late. Welsh made a considerable impression with her first novel, *The Cutting Room*: while the book utilised the conventions of the crime thriller, Welsh was clearly a literary novelist, and that balancing act is maintained in her subsequent outings. However, everything is thrown into the baggy delight that is *The Bullet Trick*: from the down-at-heel, sensuous pleasures of the burlesque scene to sharply realised locales (Glasgow gin joints, seedy Soho nightclubs and Berlin alleys – the author said at the time of publication that she was learning German in painfully slow fashion, but her grasp of the German settings here is second to none). Her shabby protagonist is Glaswegian conjurer William Wilson. He has been glumly watching his life go into a downward spiral and is desperate for a change, but he begins to tentatively believe that his luck may be improving when he finds himself signed up for a series of cabaret jobs in Berlin. The move from Glasgow comes at a particularly opportune moment, as Wilson has several people he'd rather not see again. The decadent charms of underworld Berlin initially look like the answer to a prayer, as Wilson plunges into a heady world of sexually available showgirls and persuasive conmen. But as his past (inevitably) begins to catch up with him, he finds the dividing line between reality and a more threatening nightmare world growing blurred. And, before long, he finds himself knee deep in paranoia and fear.

Those who want their books overloaded with lowlife atmosphere will plunge gratefully into the delights on offer here – but if your taste is for carefully refined prose and delicate effects, Louise Welsh is not for you. The other group of readers who should steer clear are those who believe that sexuality should not be confronted head-on in a novel: Welsh takes no prisoners in the area of the erotic – but how could she do otherwise when *Cabaret*-style Weimar decadence is on the menu? However, she is never a writer who is out for the easy effect by shocking the reader: the use of sexual violence here is handled responsibly, avoiding exploitation while not being afraid to tackle the subject with eyes wide open.

On the Isle of Lewis, villagers are stocking up on winter fuel in the usual fashion – cutting up peat. But they make a macabre discovery – one that is frequently made across Europe. Peat has the property of keeping bodies in a remarkable state of preservation over the centuries, such as the body found here – the Lewis man. But the assumption that this body may be millennia old is dispelled when a tattoo is discovered – one referring to Elvis Presley. This wonderful touch is one of the many praiseworthy things about **PETER MAY**'s exceptional *The Lewis Man*, which shows that its equally accomplished predecessor, *The Blackhouse*, was no flash in the pan. May has a prodigal inventiveness, which springs off every page. Saturnine copper Fin Macleod has left the force and has made his way back to his ancestral home. As well as terminating his career, he has left his wife in Edinburgh and has doggedly set about the task of restoring his parents' rural croft to a liveable state. Unsurprisingly, Fin is soon involved in what appears to be a murder case (crime readers will struggle to think of a single novel in which a retired copper is successfully able to leave his old career behind him). The peat-preserved body undergoes DNA tests, and is found (in an unlikely development) to share a family connection with the father of Fin's girlfriend when the detective was a boy. The old man, Tormod, is suffering from progressive dementia – and has, in fact, claimed that he was an only child. But the body in the bog gives the lie to this statement, and Fin finds that the dark past has an awkward way of resurfacing – both for him and for the father of his ex-sweetheart.

This is terrific stuff, and a reminder that when a crime novelist of authority sets his sights high, the results can be as persuasive as the best writing in any genre. Particularly effective here is the parallel narrative of the old man Tormod's own story, conveyed to us with all the confusion of a drifting mind, but still as utterly compelling as the main strand of the novel. Fin, as in the previous book (and, indeed, in the final entry in the trilogy), is something special in the field of fictional coppers, and *The Lewis Man* itself is a very distinctive novel.

Every new crime debut is inevitably trumpeted by its publisher, though many such books fall neglected by the wayside. But every so often, a book comes along which not only justifies the publisher's hyperbole but has critics attempting to come up with new adjectives to praise it. Recent examples include Belinda Bauer's *Blacklands* and Attica Locke's *Black Water Rising* – along with **MALCOLM MACKAY**'s debut, *The Necessary Death of Lewis Winter*. This book burst upon the scene in 2013 with the impact of a hand grenade, uneasily placing the reader in the mind of a hitman. Using the familiar trappings of the crime novel, the book was still utterly original, and it was clear that a major new voice had appeared, virtually fully formed. What made that novel particularly impressive was its terrifyingly laidback, authentic toughness – surprising, coming from a quiet, unassuming 30-year-old author from Stornoway (where Mackay still lives). And as if to put paid to the notion that a second novel after a powerful debut invariably disappoints, *How a Gunman Says Goodbye* was, if anything, even better than its remarkable predecessor.

In the second book, we're back in the Glasgow underworld, where life is cheap and criminal organisations are constantly engaged in ruthless face-offs with each other. Frank MacLeod, a man who has long practised his callous trade as a gunman, is perhaps no longer the best in the business. Something of a legend in his circle, he has been doing his bloody work for the Glasgow gangs for over 20 years, but now his skills are in decline. Frank is over 60 and is dealing with the inconvenience of a hip replacement. Is it time for his youthful protégé, Calum MacLean, to step into his shoes? The two men have been friends, but events are conspiring to put that friendship to the test – and the results will not be pretty. The real achievement here is how Mackay has built on the dark and vivid vision of the Scottish criminal world that made his first book so memorable. Crucially, he has not forgotten the importance of pithy characterisation, particularly where his relentless protagonists are concerned. Subsequent work has proved equally intriguing, and the author is being hailed as a new star of Tartan Noir – Stuart MacBride and co. may have to look to their laurels.

Slowly but surely, the capable Scottish writer **ALEX GRAY** has been building a reputation in the crime fiction arena, and *Keep the Midnight Out* is one of her very best books. The series featuring her protagonist Detective Superintendent William Lorimer has gone from strength to strength; here he finds himself confronted with something reminiscent of a 20-year-old case that he failed to solve as a fledgling detective constable. The body of a young redheaded man is washed up on the shore of the Isle of Mull, bound in a grotesquely unnatural position. While trying to avoid treading on the toes of the local police, Lorimer finds – as so often in crime fiction – past and present colliding with incendiary results. Lorimer, as before, is a sharply characterised figure.

For a time, his publishers bracketed the sardonic **CHRISTOPHER BROOKMYRE** under the generic heading of Tartan Noir, and certainly his books deliver the gritty diversions that such a label suggests. But Brookmyre was always keen to stretch the possibilities of the crime genre – and his Scottishness was a long way from that of his crime-writing confrère Ian Rankin. Brookmyre has always been more than ready to tread on the toes of the politically correct while outraging those of a conservative bent, but his ideas are never pushed in our faces at the expense of the narrative.

A Tale Etched in Blood and Hard Black Pencil has many of the familiar Brookmyre fingerprints – satirical wit and a murder investigation conveyed with uncompromising detail among others – but it is also an attempt to do something new. And for those not totally under the Brookmyre spell, this might be something of a problem. Detective Superintendent Karen Gillespie is investigating a botched attempt near Glasgow to burn a pair of corpses. The two suspects turn out to be fellow pupils of Karen in her schooldays, and the man representing them is also one of her contemporaries, now a successful lawyer who has worked on celebrity cases. Everybody involved has reason to regret taking part in this grisly spin on a Friends Reunited scenario, and Karen is forced to wonder: can criminal acts in adulthood be traced back to playground traumas? While all this is handled with cold-eyed assurance, it's quickly clear that, for all the authenticity of the present-day murder investigation, Brookmyre is most interested in writing a novel about the cruelties and betrayals of childhood. The flashbacks to Karen at school clearly claimed much more of the author's attention. These scenes are vigorously handled; Karen's childhood humiliation at wetting herself is given as much force as any event in her police career. Perhaps the comic episode involving some spectacular farting is a tad adolescent, but characters such as a monstrous neo-Dickensian schoolmaster definitely represent Brookmyre on fine form. And the changes that time brings about in school friends is something we can all relate to.

Is **DENISE MINA** becoming blasé about the crime fiction awards that routinely come her way? And the concomitant praise? The process was accelerated by *The Red Road* – a novel that reminds us that she is not only one of the finest practitioners of the modern art of crime, she is also a social commentator of perception and humanity. *The Red Road* begins in 1997, with 14-year-old Rose Wilson being pimped by her 'boyfriend' (using the term loosely), when she compromises her already ignoble life by committing two desperate crimes. Rose is arrested, and defence lawyer Julius Macmillan decides to take her case. Although she ends up in prison, she is visited by her sympathetic counsel, accompanied by his son Robert. After her rehabilitation, she joins the Macmillan household and even acts as nanny to Robert's children as well as becoming Macmillan's assistant in his law practice when darker corners need to be probed.

Unsurprisingly, all of this is handled with the assurance we expect from Mina, who is second to none in the creation of damaged female protagonists – and Rose is one of her most fully rounded and convincing creations. But then the novel moves to the present, where a deeply unpleasant arms dealer, Michael Brown, is involved with a murder in the eponymous Red Road flats, and detective Alex Morrow is a witness in the case. At the same time, a well-heeled Scottish lawyer waits in a castle on Mull, knowing that an assassin is en route to kill him; he has sold out his own father, and his days are numbered. These disparate elements (and a host of others –

Mina is always spendthrift in her plotting) are brought together with authority, intricately drawing us into a narrative that engages with a variety of issues, all equally provocative. Concealed beneath the surface is an agenda that has been a consistent element of Mina's work over the years: a passionate concern for the vulnerable and damaged in society – and a rage at injustice. Our sympathy is both invited and tested in the most rigorous of fashions, and it is to Mina's credit that she is never sentimental towards her victims. And if the unpleasant characters here are writ larger than we are accustomed to with this writer, their unspeakableness serves the function of galvanising our responses to a complex, crowded novel.

In a short space of time, **JAMES OSWALD** has demonstrated his mastery of the contemporary crime novel, with such books as *Natural Causes* (the first entry in his series featuring Inspector McLean) proving to be a debut of real authority. Some five books later in that sequence, *Prayer for the Dead* made it clear that Oswald still has command of the thriller genre. The body of a missing journalist is discovered in the sealed catacombs of Gilmerton Cove, the apparent victim of a grim Masonic ceremony. His throat has been cut, and the walls daubed with symbols written in his blood. With its macabre and occult overtones, this case is a natural for Inspector Tony McLean, but even before his investigation is fully underway, another corpse turns up – once again displaying no forensic clues. While McLean himself may be cut from a familiar cloth, this is terrific stuff with lashings of pace and atmosphere.

TF MUIR is an uncompromising and gritty novelist whose writing is both astringent and focused. In *The Meating Room* (the fifth DCI Gilchrist book), these characteristics are strongly in evidence. When Thomas Magner's business partner is found dead in his car on the outskirts of St Andrews, the evidence points to suicide. But Magner, a wealthy property developer, is being investigated for a series of alleged rapes that took place almost 30 years earlier. In total, 11 women are prepared to go to court to testify against him, but one by one they withdraw their complaints until only five remain. With the Procurator Fiscal now reconsidering her case, one of Magner's remaining accusers is found brutally murdered in her home. Even though Magner's alibi is rock solid, DCI Andy Gilchrist is convinced he is somehow responsible. But as Gilchrist and his sidekick DS Jessie Janes dig deeper, they begin to expose Magner's murky past, and uncover a horrifying secret that has lain dormant for decades.

In the space of four or five books, **CRAIG ROBERTSON** has established his place in the crime field, showing an unerring command of narrative. The encomiums he received for his earlier books were echoed for 2014's *The Last Refuge*, which initially appears to be firmly located in the Scandicrime genre but is shot through with the author's own highly individual personality. John Callum has moved to the hauntingly desolate Faroe Islands, keen to put his troubled past behind him. The community on the islands is close-knit, but Callum finds it relatively easy to integrate himself – his only problems involve the nightmarish dreams that disturb his sleep. But then the quotidian life of the islands is shattered by an unusual occurrence: a murder. Denmark sends a specialist team of detectives in order to help the out-of-their-depth local police, and Callum is to discover that the relationship he has built up with his fellow islanders is as insubstantial as gossamer. They begin to close ranks, and he finds himself on the outside. His real anxiety, however, is caused by the hint that is coming to him through his nightmares: he himself might possibly be the killer. Those who have read earlier books by Robertson will not be at all surprised by the authority with which he delivers his cool but involving tale. The accoutrements may appear to be those of Scandinavian crime fiction, but this is in fact something very individual – and readers will find that it is quite unlike most other crime novels they have encountered.

'Now for a header into the cesspool,' George Orwell once wrote of British crime writer James Hadley Chase, whose *No Orchids for Miss Blandish* Orwell saw as reprehensible compared with the lightweight charms of the Raffles books. The rigid class structures of the latter seemed not to worry him, but he was outraged by the 'general brutality' of the Chase novel, with its casual killings and woundings, an exhumation and the flogging of the heroine. Were he still alive to cast a cold eye over the crime fiction of the twenty-first century, what would Orwell make of the novels of **STUART MacBRIDE**, a writer who makes Chase look like Enid Blyton?

MacBride is one of the signature writers of the Tartan Noir school, with a string of abrasive bestsellers to his name. His protagonist, the tough DS Logan McRae, moves through an Aberdeen that sometimes seems like an anteroom to hell. The novels are written in a scabrous prose that traverses the darkest recesses of the human psyche, but does it with a sardonic black humour that renders everything strangely exhilarating (although it's unlikely that Orwell would agree). *A Song for the Dying*, however, is the second appearance of a character who previously surfaced in *Birthdays for the Dead*, the disgraced copper Ash Henderson. And if you'll forgive a second simile, Ash makes Logan McRae look like Jane Marple. While Logan is at least able to function within the rules of the police force, Ash is from another era, unsparing in his dealing with the lowlife scum who are his daily workload. Politically correct he ain't.

Henderson has been serving time but is released to investigate a series of gruesome killings committed by a sadistic murderer who has been given the name 'The Inside Man'. The killer's speciality is to operate on his victims, inserting a cheap plastic doll into their stomachs before dumping their bodies; a vertiginous climax is in the offing. MacBride has made it clear that he is not interested in attracting readers with delicate sensibilities, but those who respond to the most visceral crime fiction (and those not alienated by its author's truly stygian view of human nature) will find not only the requisite excitement but a lively cast of characters and a pungent sense of place – although the invented town here, Oldcastle, is not as successfully evoked as the real-world Aberdeen. And there's Ash Henderson himself, mesmerisingly ruthless on the page – but perhaps someone to avoid if he actually walked the streets.

Bagging the much-desired Crime Writers' Association Dagger for best crime novel with the remarkable *Raven Black* is only one of **ANN CLEEVES'** achievements. Two TV series adapted from her books have gleaned keen followings: *Vera* with Brenda Blethyn and *Shetland*, with detective Jimmy Perez played by Douglas Henshall.

Cleeves is a well-known aficionado of Scandinavian crime fiction, and she is able to transmit that Nordic feeling into her own exemplary work.

If you doubt this encomium to Cleeves' writing skills, you should pick up *Blue Lightning*, a cogent demonstration of her considerable narrative grasp and (her ace in the hole) persuasive evocation of atmosphere. Her Shetland detective Jimmy Perez is not looking forward to his journey to Fair Isle. It is famous for being a very tight-knit community, which does not extend open arms to incomers. As Jimmy knows, the islanders are a hardy breed – and they need to be, as winter approaches with its inevitable storms, making an already insular community close in further upon itself. It is in this pressure cooker atmosphere that murder takes place (this is an Ann Cleeves novel, after all) and the body of a woman is found with her hair laced with feathers. With the locals in a furious and fractious mood, it's up to Jimmy to investigate the killing as quickly and efficiently as he can; not an easy task, as he has no resources to call on except his own. And as the clock ticks, the inevitability of another murder looms ever larger.

As in Ann Cleeves' earlier Shetland mysteries, the trick here is to utilise the apparatus of the Christie-style murder mystery (most notably the cloistered, cut-off setting) and reinvigorate it with a healthy dose of plausible contemporary psychology. This Cleeves does splendidly, and even though Jimmy Perez may be a familiar kind of figure to those who read a great deal of crime fiction, there are still some canny changes that the author is able to ring on the formula. Best of all, though, is the skill with which she evokes the experience of being on these dangerous islands, and readers will be delighted that this series is continuing in parallel with her books featuring the indomitable Vera Stanhope (of which *The Moth Catcher* was the most recent at the time of writing).

LIN ANDERSON's second novel, *Torch*, was also the second to feature forensic scientist Rhona MacLeod (following the character's first appearance in the highly impressive *Driftnet*). It's another pared-down narrative that wastes not a word, but succeeds in being a thoroughly compulsive read. Edinburgh is being plagued by an arsonist, and MacLeod along with her distinctly non-PC partner Severino MacRae – a man not given to worrying about the tender sensibilities of those around him – need to work quickly before the firebug lays waste to the city's Hogmanay festival. As with so many of Anderson's books, this is crime fiction that delivers exactly what it says on the tin and its sheer momentum is matched by its ruthless stripping away of any fripperies.

ALLAN GUTHRIE has said that he is strongly influenced by American noir fiction – especially James M Cain and his mid-twentieth-century literary descendants such as David Goodis, Jim Thompson and Chester Himes – but his native Scottish influences are clear too. He is a writer of crime fiction as opposed to detective fiction, police investigations rarely having more than a peripheral role in any of his books. His vivid tales of Edinburgh's underbelly are written from the viewpoints of criminals and victims, and told in prose that is spare, hard-hitting, and full of explicit violence, absurdity and black humour. His debut novel, *Two-Way Split* – which was the Theakston's Crime Novel of the Year in 2007 – tells the story of an ex-concert pianist turned armed robber with mental health problems who's secretly off his medication. On the day of a robbery, he finds out that his wife and a fellow gang member have been sleeping together. This is modern Scottish Gothic, with more than a passing nod to Stevenson and Hogg. While personal identity crisis lies at the heart of *Two-Way Split*, Guthrie's second novel, *Kiss Her Goodbye*, looks at the nature of fatherhood. The novel opens with Joe Hope, an enforcer for a loan shark, discovering that his teenage daughter has killed herself. The rest of the book focuses on Joe's attempt to make sense of her death. Joe Hope is hardly a likeable character, but Guthrie stresses empathy over sympathy. *Kiss Her Goodbye* was nominated for the Edgar, Gumshoe and Anthony awards in the US. More recent work has forcefully maintained the early momentum.

MC BEATON was born in Glasgow and began her professional life as a bookseller, but subsequently became a journalist on the Scottish *Daily Express*, where she reported mostly on crime, and later moved to Fleet Street and the offices of the London *Express*, where she became their chief female reporter. Her fiction career began with Regency romances, writing over a hundred such titles under her maiden name of Marion Chesney. But she tired of setting every story within the years of 1811 to 1820, and began to write detective stories. On a holiday trip from the USA to Sutherland in Scotland, a course at a fishing school inspired the first Hamish Macbeth novel, the quirky series about a policeman in the Highlands that is a particular crime readers' favourite. Moving to the Cotswolds, she later created the long-running Agatha Raisin series: notably 'cosy' but beguiling.

With seven crime novels published over ten years (2006 to 2015), **DOUG JOHNSTONE** has ploughed something of a lonely furrow in the Tartan Noir community. Not interested in police procedurals, spies or secret agents, Johnstone is one of the few British writers dealing solely in the noir of the domestic, looking at everyday men and women and the split-second wrong decisions they make that can lead their lives to unravel. His novel *The Jump* is typical. Ellie, a middle-aged woman still mourning the suicide of her teenage son, discovers another boy about to kill himself by jumping from the Forth Road Bridge. She talks him down, seeing a shot at redemption, but in reality that action leads her life down a terrible and bloody path. This penetrating examination of suicide and the grief of those left behind is tackled with a cogency worthy of any 'literary 'novel on the subject – but without short-changing crime fiction aficionados. Like many of Johnstone's books, *The Jump* deals primarily with the people committing the crimes, and looks at how the ripples of their actions spread out to cause mayhem within the wider community. And in *Gone Again*, Johnstone's most commercially successful book, a father has to deal with his young son while trying to find out what has happened to his missing wife. The success of Johnstone's books lies in the deliberately narrow focus: he hones in on the brutal everyday details of having to cope with extreme situations, and the reader therefore can't help but wonder what he or she would do in the central character's situation. It's not comfortable reading, but there is something compelling about it all the same, as if the reader is forced to follow the story through the slits of their fingers.

MARSALI TAYLOR's books are set in Shetland – specifically, the west side of Mainland and the sailing area known as Swarbacks Minn. The first book in the Cass Lynch series is *Death on a Longship*, in which sailing enthusiast Lynch has landed her dream job, as the skipper of a replica Viking longship being used to shoot a Hollywood film on location in Shetland. Back in her home waters after 15 years, Cass finds herself drawn back into the community, where her father is involved in creating a huge windfarm, and her school friend Inga is part of the protest group. The filming seems to go well – until a rock rolled downhill narrowly misses the star. Then Cass finds a body on her deck… This series focuses on country life in Shetland, weaving in the places and habits that are a legacy of the Vikings who once ruled the isles, the beauty of the landscape, and the distinctive dialect and folklore heritage, but it also provides a glimpse into modern Shetland: the wealth brought by oil, the fight against centralisation, the tug between money and environment (the projected windfarm in the book is inspired by real life), and – remembering that Shetland is 22,000 people living 200 miles out in the North Sea – the difficulties brought about by the council's austerity measures in an isolated community.

The Hanging Shed was a massive success even before its print incarnation hit the bookshops, proving that new technology cannot be ignored even in the largely technophobic world of books. Until a few years ago, **GORDON FERRIS** was completely unknown; the Kilmarnock-born Ferris didn't inaugurate his writing career till the age of 50, but his fourth novel became one of the most downloaded Kindle books in Britain. However, *The Hanging Shed*, and the other books in the series featuring reporter and ex-policeman Douglas Brodie, are set in the 1940s, so don't fulfil the remit of this survey. *Money Tree* is a departure for Ferris, a literary thriller set among the glittering canyons of New York and the seething alleyways of New Delhi. At its heart is the story of a destitute woman in a dying village in central India, and her struggle against the daily embrace of usury. Into her fraught existence blunder two Westerners: a world-weary American reporter living off the faded glory of a Pulitzer Prize, and a hard-bitten Scottish banker wrestling with her late-developing conscience. As the tension mounts, their three storylines interweave and fuse in a strong and moving climax. In pointing up the gulf between rich and poor, and the misguided efforts of Western institutions to meddle in developing countries, Ferris pays homage to Professor Yunus, winner of the 2006 Nobel Prize for Peace and founder of the Grameen Bank in Bangladesh. The book is the first novel in his new *Only Human* series – novels tackling some of today's global challenges.

GILLIAN GALBRAITH's *Dying of the Light* starts arrestingly. On a cold night in Leith, a policewoman's torch shines on the face of a body in a wintry cemetery. It is the corpse of a prostitute, the first victim of a serial murderer. As so often in such cases, the threat to the women plying this trade is not sufficient to keep them off the streets, and DS Alice Rice looks into their activities on the back streets. And she soon finds herself in considerable danger. Alice Rice may have joined a very crowded profession – that of the tough female copper – but the auguries were good for Rice and her creator, who earned the praise of Alexander McCall Smith for her debut novel *Blood in the Water*. In the later, and equally impressive, *Troubled Waters*, a young disabled girl finds herself distressed and lost one cold night in Leith, and cannot find her way home. Shortly after her disappearance, a body is washed up on Beamer Rock, a small island in the Forth which is being used as the foundation for a new bridge. Testing all her sorely overstretched skills, Rice (now an inspector) finds herself dealing with not one but two deaths when a second body is found at the edge of the estuary. Is there a connection between the victims? The answer to that may be easy (when has there not been a connection in all the annals of crime fiction?), but there are narrative surprises aplenty here, in a book in which the storytelling ethos is ironclad. This is Scottish crime writing of real accomplishment, at times matching the most acclaimed names in the Celtic genre.

The **QUINTIN JARDINE** novel sequence that features the tough copper DCC Bob Skinner has marked itself out from the competition by pithy, idiomatic writing and some razor-sharp characterisation. In such books as *Murmuring the Judges* and *Skinner's Ghosts*, a growing league of Jardine readers grew to anticipate the challenges the author would put his protagonist through (as in *Head Shot*, where Jardine dropped Skinner into a very dangerous USA). In *Stay of Execution*, he was back on his home turf as a series of ruthless killings make Edinburgh a very fraught place – particularly as the Pope is scheduled to visit the city. As Skinner looks into the deaths (a small businessman, found hanged; a musician dying under the wheels of a car), he begins to realise that stopping a major killing may be more difficult than simply nailing some criminals – the ramifications of this case are dark and far-reaching. Jardine at his edgy best.

When Val McDermid grants an imprimatur to a writer, it's sensible to listen. **CARO RAMSAY**'s *Absolution* was a recipient of the McDermid largesse, and this was an undeniably caustic debut novel. The Glasgow locale may have been well-trodden territory for aficionados of Tartan Noir (and hard-edged Scottish crime writing is a crowded field), but Ramsay shows that there are fresh excavations to be made. 'The Crucifixion Killer' is murdering luckless female victims, leaving them to bleed to death with their arms outstretched. The case is a tough one for DCI Alan McAlpine and his colleagues – and not just because of the necessity of quickly tracking down a brutal killer. In 1984, McAlpine was a copper on the beat, tasked with guarding a woman whose face had been disfigured by an acid attack. Disaster followed this assignment, and McAlpine has been living with the consequences ever since. But as he gets closer to the truth about this more modern monster, the past (unsurprisingly) makes a grim return.

The world was obviously ready for **ALEXANDER McCALL SMITH**. Although the crime genre had long been plunged into a welter of blood and violence by stylists as different as Thomas Harris and Mo Hayder, there were those who hankered for the more genteel mysteries of the Agatha Christie era, replete with quaint detectives, ingenious plots and a marked avoidance of eviscerated victims. The phenomenal success of McCall Smith's novels has demonstrated that publishers underestimate the spending power of this market at their peril. The author is notably out of sympathy with the sex, violence and unblushing language of contemporary crime novels, and his *No. 1 Ladies' Detective Agency* series harks back to a more sedate age, with their amiable protagonist, the generously proportioned Precious Ramotswe, fulfilling Marple-like duties in a sultrily-rendered (if anodyne) Botswana setting. The author, however, lives in Edinburgh, home to Ian Rankin's tough copper, Rebus, who represents – one might guess – everything in crime fiction that McCall Smith is reacting against. And to the surprise of his army of readers, McCall Smith inaugurated a series set in his home town with *The Sunday Philosophy Club*, featuring a new non-affiliated female detective, the philosopher Isabel Dalhousie. This was a pleasing novel, full of imaginative touches and pithy characterisation – notably of McCall Smith's new heroine. In the second outing for Isabel, *Friends, Lovers, Chocolate*, she once again called upon her philosophical skills to crack some complex mysteries. She has found herself having ambiguous feelings for a young man, Jamie, who was going to marry her niece Cat. Her attraction to the young man means trouble – Cat is holidaying in Italy, and Isabel has agreed to take over the running of the latter's delicatessen. One of the customers, she discovers, has recently had a heart transplant and is experiencing phantom memories that he believes belong to someone else. As Isabel investigates, she once again finds that her gift for philosophical discourse – and extrapolating facts – puts her in the path of danger.

McCall Smith's publishers must have wondered if his Dalhousie outings would seduce those impatient for him to get back to the plump Precious. The books' appeal is more subtle than that of the earlier series: the pleasures come from the aperçus on a whole variety of issues – the eternal problems between men and women, the seductive appeal of the Wildean approach to temptation (in this case, whether or not to give in to good-looking Italians or high-calorie confection). Not a book for those seeking stronger meat, but beguiling enough for readers with a taste for literary chocolate.

In *Who Robbed the Dead?* by **TANA COLLINS**, DCI Jim Carruthers and DS Andrea Fletcher are conducting an investigation into the brutal death of a young man when the peace of Fife is shattered by an explosion. What connects the tattoo of a bluebird on the dead man, threatening letters to a controversial politics lecturer and the shooting of a young woman over 40 years before? The investigation takes an unwelcome turn for Carruthers when the former colleague he blames for his marriage break-up is sent to Scotland to help with the investigation. Meanwhile, Andrea Fletcher has received shocking personal news. Can Carruthers and Fletcher locate and save the life of a man who has spent 40 years living in fear? Or will this man be tracked down by a shadowy figure hell-bent on revenge for an event that changed the course of British political history? This is the first novel in the Jim Carruthers series by the talented Collins, set in and around the historic town of St Andrews, a part of Scotland close to the writer's heart.

ALISON BAILLIE's *Sewing the Shadows Together*, set in Edinburgh, the Outer Hebrides and South Africa, is about loss and the question of whether we ever really know the people closest to us. More than 30 years after the murder of 13-year-old Shona McIver in Portobello, the seaside suburb of Edinburgh, the tragedy still casts a shadow over the lives of her brother Tom and her best friend Sarah. Tom's family emigrated to South Africa after the tragedy, where he drifted aimlessly, with short-term relationships and dead-end jobs. Sarah seems to lead a perfect family life, but is haunted by memories of her friend's death. On Tom's first visit back to Scotland to scatter his mother's ashes, they meet again at a school reunion and feel an immediate connection, but when DNA evidence shows that the wrong man was convicted of the murder, their relationships and emotions are thrown into turmoil. Tom uncovers secrets from the past and Sarah's golden life begins to crumble as suspicion falls on family and friends.

JAY STRINGER likes to find his stories in the voices of people who are usually left on the fringes of mainstream society. This was shown with his Eoin Miller trilogy, starting with *Old Gold*, which used a Romany protagonist to explore social issues, including immigration, human trafficking, police corruption and sexual assault. His writing clearly owes a debt to American crime writers such as George

Pelecanos, and Stringer also cites the works of Sean O'Casey and George Orwell as major influences. After writing a series of hard-boiled novels set in his native West Midlands, Stringer moved in a more comedic direction with his later *Ways to Die in Glasgow*.

MATT BENDORIS, when not holding down the day job as a journalist, is proving himself to be a talented writer of crime fiction, with his debut novel *Killing with Confidence* instantly establishing him; subsequent books demonstrated that his first novel was no fluke. Strong narrative skills and an acute sense of place are notable characteristics. Bendoris has worked in newspapers since he started writing a pop column for the Glasgow *Guardian* in 1989. After a spell in London, he returned to Scotland in 1996, where he has been chief features writer for the Scottish *Sun* ever since. In 2007, when his office relocated to Glasgow city centre, Matt tentatively began writing a crime novel, tapping out the chapters on the tiny keyboard of his Blackberry on the train during the daily commute. The result was *Killing with Confidence*, which focuses on a serial killer who uses self-help, motivational material to become a better murderer. His follow-up, *DM for Murder*, was written in much the same fashion, although this time the bulk of it was done on an iPhone due to his employer upgrading their smartphones. It also features his two principal characters April Lavender – an ageing, overweight, technophobic journalist – and her younger colleague Connor 'Elvis' Presley. The third April and Elvis instalment is *Wicked Leaks*.

RUSSEL D McLEAN has created a memorable private eye protagonist in J McNee (first name unrevealed), whose stamping ground is a vividly drawn Dundee. *The Good Son* is a typically idiosyncratic entry, with McNee up against a ruthless criminal influence that stretches from London to Scotland, while the later *Father Confessor* has McNee defending the honour of a deceased policeman friend. McLean's work bristles with inventiveness and imagination, with McNee a winningly sardonic antihero. McLean credits his major influences as being mainly American writers, moving the tropes of private eye fiction to a Scottish setting in several of his short stories and five novels. The five McNee books (beginning with *The Good*

Son in 2008 and ending with *Cry Uncle* in 2014) are concerned with family, guilt and the almost paternal relationship between local crime lord David Burns and private investigator McNee. While each book stands alone, together they form a longer arc, detailing McNee's journey from damaged antihero to conflicted pawn in a game played between the local police and Burns himself. There may be other work featuring McNee in the future, but for now McLean is looking to work on other projects in new locations.

Other writers and key books
TONY BLACK: *Truth Lies Bleeding, Paying for It*
KAREN CAMPBELL: *Shadowplay, The Twilight Time*
SJI HOLLIDAY: *Black Wood*
DOUGLAS LINDSAY: *Murderers Anonymous, The Cutting Edge of Barney Thomson*
SINCLAIR MACLEOD: *The Reluctant Detective*
MICHAEL J MALONE: *A Taste for Malice, Blood Tears*
KEN McCLURE: *Deception, Hypocrites' Isle*
KEITH MILES: *Bullet Hole, Double Eagle*
LOUISE MILLAR: *The Hidden Girl, City of Strangers*
DOUGLAS SKELTON: *Devil's Knock*
ANNA SMITH: *Betrayed, Screams in the Dark*
ALINE TEMPLETON: *Evil for Evil, Cold in the Earth*

Ireland

The North and the Republic

Although the credit crunch caused the odd hiccup, the city of Dublin maintains its frenzy of property development. Walk through such areas as James Joyce's 'Nighttown' these days, and you'll see something rather different from the locale he celebrated: the working girls may still be there, but there are fewer of them and cranes now loom above the narrow streets, preparing the way for the proliferating wine bars, coffee shops and upscale couture houses. But Dublin's basic identity seems to remain inviolable, however much her face may change – and it is this struggle between the old and the new that is powering some of the most provocative fiction being written in Ireland today. Interestingly enough, as **ALAN GLYNN's** *Winterland* comprehensively proves, it's the not entirely respectable genre of crime fiction that is throwing up some of the most incisive evocations of this protean city.

The central character, the tenacious Gina Rafferty (who takes on some very powerful and dangerous people), may have wandered into *Winterland* from a Martina Cole novel, but the territory here couldn't be further from the East End of London, either geographically or in terms of the author's ambition; despite its popular pedigree, this is something of a state-of-the-nation novel. From the violent opening in a smoking section of a Dublin pub – where the dialogue has an authentic snap, maintained throughout the novel – Glynn keeps his narrative exuberant and fleet-footed. A young drug dealer, Noel Rafferty, is shot in a beer garden, and the police are happy to file it under gangland killings – one less thug to worry about. But on the same evening, Rafferty's uncle (who shares his nephew's name) also loses his life in a suspicious car accident. Coincidence or conspiracy? Gina Rafferty, Glynn's heroine, isn't buying the official explanation of either death, and undertakes some amateur detective work. But she quickly realises that she is up against some influential opponents – movers and shakers in a world of crooked property deals and corrupt political influence. She discovers that her brother (the Rafferty who died in the car crash) was involved with the construction of a massive skyscraper together with a property developer, Paddy Norton, whose ambition is to transform Dublin into something like downtown Chicago. The real crimes in Glynn's provocative and richly textured novel are not necessarily the killings, but the unfettered exercise of greed and political self-interest.

The names of certain crime writers are uttered with due reverence, and for a long time, **KEN BRUEN** has been a writer spoken about by both his fellow scribes and his devoted readers with great affection. Among his many skills, perhaps his most notable is the astonishing consistency he has shown over his series of books. The Galway-born author's Jack Taylor series has bagged both Shamus and Crime Writers' Association awards – not to mention critical acclaim. *Cross*, the sixth in the award-winning private eye series, is a first-rate entry, played out against a slowly – and sometimes reluctantly – modernising Ireland and Galway City. The author's PhD in metaphysics is reflected in the mental processes of Jack Taylor, and Jack's frequently alienated state is one of the many unusual aspects of these very individual novels.

It's always a gift for a crime writer when his series character enjoys a successful TV incarnation, as **COLIN BATEMAN** has done with his Martin Murphy books. Or is it? James Nesbitt has made the character very much his own on television, but every reader will have their own conception of Murphy when they read the cleverly written novels. In fact, it's probably best to forget the face of the actor involved and let the author work his particular magic. There is a serious point at the heart of *Murphy's Revenge*: who defines the moral imperatives if it is possible to track down and kill the person who murdered a loved one? A support group for relatives of murder victims – Confront – counsels empowerment through therapy, but someone is choosing to murder the killers involved. Martin Murphy joins the group undercover, but finds it impossible to remain aloof when his own past is wrenched into the investigation. What makes all of this even more involving than one might expect from the reliable Bateman is the insidious way in which he confronts the reader's own prejudices. Surely the scum who have murdered loved ones deserve no more pity than they gave to their victims? The moral equivocation forced upon the unwilling Murphy strengthens Bateman's narrative.

Slowly but surely, Bateman (who went for a time under just his surname, a strange ploy his publishers have wisely abandoned) has been building a loyal army of fans, eager for all they can get of his sardonic and idiosyncratic writing. Bagging the Betty Trask Prize with his first novel *Divorcing Jack* was not the passport to oblivion such early success can often be; in fact, it was an open sesame for what has been a very healthy career. This first book introduced Bateman's feckless hero, Dan Starkey. By the time of *The Horse With My Name*, Starkey has not made a success of his career in journalism and is living in a run-down Belfast flat. He spends most of his time in the pub, his only activity being worrying about his collapsed relationship with his wife Patricia (who has found herself a new lover). But when his friend Mark (who moonlights as 'The Horse Whisperer', an online tout) asks him to look into the activities of Geordie McClean, the prime mover in Irish American racing, Dan finds himself in very deep waters – and yearning for the balmy days when no one cared what he did. Dan is a wonderfully rounded comic creation, and the ever-surprising narrative has all the bite and incident of Bateman's best work. If you like the hard-edged wit of Irvine Welsh but find all the drugs a little hard to take, Bateman may well be the writer for you.

So many debut crime thrillers have been appearing over the last few years that it's harder and harder to keep up. But **LIZ ALLEN**'s intelligently written *Last to Know* was a book that really deserved to rise above the throng. Her heroine Deborah Parker is a fresh recruit at the prestigious firm of solicitors Jennings and Associates, trying to make her mark in a challenging legal world. A plum job drops in her lap: she is to defend the scion of one of Ireland's leading crime figures. The issue is rape – a particularly savage one – which makes her uneasy, and Deborah soon finds that her big break is actually a recipe for disaster: her whole life is turned upside down and she finds herself part of a world that is very different from the one she is used to. It's a standard thriller ploy to drop your hero or heroine into a maelstrom of danger and suspicion, watching in horror as their life implodes around them, but Allen brings off the device with more panache than most, and the Irish criminal underworld is created with salty, threatening authenticity. A key element here, of course, is the beleaguered heroine, and Deborah Parker is sympathetically characterised – we share her fears, get annoyed at her (frequent) missteps and identify with her successes. Similarly, the various Irish heavies Deborah comes up against are vividly created, from the brutal to the more dangerous intelligent kingpins.

The Northern Ireland novelist **STUART NEVILLE** enjoys the heavyweight imprimatur of American crime-writing legend James Ellroy – with such encomiums as 'This guy can write!' The Celtic onslaught on crime fiction continues apace, with Neville making a mark as a very individual talent. Apart from a sure grasp of the mechanics of suspense, Neville's real coup in such books as *Stolen Souls* is to present a markedly multifaceted protagonist – prey to ghosts from Ireland's troubled and violent past – about whom the reader is frequently obliged to change their mind. Comparisons may be made with other writers, but Neville is very much his own man. In 2015, *Those We Left Behind* saw the start of a completely new set of characters, a new location and a new style of writing. Gone is the growing pile of bodies, gone the male-dominated cast of characters, replaced instead by the brilliant and complicated DCI Serena Flanagan, a detective just back to work following her treatment for breast cancer. *Those We Left Behind* is not just about the whodunit, but about the ripples that crime creates and the impact it has on the remaining family, on the inspectors who work on the case, and on the perpetrators themselves.

In *Crazy Man Michael* by **JIM LUSBY**, DI Carl McCadden is being tipped to head up a new unit – the Murder Squad – which the Irish

Minister for Justice is planning to form. The unit will have exclusive responsibility for tackling homicide throughout the Irish state, and the first assignment will be to investigate a group of unsolved murders of women. But as McCadden readies himself for this high-powered job, he encounters an undercover policeman called Wallace who has a strange story to tell – and, what's more, he is being pursued by Special Branch. McCadden realises that it would be far more sensible to avoid the trouble that Wallace brings with him, but, inevitably, he is soon deep in a very dark business that threatens everything he has worked for. Jim Lusby has steadily developed his McCadden character through three previous thrillers, all rich in atmosphere and crammed with the kind of assured plotting that is found too rarely these days. *Making the Cut* was a powerful debut that the author succeeded in building upon, but *Crazy Man Michael* is possibly the most complex in the series. By dividing his hero's sympathies, Lusby presents him, and the reader, with a host of difficult moral decisions that give a keen edge to the plot. Some of the revelations (including corruption in high places) are familiar, but it is more and more difficult for authors to avoid treading these familiar waters. The point is: can Lusby ring enough changes to make his novel stand out from the crowd? And on that score, there is little room for debate – this is a richly textured tale.

The phrase 'If you've got a winning formula, why change it?' is clearly one that the writer **CHRIS EWAN** doesn't agree with. He made a mark with the titles in his witty and entertaining crime series *The Good Thief's Guide*, all of which enjoyed critical acclaim and respectable sales. So – one might legitimately ask – why rock the boat with an entirely different kind of book? The answer to that is simple – in their very different way, his more recent novels, set in the author's own Manx/Irish Sea territory, are proving to be just as accomplished as the earlier series. *Safe House* dealt with governmental corruption and international terrorism. And impressive though it was, *Dark Tides* was even better, this time drawing on the Isle of Man Halloween convention of Hop-tu-naa.

Claire Cooper is just eight years old when her mother disappears without trace during Hop-tu-naa. The years do little to assuage her loss, until Claire, now a teenager, finds herself part of a group of five friends who celebrate Halloween with foolhardy dares. Claire is a participant, but she is more mature than her friends and her presence changes the nature of the group. Then one of the pranks takes a very grim turn, and the group is torn apart. Six years pass, and one of Claire's friends dies in what appears to be an accident on the night of Hop-tu-naa. Claire has now become a police officer, and she is not convinced that the death was accidental – and what is the significance of the single footprint found near the body? After another Halloween death and another footprint, Claire begins to fear that somebody is seeking revenge – and the secret to the identity of the killer clearly lies in the past.

If the above scenario – prank goes wrong, body count begins – sounds familiar from a hundred films, well, yes, it is. But such is Chris Ewan's skill that this is a compelling piece of work. Ewan utilises the more sinister aspects of Manx folklore, forging from them a truly atmospheric thriller, about which one is forced to use one of the oldest clichés in the reviewer's handbook: it is impossible to put down. If Ewan chooses never to go back to his lighter *Good Thief's Guide* series and continues to produce novels like *Dark Tides*, readers will have little cause to complain.

Authors tend to like to have their egos stroked, and **ANTHONY J QUINN** has been enjoying such attention more than most for his remarkable novels. In *Border Angels*, a charred corpse and a set of footprints in the snow direct Quinn's protagonist Inspector Celcius Daley into the dark world of people trafficking. Daly is on the trail of a missing woman, Lena Novak, who has disappeared one winter's night along the Irish border, leaving behind only the bodies of two men. Soon, Daley finds himself working with a prostitute and a hitman in an increasingly dangerous chase – one that leads to a refuge for people who do not want to be found. Like many writers resident in Ireland, Anthony Quinn is influenced by the great American crime writers – and *Border Angels* shows that he clearly belongs in their august company.

British crime fiction was once full of boring, characterless policemen (usually wearing a gabardine and trilby), shuffling in to solve crimes committed by far more colourful criminals. And how impatient readers were to get back to the malefactors! The breed, however, was comprehensively consigned to the dustbin by a new kind of copper, one who bends the rules to get the bad guy. This maverick cop soon calcified into cliché in its turn, so it's a cause for celebration that such writers as **GENE KERRIGAN** (author of *Little Criminals*, much acclaimed by the likes of Roddy Doyle) can still produce something fresh and radical with the concept.

In *The Midnight Choir*, DI Harry Synnott of the Dublin Garda has under his belt several high-profile cases. He is a policeman with uninflected views on the difference between right and wrong – and he is unforgiving when he encounters corruption among his fellow officers. Harry is aware that a glitzy promotion is in the offing, but he's also aware that he first has to close his investigation into an armed robbery – and he knows who the perpetrators are. He needs a lever to crack the case, and it comes his way in the figure of the desperate young Dixie Peyton. She is the widow of a petty criminal, and in her efforts to regain custody of her son she has taken to mugging. She accidentally stabs a tourist with a syringe that she claimed was full of HIV-infected blood, though this is a bluff. Dixie is perfect cannon fodder (after all, anything that could hurt the tourist trade in Dublin is frowned upon by Harry's bosses), and as Harry and his fellow cops work through the usual line-up of rapists and thugs, he begins to feel that a sacrifice on the altar of his career might be justified if it can get him the breakthrough he wants… and that sacrifice is Dixie.

Little Criminals marked Kerrigan out as a truly ambitious crime writer, with a dextrous use of language married to some masterful plotting. While working in a different genre, he has something of Joyce's ability in conjuring up a very vivid picture of Dublin – but this modern city is completely different from the one Leopold Bloom wandered through; the boarded-up shops and vicious petty thugs are artfully counterpointed with the cosmopolitan gloss of a European city on the up. But what really tells here are Kerrigan's notions on the limits of justice. The destruction of lives wrought by self-styled 'righteous' men is the theme in microcosm here, but it's possible to speculate that Kerrigan is drawing parallels with righteous men on the world stage, unconcerned by the destruction their virtue carries in its wake.

The versatile **GRAHAM MASTERTON** has adopted a career trajectory very similar to that of his colleague Peter James. Both men made their mark decades ago as British horror novelists of some distinction, before turning to the more lucrative genre of crime fiction, so it's hardly surprising that it is Peter James who supplies the encomium: 'One of the most original and frightening storytellers of our time.' In Masterton's fourth novel in his Katie Maguire sequence, *Taken for Dead*, an Irish wedding is in lively form in County Cork with a ceilidh band accompaniment. But when the cake is cut, a macabre discovery is made: the severed head of the local baker. Katie Maguire of the Irish Garda has no leads until another businessman disappears. Combining Graham Masterton's two skills – crime and horror – this is proof that career changes can be successful.

TANA FRENCH possesses one thing many writers would kill for – impeccable word of mouth among readers and critics. There are few aficionados of crime fiction who do not speak approvingly of her work: in fact, more than approvingly – with massive enthusiasm. Her novel *The Likeness* started with a conversation in a pub involving the notion that everyone has a double somewhere in the world. She began to speculate: what would it feel like if you and your double made friends? Or what if you couldn't stand each other? Would you have other things in common, beside that shared face? In a mystery novel someone has to die, so French's concept was that her protagonist meets her double when it is too late – she is already dead. But her protagonist, Cassie, is the only person who can find out who her double was and what happened to her, and the only way to get to know her is to *become* her. Detective Cassie Maddox, who first appeared in *In the Woods*, shows up at a crime scene and finds a victim who not only looks like her but is using her old undercover identity, Lexie Madison. She ends up going back undercover as Lexie to tempt the killer out of hiding to finish the job. But Cassie's at a very fragile moment in her own life, and Lexie's world is a very tempting one: a tightly knit group of friends sharing a huge, beautiful, ramshackle house in the countryside outside Dublin. Gradually, she starts to fall deeper and deeper into Lexie's life and to lose hold of her own. In many ways, this is a book about identity, and what a tricky, vulnerable thing it is. French has said that most of us have had at least one moment when we want to simply leave our own lives behind, just put them down and walk away. In *The Likeness*, some of the characters actually follow that impulse: they try to erase their old selves and start over from scratch. But it's a dangerous thing to do. French's other novels are equally ambitious and gripping.

The best crime writers, such as **BRIAN McGILLOWAY**, are adroit at bringing thorny issues to a general readership. And in *Bleed a River Deep*, the Irish-born author takes his Garda Inspector Benedict Devlin away from the locales of earlier books to a new setting: the opening of a gold mine in Donegal. Elements here include pollution in a local river and the treatment of illegal immigrants in Ireland, and McGilloway develops the relationship between Devlin and his Northern counterpart, Jim Hendry, in a highly satisfying fashion. The book is a reminder of just what an accomplished crime scribe McGilloway is – and how his skills keep on growing.

The acclaim that greeted **DECLAN BURKE**'s adroit *Absolute Zero Cool* was replicated for *Slaughter's Hound*, which arrived bearing praise from no less than Lee Child (as well as a striking jacket that rather cheekily lifts motifs from the designer Saul Bass – but then everyone does that). Burke's protagonist, the world-weary Harry Rigby, is witness to a suicide – a suicide that may be part of an Irish epidemic. And in Harry Rigby's Sligo, life can be very cheap, as Harry is reminded in the most forceful of terms. Those familiar with Declan Burke's work will know what to expect here: that wry and sardonic authorial voice, married to a particularly idiosyncratic command of dialogue. In some ways, perhaps, it's the latter (as in *The Lost and the Blind*) that marks Burke out from what is rapidly turning into an unstoppable juggernaut of Irish crime fiction.

In *The Priest* by **GERARD O'DONOVAN**, the streets of Dublin throb with fear as a ruthless killer cuts a swathe through his victims. Before each assault, he makes the sign of the cross. A visiting politician's daughter is attacked and left for dead, her body burned by a heated cross. It's up to DI Mike Mulcahy to track down a ruthless murderer, the eponymous 'Priest'. As the divine mission of the killer proceeds bloodily, Mike finds himself dealing with both a hostile media and a highly intelligent nemesis, with only journalist Siobhan Fallon to help him bring a truly monstrous figure to justice. This book showed that O'Donovan was a name to watch, which was proved subsequently by *Dublin Dead*. The tenacious Fallon is attempting to track down a missing girl, while Mulcahy discovers a connection between Ireland's biggest ever drugs haul and the killing of a Dublin gangster in Spain. More people will die, as the duo begins to uncover some very nasty secrets from the past. O'Donovan's wonderfully evocative sense of locale, breakneck pacing and strong characterisation mark out *Dublin Dead* as something special in the crowded field of modern crime, and he ensures that the streets of Dublin are always a scary place in his memorable novels.

The galvanic *Black Cat Black Dog* by **JOHN CREED** (a pseudonym of Eoin McNamee, mentioned below) is as stylishly written as it is filled with kinetic action. Creed's *The Sirius Crossing* introduced his resourceful ex-spook Jack Valentine, and provided an exhilarating experience – but not at the expense of carefully honed prose, and that, thankfully, remains the case with this outing, even if Creed takes slightly longer than before to exert a real grip.

On a beach in County Antrim, a set of dog tags is discovered, appearing to belong to a sailor who vanished in the 1950s. Jack Valentine may have renounced his previous life as a spook, but he is drawn once again into a dangerous mystery. The mix here involves a WWII arms dump in the North Sea and an American mission to Iraq that went disastrously wrong in the early 1990s. As Jack gets deeper and deeper into his old familiar universe of violence and betrayal, he finds that Northern Ireland is still prey to some of the sinister individuals he knew in the past. But there is a frightening global agenda at work here and perhaps it would be best for Jack simply to walk away – not something he's very good at.

Those who have read Creed's earlier books will know what to expect, and will be more than prepared to put up with the extra time the author takes to lay out his stall. In fact, this is some very canny work on Creed's part that more than pays dividends as his convoluted plot unfolds.

Under his real name, **EOIN McNAMEE** produces disturbing journeys into the benighted soul of his native country. The *Blue* trilogy of books is based on real-life murders – but, as they took place before the Troubles, they are not within the remit of this study – while his extraordinary debut novel, *Resurrection Man*, detailed the bloodletting of the UVF gang the Shankill Butchers in the Belfast of the 1970s.

With such books as *The Cold Cold Ground*, comparisons have been drawn with David Peace's blistering *Red Riding Quartet*, specifically suggesting that the talented **ADRIAN McKINTY** is doing for Northern Ireland what Peace did for Yorkshire. And these comparisons are not far-fetched: it would seem that the effortless grasp of genre that the author demonstrated in earlier books, such as the powerful *Dead I Well May Be*, is matched by a prodigious literary reach which is every inch the equal of its ambition. In *The Cold Cold Ground*, the first in the series featuring DS Sean Duffy, the detective is promoted and posted to Carrickfergus CID, where he finds himself with a challenge involving two very different cases: what appears to be the county's first serial killer and a young woman's suicide (which may well be murder). Things are complicated by the involvement of one of the victims in the IRA. This is powerful and pungent writing that takes on social issues along with its storytelling impetus.

JOHN GORDON SINCLAIR has successfully made the transition from actor to novelist – from the gangling youth of *Gregory's Girl* to a hard-boiled middle-aged crime writer. *Seventy Times Seven* is set in 1992. Professional hitman Danny McGuire has a job: to kill the 'Thevshi', the Ghost, who has been acting as a mole within the Republican movement of Northern Ireland. But the Thevshi knows who murdered Danny's brother, and Danny will need to speak to his victim before he kills him. And there is a third figure in the equation, as ruthless as either of the people he is up against. The American locations are a clue to an element in the stew that Sinclair has concocted: US maestro Elmore Leonard, whose peppy dialogue and delirious plotting are echoed here. But Sinclair is the real thing – a full-throttle writer of energy and inventiveness. Sinclair's second book, *Blood Whispers*, was set in his native Scotland.

Given the rude health of Irish crime fiction, it becomes harder and harder to point out who are most striking of the current writers – there are a hell of a lot of candidates. But in any such criminal beauty contest, **DECLAN HUGHES** would quickly assume pole position. Hughes is a writer of real authority and power, as demonstrated in his skilfully written novels featuring tough private eye Ed Loy. The surname of his Dublin-based Irish-American sleuth is a nod to Dashiell Hammett's imperishable gumshoe Sam Spade in *The Maltese Falcon*: a 'loy' is a traditional Irish spade. Signature books include *City of Lost Girls* and *All the Dead Voices*; a good starting point is the lively *The Colour of Blood*. The writer is also a playwright and screenwriter, and has served as writer-in-association with Dublin's Abbey Theatre.

IAN SANSOM writes two series with very different locales, but the tongue-in-cheek *Mobile Library* novels are set on the north coast of Northern Ireland – hence his inclusion here. The most representative book is probably the first in the series, *The Case of the Missing Books*, which introduces the librarian (and unlikely detective) Israel Armstrong and his eponymous mobile library. However, the period-set *County Guides* sequence is set – or will be set – in every corner of England. Sansom's plan is to write a book about every historic county, and once he has covered England he is planning to turn his attention to Scotland, Ireland and Wales.

Other writers and key books
GERARD BRENNAN: *Wee Rockets*
SINÉAD CROWLEY: *Are You Watching Me?*
MATT McGUIRE: *Dark Dawn*
SAM MILLAR: *Dead of Winter, Bloodstorm*

A world elsewhere

British writers, foreign settings

In a very short time, **STAV SHEREZ** has become established as one of the most idiosyncratic and entertaining of crime writers. In *The Devil's Playground*, the mutilated body of a tramp is found in a park in Amsterdam, and Dutch copper Ronald Van Hijn thinks he has found another victim of the serial killer currently plying his trade in the city. From material on the body, the canny detective tracks down a man called Reed, who gave the vagrant shelter in London some time before. Reed becomes as intrigued as Van Hijn when he discovers that the encounter he had with the dead man was no accident, and begins to uncover the victim's secret life – one that stretches back to the grimmest events of the Second World War. As a debut thriller, this is something special – the assurance with which the baffling narrative is dispatched by Sherez seems more like the work of a seasoned pro than a tyro novelist. Both Reed and Van Hijn are persuasively realised characters, and the final revelations involving the Nazi death camps have considerable force. The more recent *Eleven Days* is a demonstration of just how consistently Sherez has maintained his very high standards. And a final encomium: his work is subtly and pleasurably different from that of his confrères.

If you relish that delicious chill of fearful anticipation while reading a thriller, *The Farm* by **TOM ROB SMITH** will be right up your alley. The young author's debut novel *Child 44* burst upon readers with the impact of a grenade, and that riveting tale of an investigator in Stalin's Russia led to an inevitable big-budget movie starring Tom Hardy and Gary Oldman. Smith has perhaps struggled with subsequent offerings to recapture the impact of that first book, but *The Farm* is quite unlike his earlier period novels and takes a very different direction. We are no longer in the totalitarian Russia of the past, but moving between modern-day London and Sweden – Smith is in fact half-Swedish, and is able to draw on his personal legacy. This is a literary thriller with penetrating psychological undertones.

Daniel has imagined that his parents were leading a comfortable existence on a Swedish farm, until he receives a distressed call from his father. He discovers that his mother has been committed to a mental hospital but has escaped. Then Daniel receives a second phone call, this time from his fugitive mother who is making her way to London and desperate for him to hear her side of the story. Daniel's problems are acute: is his mother the victim of a massive conspiracy as she claims? Or was his father right to commit her to an asylum? As the canny reader might imagine, in a 350-page thriller, it's not hard to guess which of these two scenarios is the most likely. And as Daniel tries to unpick the truth about the trauma of his family, he learns of a grim crime in which his father may be involved.

To say that Smith has moved his writing on to a new plane of achievement understates the case here, and he finds something new and radical to do with a well-worn thriller device of the past having a devastating effect on the present. There is a keen attention to the conflicts within his troubled hero, as he realises that much of what he believed about his family is a lie, and the consequences of dealing with betrayal and corruption are handled with steely authority. Smith has chosen to write about a gay protagonist here, but *The Farm* is a novel that can speak to all of us, whatever our sexuality.

Let's face it, it's much easier to pick up a thriller by an author whose work we know well, rather than taking a chance on a debut novel by someone we've never heard of. But sometimes playing safe is the wrong option – as was proved by ignoring **NICK STONE**. *Mr Clarinet* was a book that came weighted down with some heavy pre-publicity hype from his publishers, clearly hoping that Stone would be the Next Big Thing. Certainly, his biography is unusual: born in Cambridge to a Scottish father and Haitian mother, with a great-grandfather who used voodoo remedies, Stone was sent to live in Haiti with his hard-drinking, gun-brandishing grandfather. After university, he was back in Haiti when the country went down another bloody path. But all of this didn't guarantee that he could turn out a novel as interesting as his life had been. However, a few pages of *Mr Clarinet* are enough to prove that Nick Stone was indeed the find that his publishers were clearly hoping for. For a start, Stone's scene-setting is a revelation: a pungent, massive Haitian canvas against which the terrifying narrative plays out. Miami private investigator Max Mingus will pocket $10 million if he can track down Charlie Carver, scion of an extremely rich family. Charlie has gone missing on the island of Haiti, where many young people have disappeared. And it's here, of course, that Stone is able to make impressive capital from his years in this violent and exotic country. As Max digs ever deeper into the mystery surrounding Charlie Carver, he finds that voodoo is not just a come-on for the tourists in modern Haiti, but an extremely sinister and forceful presence, behind which hovers the mysterious figure of Mr Clarinet, who the natives believe has been luring children away from their families.

All of this is dispatched with great brio by Stone, who never gives the slightest impression of being an apprentice novelist. Many elements are stirred into the heady brew: black magic, Baby Doc Duvalier, the cocaine trade and the incipient civil war in the country among them. Stone even persuasively draws parallels between the 1994 American invasion of Haiti and the then current Iraq situation. If he doesn't pull together every strand in this ambitious enterprise, few readers will have cause to complain when the experience of reading *Mr Clarinet* is so exhilarating. More recent work (such as 2014's legal thriller *The Verdict*) is less ambitious.

If you're tiring of the frigid climate of Scandinavian crime fiction, a welcome antidote may be found in **JASON WEBSTER**'s sultry, and elegantly written, Max Cámara series, of which *The Anarchist Detective* is the most accomplished. The publishers evoke Donna Leon as a comparison, but Webster is very much his own man, and his dyspeptic Spanish detective is a very different kettle of fish to Leon's Brunetti. In *The Anarchist Detective*, Cámara is in an elective exile in Madrid, with a view to cultivating his cordon bleu skills (and enjoying some erotic indulgence with the seductive Alicia). But, of course, the day job exerts its hold again, and he is drawn back to his grim home town of Albacete, a place he has struggled to forget. Back on familiar territory, he is soon knee deep in betrayal, lies and the ugly residue of the Civil War, still poisoning lives.

If the utterly enthralling first volume in **JAKE WOODHOUSE**'s Amsterdam Quartet, *After the Silence*, is any indication, this looks set to be one of the key sequences in modern international crime fiction, with Amsterdam itself a major character – as it was in the novels of Nicolas Freeling. The subsequent *Into the Night* takes readers into the criminal underworld of Amsterdam with Inspector Jaap Rykel. A woman has been pushed under a train by a man in police uniform, sending the citizens of Amsterdam into a frenzy. The situation is further exacerbated by a serial beheader posting pictures of his victims on Twitter. Disturbingly, each victim carries a picture of Jaap, and, as the investigation unfolds, we follow Rykel into a dark world of violence and menace.

Immense popularity can come with a price in the world of books. Dan Brown can shrug off the now-customary dismissal of his writing skills, success being the best revenge. But it is harder if you toil in similar territory further down the bestseller lists and glean the disdain without the remuneration. **SIMON TOYNE**, thankfully, has largely been spared cutting comments, even though his books are in that familiar mould: breathless, picaresque page-turners with plots underpinned by the threat of some cataclysmic event (in *The Tower*, strange weather phenomena and mass migrations suggest the End of Days). Toyne must be well aware that there are people who will find such synopses off-putting precisely because of the *Da Vinci Code*-like associations, but he is no doubt hoping to channel the American writer's Midas touch. In fact, Toyne deserves it: he may trade in the familiar elements (his Robert Langdon figure is tyro FBI agent Joseph Shepherd), but he delivers his outrageous plot with a far more intelligent use of language than his publishing model.

A catastrophe hits NASA's deep space search programme – it is wiped clean, replaced by a minatory announcement: 'Mankind must look no further.' The warning is greeted with scepticism, but not by the FBI's Joseph Shepherd, tasked with investigating the destruction of the programme. At the same time, ex-crime reporter Liv Adamsen relocates from the Turkish city of Ruin to an oilfield in Syria. The development is abandoned, but an oasis forms around her new dwelling – along with a nameless danger. All around are suggestions of Armageddon: a hideous plague is beginning to spread (emanating from the citadel in Turkey that Liv Adamsen left behind), and the weather is behaving in a terrifying fashion that cannot be accounted for by global warming. The signs are that all human endeavour is drawing to a close, unless a handful of determined individuals can avert doomsday.

The pleasures of *The Tower* do not lie in the writing, literate though it is. The author (who worked in television for two decades) knows that in this sort of book sheer narrative gusto is far more valuable than nuance, and everything is presented in poster colours. But that is not a criticism. High-concept thrillers may be ten a penny, but Toyne rises above the competition to deliver something that is both confident and cinematic.

Those in the know (in crime fiction terms) are well aware that **MARTIN WALKER**'s weathered detective protagonist Bruno is something special. The companionable Walker has an impeccably solid journalistic background and is the author of several acclaimed works of non-fiction, including *The Cold War: A History*, along with a historical novel, *The Caves of Périgord* – but none of this guaranteed a winning streak in the crime fiction genre. However, *Bruno, Chief of Police* proved to be a superb crime debut, full of unusual touches and characterised with great skill. Walker's hero, Captain Bruno Courrèges, heads a small force in the town of St Denis in the Périgord region of France – which means that Walker could channel elements from his earlier novel set in the region. He is an unorthodox detective: he doesn't carry the gun he owns, and barely needs to arrest people. But suddenly chaos reigns in the town as inspectors from Brussels target the rural market, making many enemies. Bruno is concerned by the fact that this phenomenon is invoking memories of the town's ignoble Vichy France past. Then an old man from a North African immigrant family is murdered...

MICHAEL GREGORIO is the joint moniker of a husband-and-wife team: Liverpool-born Michael G Jacob and Italian Daniela De Gregorio. The duo are best known for their highly praised series of Gothic thrillers set in the Prussia of Immanuel Kant – with titles such as *Critique of Criminal Reason* and *Unholy Awakening* – but they have recently turned their hand to contemporary crime fiction. In *Cry Wolf*, the first of a new series, Sebastiano Cangio, a ranger in a national park in idyllic Umbria, sees tell-tale signs of the nightmare he has left behind in his native Calabria. An *'Ndrangheta* mafia clan is moving into the earthquake-torn area, bringing violence, drugs and corruption. In this dramatic, fast-moving tale, Cangio alerts the local authorities, but to no avail. In doing so, he becomes the target not only of the *'Ndrangheta* but also of the greedy politicians and bent cops who are already on the wrong side of the law. *Think Wolf* is the second novel in the series.

CARLA BANKS' *The Forest of Souls* is a powerful and compelling piece of work, in which the heroine is taken to the furthest extremes of human behaviour and forced to confront the darkness at the heart of the soul. Helen Kovacs has been researching the Nazi occupation of Eastern Europe, though she has chosen to keep her research from her close friend Faith Lange. But then Helen is killed, much to Faith's horror. At first, Faith believes that the police have found the murderer, but then she begins to suspect that the man in custody is not the man who killed her friend. At the same time, the journalist Jake Denbigh has been led to believe that there is more to Helen's murder than meets the eye; Jake has discovered that, among the supposed concentration camp victims who escaped from Minsk, several war criminals disguised themselves. It would appear that Faith's much-loved grandfather Marek may be one of these. But who is responsible for Helen's death? Someone from this dark past, or a totally unexpected (and well-hidden) source. What makes Banks' novel so forceful is the strength of its dual narrative. As Faith delves into the secrets of her own family, Jake travels to the mass graves in the Kurapaty forest in Minsk, on a related – but even more dangerous – quest. This is psychological thriller writing of a high order.

Crime Writers' Association Daggers for best crime novel are sometimes controversial, but nobody argued with the award bagged by **HENRY PORTER** for *Brandenburg*. This has all the ambition and assurance of Porter's earlier books, with an even more assiduously realised time and place: the fall of the Berlin Wall and the collapse of communism. Porter's protagonist is a Dresden academic who is also an agent for MI6. It's a richly drawn portrait of an epoch, crammed with authentic detail.

ZOË SHARP created her no-nonsense heroine Charlie Fox after receiving death-threat letters as a photojournalist; Sharp herself, like her heroine, is notably no-nonsense. The series of thrillers, which started with *Killer Instinct*, sees the resourceful Charlie become a close protection officer working for the man who was her training instructor in the army, and finds her on assignment in a variety of (usually American) settings. Sharp's US-set work has been nominated for the Edgar, Anthony, Barry, Benjamin Franklin and Macavity Awards in the United States, as well as twice for the Crime Writers' Association Short Story Dagger.

With its heady mix of Sudanese killers, ruthless and corrupt business types and a biotech firm with blood on its hands, **ALEX BLACKMORE**'s *Lethal Profit* is nothing if not busy, but the author manages to keep its labyrinthine plot in apple-pie order. When Jackson Scott vanishes after uncovering some inconvenient facts about a biotech company, it's up to his sister Eve to track him down. Her investigation begins in Paris, but soon she is immersed in a violent global conspiracy that threatens not just her own life but the lives of many others. This is immensely lively fare, delivered with a skill that belies the fact that this is the author's first novel.

The inexorable ascent of **ROBERT HARRIS** as one of the UK's most important popular novelists has been an unusual phenomenon, quite unlike the career path of most of his peers. His breakthrough book was, of course, the powerful *Fatherland* in 1992, with its dark alternative view of history, in which Germany was the winning nation in the Second World War. A sequence of striking and genre-bending novels followed, for which the sobriquet 'thriller' no longer seemed sufficient: *Archangel*, *Enigma* and the much-acclaimed *The Ghost*, memorably filmed by Roman Polanski. But if there is one thing that has marked out Harris's career, it is his wholly admirable refusal to be typecast with regard to category. The thriller may be his natural home, but Harris has also shown an immense skill in dealing with historical subjects and the past in impressive novels such as the ambitious *Pompeii* and *Lustrum*.

The central character in Harris's *The Fear Index* is celebrated in the coteries of the ultra-rich, if unknown to the general public. Dr Alex Hoffmann is a scientist: a genuinely visionary character who can create from computer software the equivalent of what Mahler could spin from the staves on a sheet of music paper. Hoffmann's genius has been to create a groundbreaking form of artificial intelligence, and, aided by his partner, an investment banker, he has found a way of reading human emotions, facilitating a way of predicting movement in the financial markets – his Geneva hedge fund has already produced billions in profit. But then everything begins to go grimly wrong. Hoffmann, lying asleep with his wife, is unaware of an intruder who has managed to get past the security of their luxurious lake house and who sets in motion a nightmare that, in its vaunting paranoia, makes Orwell's *Nineteen Eighty-Four* look like a fairy story. In fact, Orwell's influence on this characteristically efficient novel is but one element here: Mary Shelley's *Frankenstein* may similarly be detected (in the form of a creation that achieves autonomy and ends up threatening its creator), and perhaps there is a hint of Stanley Kubrick and Arthur C Clarke's malign computer HAL 9000 from *2001: A Space Odyssey*.

The pseudonymous **AD GARRETT** (actually the much-respected crime writer Margaret Murphy and forensic specialist Professor Dave Barclay) made a notable mark with *Everyone Lies*, a highly individual forensic thriller. And the team's second book, *Believe No One*, is (if anything) even better. DCI Kate Simms is on placement in the United

States with St Louis PD, reviewing cold cases and sharing expertise with forensic expert Professor Nick Fennimore. A call for help from a rural sheriff's deputy takes Fennimore to Oklahoma, where he discovers a mother is dead and her child has disappeared – what's more, they're not the only ones. How many more young mothers have been killed, and how many children are unaccounted for? There may be serial murders to be unearthed across two continents and two decades. The two British authors travelled to America's Midwest to research the novel, and their experience of the vastness of the landscape resonates throughout the mesmerising narrative of *Believe No One*.

The surface brilliance of her highly accomplished thriller is mesmerising enough, but **JOANNA HINES'** combination of adroit characterisation and nimble plotting lifts *Angels of the Flood* above most contemporary crime writing. While the premise is fresh (the heroine, Kate Holland, finds herself drawn into a dangerous mystery after she receives a priceless Italian painting), the real strength of the novel is its vivid evocation of Florence during the disastrous floods (30 years before Kate receives the painting) and the very different Italy of the late 1990s. Hines knows her locales, and her writing is as good as a holiday under Mediterranean skies. *Angels of the Flood* is something of a treat: an intelligent and original piece of writing.

If you are someone who enjoys being led down the darker alleyways of Italy by **DAVID HEWSON**, reading *Carnival for the Dead* will be something of a bittersweet experience. Yes, it's every bit as atmospheric and engaging as anything in the writer's Nic Costa series, although another of his favourite characters, forensic pathologist Teresa Lupo, moves centre stage in this book. And, yes, the central mystery is every bit as intriguing, with a solution locked deep in the fabulous artistic heritage of Venice and unravelled with the satisfying precision that we know the author delivers so adroitly. But we may feel a certain sadness, as this was the last of Hewson's Italian novels.

Beyond the tourist traps of San Marco and the Rialto, the Venetian past leaves shadows invisible to visitors but that are standard terrain for such professionals as Teresa Lupo. As the city is transformed into a magical place by the Carnival, Teresa is investigating the strange disappearance of her aunt Sofia, a lively and unconventional figure. Her search takes her into ever more dangerous territory, and here Hewson tips his hat to some of the great chroniclers of sinister Venice, such as Daphne du Maurier. As so often with Hewson, the tangled history of Italy wreaks a powerful influence on the characters, and the revelations in *Carnival for the Dead* are as extraordinary as anything the writer delivered previously.

Perhaps the reason for abandoning Italy was that Hewson landed a choice assignment – something of a challenge. He agreed to deliver two books based on the cult Danish TV series *The Killing*, working with the creative team of the programme and sanctioned by the original writer, Søren Sveistrup. Following the bestselling results, Hewson then set his sights on the Netherlands. The first book in his Amsterdam-based Pieter Vos series, *The House of Dolls*, has been optioned for Dutch television, and *The Wrong Girl*, the second in the series, proved to be among his best work. For these books, David Hewson may be taking us into a chillier Northern Europe, but let's hope that he'll be stamping his passport in warmer climes again before too long.

CRAIG RUSSELL's detective Jan Fabel operates in Germany, and a return to duty on the Hamburg murder squad leads to an encounter with a particularly terrifying killer in *A Fear of Dark Water*, winning kudos from the likes of Mo Hayder. An environmental summit is due to begin in the city when the weather turns turbulent. As the floodwaters disappear, a body is found, decapitated. In his initial investigation, Fabel thinks the dead person was the victim of a serial murderer and rapist who tracks down his prey using social network websites. However, this explanation begins to seem inadequate when the detective's investigations uncover a clandestine cult with an environmental agenda.

Many non-Italians have chosen to set their crime fiction in Rome, but **CONOR FITZGERALD** has proved that he is easily the equal of any of his predecessors. In *The Dogs of Rome*, Arturo Clemente is killed on a hot summer morning in his Rome apartment. He is a man of interest, married to an elected member of the Senate, and worthy of the most intense police investigation. When detective Alec Blume arrives, he finds that a suspect is already in the frame. And when Alec begins to question the accepted view, he discovers (as has many a policeman in Italy before him) that political influences are not to be argued with.

SAUL BLACK (whose real name is Glen Duncan) is another British writer who has the full measure of the US locales in which he sets his tense narratives. *The Killing Lessons* arrived festooned with cover blurbs from some heavyweight names – Jeffery Deaver, Lee Child and Linwood Barclay – leading readers to assume that the author was American. In a brutal scenario, two killers are behind the rape, torture and murder of seven women in the space of three years, always leaving an inexplicable item inside their victims, such as an apple or a ceramic goose. On their tail is San Francisco homicide detective Valerie Hart, struggling with the bottle. Duncan, before becoming Black, was a literary novelist, and he channels those skills into a well-written entry in an overpopulated genre.

Word-of-mouth approval for any new title is something that publishers desperately seek but are unable to guarantee. His publishers, however, must have been rubbing their hands when the phenomenon kicked in resoundingly for **THOMAS MOGFORD**'s *Shadow of the Rock*, which arrived festooned with praise from the likes of William Boyd. Gibraltarian lawyer Spike Sanguinetti comes home to discover old friend Solomon Hassan on his doorstep. The latter is on the run from the police, after being accused of a savage killing in Tangiers. The Moroccan authorities want to extradite him, and Spike agrees to travel to Tangiers to intervene... which is how Spike's troubles really begin. This is an economically written thriller that delivers on every level. The third book in the Sanguinetti sequence, *Hollow Mountain*, is similarly vivid, with almost all of it set on the Rock, while *Sleeping Dogs* (the fourth) adds a further layer of narrative sophistication.

Almost at the same time that Malcolm Mackay's *The Necessary Death of Lewis Winter* created waves in the world of contemporary crime fiction, another novel had an even more sizeable impact. But **TERRY HAYES'** *I Am Pilgrim* is a much more substantial work, weighing in at 700 pages. What is most surprising here is perhaps the utterly individual tone of voice – something all too rare in modern crime fiction. 'Pilgrim' is the code name for a man who does not exist. The adopted son of a rich American family, he has been in charge of a clandestine espionage unit and has written a book on forensic science, a book that will help NYPD detective Ben Bradley to find him. A remarkable – and unmissable – novel that deserved its success.

Few crime novels deserve to be called operatic – in the sense of being larger than life, with emotions etched in the most striking of colours – but **KT MEDINA**'s remarkable debut certainly qualified for the adjective. Painted on the most ambitious of canvases, *White Crocodile* takes the reader into a Cambodia that suggests the fraught psychological territory of Joseph Conrad's Africa in *Heart of Darkness*. In Battambang, not all danger is located in the lethal minefields; young mothers are being abducted. Some are discovered gruesomely mutilated, their abandoned babies by their side. In this superstitious society, people live in fear of the 'White Crocodile', a creature that means death for all who encounter it. In England, Tess Hardy has found some equilibrium in her life after severing relations with her abusive husband Luke. Then she receives a call from Cambodia, where Luke is working as a mine-clearer, and Tess realises he has changed. But there is to be no reconciliation; a fortnight later, Luke is dead. Despite her better judgement, Tess sets out for the killing fields to find out what happened to him. Medina has the full measure of the sweltering Cambodian locale, and her own experience in the Territorial Army (as well as working for the information group Jane's) has been parlayed into her novel with great skill. The descriptions of the minefields of Cambodia – along with those who undertake the terrifying job of finding and disarming mines and IEDs – demonstrate the author's personal sympathy for this damaged country where thousands of individuals are still maimed and killed by these relics of a bloody war; it might be argued that Medina's anger is the backbone of the novel, lifting it out of the crime category into something more complex and ambitious. But, in fact, the real skill of *White Crocodile* lies in its vulnerable but tenacious heroine Tess Hardy, the perfect conduit for the reader through a novel that is unyielding in its grip. The myth of the White Crocodile still exists in Cambodia today, and Medina's use of this belief as the story engine has allowed her to produce both a strongly written thriller and a passionate meditation on the West's exploitative attitude to a benighted country. Her second novel, *Fire Damage*, under the name Kate Medina (and mentored by Mo Hayder), represents a change of pace, with psychologist Jessie Flynn centre stage.

The urbane Atlantic-hopping **MICHAEL MARSHALL** (who adds a 'Smith' – his real name – for his science fiction novels) has firmly established himself as a compelling practitioner of the modern science-based thriller: his elegant prose is always at the service of a supercharged narrative. In *Bad Things*, somewhat different from his usual fare, a four-year-old boy, Scott Henderson, walks out on to a jetty in Black Ridge, Washington State, and is not seen again. His father, John, is devastated but struggles on – until he receives an e-mail from a stranger who says he knows what happened to the boy. John decides to return to Black Ridge, but instead of a satisfactory solution, chaos is unleashed, and John finds himself likely to lose what little is left to him.

The inclusion of **MANDA SCOTT** in a book devoted to contemporary British crime writing may seem inappropriate given that she is one of the most talented writers of historical crime fiction in the UK. But her 2015 novel *Into the Fire* features (along with its period strand) a modern-day narrative, with French copper Inés Picaut looking into arson attacks apparently committed by a self-styled Jihadi group in the city of Orléans. The real achievement of the novel is that the parallel story set in the fifteenth century – with mercenary Tomas Rustbeard planning to kill Joan of Arc – does not suck the oxygen from the modern-day narrative, as period sections are always wont to do in such novels. Both elements are delivered with great vividness, and the book as a whole is proof that Scott's credentials in the field, both historical and modern, are impeccable.

Crime fiction aficionados are in luck nowadays – barely a month seems to pass without a first-time novelist arriving fully formed, with all the authority of older hands. Such as (for instance) **CAL MORIARTY**, who centred her 2015 debut *The Killing of Bobbi Lomax* on an unassuming book-lover who may also be an ingenious murderer. Clark Houseman comes to the attention of Moriarty's tenacious detectives Sinclair and Alvarez when bombs go off in the US city of Abraham, killing the eponymous Bobbi Lomax and a man named Peter Gudsen. The survivor is Houseman, who turns out to be a skilled forger of literary signatures and, like Lomax and Gudsen, to have belonged to a sinister sect, The Faith. Moriarty's novel is a blistering examination of both the criminal mind and the dark secrets that lie within America's fundamentalist Bible Belt.

A body is discovered washed ashore on the beach of a rural Icelandic fishing village. In *Frozen Out* by multilingual **QUENTIN BATES**, this is the beginning of a series of events that will pile up problems for the village's police sergeant Gunnhildur. She is convinced that the death was not an accident – and she begins to investigate the hours leading up to the death. Then a second murder occurs, and Gunnhildur finds herself in a dangerous, and very different, world. The above may suggest an entry from a Nordic crime writer, but Bates is, in fact, English – although he worked in Iceland for his gap year. Bates demonstrates that he has the requisite nous to recognise that an atmospherically realised sense of place is crucial to a novel such as this. Latterly, he has been translating the Icelandic writer Ragnar Jónasson.

The consistency with which **BARBARA NADEL** has delivered highly atmospheric, sharply characterised novels in her Istanbul-set series of Inspector Cetin Ikmen thrillers is nothing short of amazing – such books as *Belshazzar's Daughter* and *A Chemical Prison* have dovetailed exemplary scene-setting with deliciously tortuous plots, with the resourceful Ikmen always struggling against seemingly intractable cases. *Petrified* begins during a particularly sultry Istanbul summer, when two bodies are found in a flat: an elderly woman and a young man. But the man died much earlier. And in the Jewish quarter, an artist seems curiously indifferent to the disappearance of his children. There are problems closer to home, too, with a colleague of Ikmen's having something like a breakdown. Ikmen, as ever, finds unexpected connections between these disparate mysteries, and is soon knee deep in the most curious case of his career, with Russian gangsters adding to the mix. With new facets revealed here in her dogged protagonist, this is Barbara Nadel at her quirky best.

For some time, **SAM BOURNE** (the alter ego of forthright journalist Jonathan Freedland) has been turning out high-concept thrillers as adroit as anything in the field, if lacking the intellectual rigour of his political writing. In *The Chosen One*, Maggie Costello is a White House political adviser working for a politician who has inspired her trust. Newly inaugurated president Stephen Baker has won over America, but a potential nemesis has appeared: the sinister Vic Forbes has details of a scandalous secret about the president, with threats of others – and one of those secrets threatens to destroy Baker's career. Then Forbes is killed and Maggie is forced to reassess her attitude to Baker, the man she so admired – could he be behind a convenient murder?

Wrap up warmly. **MJ McGRATH**'s Arctic-set outing *White Heat* may have cheekily borrowed its title from an old James Cagney film, but in every other respect it was a totally original thriller. That book made people sit up and take notice, but inevitably raised expectations for its successor. McGrath managed to match her achievement with *The Boy in the Snow*, the second book to feature her female Inuit hunter/sleuth Edie Kiglatuk.

Edie is an Arctic guide who knows every inch of the Alaskan forests, but when she is led by a 'spirit bear' (a ghostly white creature held in awe by the aboriginals) and discovers the frozen corpse of a child, she little realises the grim consequences the find will have for her. The Anchorage authorities are keen to link the death to a dangerous Russian sect, the Dark Believers – and Edie determines to make herself forget the sight of the boy's body wrapped in yellow fabric. Her ex-husband, Sammy, has entered an important and challenging dog-sled race, and Edie has agreed to help him. But while Sammy sets out on his journey across hostile territory, Edie is drawn into finding out the truth behind the death of the child. The secrets she uncovers have dark political implications – and Edie's life is soon in the gravest danger.

As anybody who has read McGrath's earlier book will know, she is an author with a quietly impressive command of character – Edie is a heroine with whom it is extremely easy to identify, however alien her lifestyle will be to most readers. But the author's real skill is in the astonishing evocation of the frigid landscape here, along with the sharply conjured details of Inuit life – and in keeping all these elements satisfyingly balanced. The burying of secrets – in both the physical and metaphorical sense – in a snowbound landscape is hardly a new idea, but McGrath makes it feel fresh. With the recent *The Bone Seeker*, this is turning into a series that readers will want to follow with close attention.

In **ROBERT WILSON**'s *The Ignorance of Blood*, Inspector Javier Falcón is caught in a turf war between Russian mafia groups. He has to track down those who set off a bomb that caused a host of deaths, and he encounters a Russian mob connection after a gruesome car crash. But things are complicated when his friend, the Moroccan Yacoub Diori (who works for the Spanish intelligence agency), is blackmailed by the very terrorist group he has infiltrated. This is the last entry in Robert Wilson's highly regarded Falcón quartet, and it's hardly surprising that this most reliable of authors has brought his Seville-based sequence to a satisfying conclusion, with the customary impeccable evocation of place.

And speaking of España, one might have thought that Spanish-set crime was territory sewed up by the likes of Robert Wilson, but **NICK SWEET** has the chutzpah to tackle the genre with *The Long Siesta*. This concise novel is set in 1998 Seville. An elderly priest has been gruesomely killed, and Nick Sweet's protagonist Inspector Velazquez quickly finds himself with a slew of trouble involving Russian gangsters (the villains *du jour*: see Nadel, McGrath et al.) and further ecclesiastical murders. Velazquez proves to be an intriguing and idiosyncratic protagonist, and (despite some infelicitous dialogue) Sweet evokes his sultry locale with vividness.

The first in a trilogy of novels set in the Faroe Islands by BAFTA award-winning script writer and author **CHRIS OULD**, *The Blood Strand* has as its principal protagonist the murder squad DI Jan Reyna. Reyna is Faroese by birth but was raised in the UK, and the fact that he is now a stranger to the landscape and culture of the Faroes means that this book is strong on a Scandinavian setting (the Faroes are part of Denmark) seen from a British perspective. Reyna's clouded past – both from childhood and because he is facing a discipline hearing at home – forms the central spine of the trilogy. He returns to the islands for the first time as an adult because his estranged father is seriously ill, but he's also come back seeking answers about his mother's apparent suicide 40 years ago. The book has a distinct flavour of Nordic Noir.

There is an honourable tradition of foreign correspondents turning to the crime and thriller genre – perhaps the most famous being Frederick Forsyth. But those ranks were recently swelled with another impressive addition: **ADAM BROOKES**, formerly the BBC's China correspondent, with assignments in Iraq, Afghanistan, North Korea and other countries under his belt. Of course, such experience (and even solid journalistic talent) does not guarantee thriller success, but Brookes displayed a complete mastery of the genre in *Night Heron*. The plot involves a Chinese spy and a British journalist, with a whole nation hunting them, and we are gripped by the sinewy narrative from the very first page. A desperate prisoner whose name is Peanut escapes from a brutal labour camp at night, braving the freezing desert of north-west China. Twenty years earlier, he worked for British Intelligence, but now must use his skills to vanish into the crowded streets of Beijing – and those streets are covered with surveillance cameras. He contacts his ex-paymasters at MI6 via ambitious journalist Philip Mangan; in return for safe passage out of China, he has a bushel of state secrets he is prepared to trade. Mangan, sensing the scoop of his career, agrees to take part in this highly dangerous adventure, but what neither he nor the escapee realise is just how significant those state secrets really are: the fate of governments is involved, not just the fate of two men on the run.

Like earlier masters of the thriller with a reporting background, Brookes knows exactly how to convey the essence of the situation in the most economic and effective way possible – and local colour is always conveyed with maximum vividness; the reader always knows exactly where they are as the tension begins to mount. More importantly, Brookes turns out to be a writer with a keen grasp of character, and his increasingly out-of-his-depth journalist hero Mangan is a nicely rounded protagonist. The author's experience of China adds great authority, and his laser-sharp portrayal of the compromised media and oppressive, omnipresent security in that country ensures tremendous authenticity. You may not want to visit Beijing after reading *Night Heron*, but you will certainly want to read more thrillers by Adam Brookes.

Admirers often make extravagant claims for their favourite authors, but discerning readers can safely say that the best thriller writer currently working in the UK is **GERALD SEYMOUR**. He is, quite simply, the most intelligent and accomplished thriller practitioner around, and even his misfires (of which there are few) are more interesting than most of the competition. His influential debut novel *Harry's Game* celebrated its fortieth anniversary in 2015. There is a lengthy list of fine Seymour novels, but let's look at *The Collaborator*. The Borellis are an institution in Naples – they are part of the vicious Camorra, and their discipline and retribution for transgressions are swift, even if the transgressor is one of the family. When so many novelists in the field are happy with shop-worn plots, Seymour always manages to create fresh and original protagonists, and weaves for them situations that are unlike anything he has come up with before. *The Collaborator* is Seymour firing on all cylinders, and his rivals can simply step aside: this writer, as so often, wipes the floor with everyone else.

Those lucky enough to have picked up **MARTIN O'BRIEN**'s debut crime novel, *Jacquot and the Waterman*, will have discovered a wonderfully inventive and involving detective story, with vivid French locales creating the perfect backdrop. O'Brien, who lives in Gloucestershire, was travel editor of *Vogue*, and it's hardly surprising that he utilised his globetrotting to produce his first crime novel. He continued the sequence about Daniel Jacquot of the Regional Crime Squad with *Jacquot and the Angel*. In this second book, Jacquot is unhappy with the work of his colleagues after a well-to-do German family living in Provence is murdered. It's a particularly grisly killing, involving a shotgun discharged over and over again at point-blank range. A gardener from the region is the chief suspect, but Jacquot isn't convinced. As Jacquot struggles with intractable facts, an enigmatic young woman appears and claims to have crucial knowledge that might crack the case. The answer to the mystery lies some 50 years in the past, when the Gestapo murdered a group of resistance fighters, and stirred into the mix are blackmail, lust and prejudice – and even Jacquot's own family.

It takes only a couple of pages before it's perfectly clear that O'Brien is no one-trick pony and that this second outing for the dogged Jacquot is quite as involving and forceful as the first. While the plotting takes the reader on a satisfyingly tortuous course, once again it's the meticulous scene-setting that really pays off here: French country life has never been so fraught with sinister atmosphere, and the beauty of the locales is shot through with the heavy legacy of the past.

The personable **ANNE ZOUROUDI**'s *The Doctor of Thessaly* is a typically dramatic, richly evocative piece with a tangible sense of place. The setting is a sweltering Greek island, awash with intrigue and deception. A doctor is attacked in a churchyard, a victim of a crime doesn't want it to be solved, a government dignitary is paying a visit – and corpulent Greek detective Hermes Diaktoros is called upon to utilise his highly unusual ratiocination skills to pull together the threads of a very confusing tapestry. His tasks involve not just the standard fare for a detective but the sorting out of fractured relationships. *The Doctor of Thessaly* is customarily diverting fare from the reliable Zouroudi, whose own personal life played out like a real-life version of the film *Shirley Valentine*, experience she has put to fruitful use.

MARNIE RICHES, whose eye-opening debut *The Girl Who Wouldn't Die* is set in Amsterdam and London, provides further proof that we are in something of a golden age for exciting new crime writing. Riches has created a wonderfully idiosyncratic heroine in George (real name Georgina) McKenzie, prone to bad judgement, and places her in an artfully constructed novel that even incorporates cogent discussions of sexuality and gender. Marnie Riches is clearly a name to watch.

There are various writers who are granted the accolade 'master storyteller' by their publishers (usually in the teeth of the truth), but one British writer unquestionably has earned (and continues to earn) such a title – the prolific and inventive **ROBERT GODDARD**. His novel *Fault Line* was advertised as a classic British mystery from the master of the triple-cross, with the intricacy of his plotting applauded – and it's hard to argue with this assessment. But what is perhaps most impressive about this assemblage of skills is the sheer consistency that the novelist has demonstrated over the years. The ever-reliable Goddard remains one of the most imaginative novelists this country has produced – a specialist in forging narratives of complete command and power. His name on the jacket is a sure-fire guarantee that the book will be very hard to put down – as with such books as *Blood Count*, which has the conflicted surgeon Edward Hammond as a strongly drawn protagonist caught up in a pursuit for answers that takes him across Europe.

The vivid *Blood Loss* is one of Irish author **ALEX BARCLAY**'s most accomplished US-set books and exerts a grip throughout its nicely-judged length. FBI agent Ren Bryce is drawn into her most challenging case when a father's work puts his daughter at considerable risk. But this is only the starting point for a complex and intriguing novel in which the things that people hide from others become the source of the most dangerous threats. What works particularly well here is the careful and adept parcelling out of information, so that the reader is always hungry for more – and always turning just one more page before switching out the bedside lamp.

When you enjoy the title 'King of the Erotic Thriller' (as veteran writer, editor and publisher **MAXIM JAKUBOWSKI** does), you have a certain reputation to live up to. Such books as *I Was Waiting For You* demonstrated that Jakubowski could lay an inarguable claim to that title with the kind of confrontational writing that marked out such earlier books as *Confessions of a Romantic Pornographer*, and which had Ken Bruen comparing Jakubowski to both Anaïs Nin and Raymond Chandler. In *I Was Waiting For You*, a young Italian woman is forced to leave her home in Rome and begins a very unsuitable relationship with a man in Paris. At the same time, ruthless assassin (and stripper) Cornelia – one of Jakubowski's signature characters – has been handed another mission. The two women's paths are sure to cross, and in the middle will be an English crime writer-cum-private eye on the lookout for a missing person. With the customary bouts of unbuttoned sex, Jakubowski takes the reader on an eye-opening trip from America to France, taking in Venice and Barcelona, before ending up with a dramatic finale. Unsparing stuff – and not to everyone's taste, of course, but it's pure Jakubowski.

NEIL GRIFFITHS' detective Daniel Wright is used to dealing with dangerous people in his Calabrian jurisdiction. In the diverting *Saving Caravaggio*, Wright is tracking down the artist's *Nativity* (famously stolen in real life in the 1960s and still unrecovered); he vows to claim it back from the Mafia. But in order to do this, Daniel has to disobey the orders of his superiors and even put his marriage on the line. Forming an association with gallery curator Francesca Natali, he finds that his attempt to recover the stolen art puts him right at the top of the Mafia hit list. What makes this one function so well is the atmospherically drawn locale. Certainly, Daniel Wright is a solid hero, but it's the sultry heat of Calabria that makes this such a persuasive read.

Before assuming his new writing name – **JACK GRIMWOOD** – certain themes defined the fiction of the cosmopolitan Jon Courtenay

Grimwood: a clash between cultures, fragmented families, the corrosive impact of memory, a hero on the edge of power without having power himself. And, perhaps most important of all, the potential for redemption. A strong sense of place runs through all the novels, showing most strongly in the Ashraf Bey mysteries, where the city of El Iskandryia almost becomes a character in its own right. This, combined with the tightness of the writing and Grimwood's refusal to avoid difficult themes, resulted in his solid critical reputation. With *Pashazade*, his first novel set in El Iskandryia and featuring his half-Berber, half-American detective, Grimwood began to write novels that are crime fiction first, and everything else afterwards. Two other Ashraf Bey novels followed (*Effendi* and *Felaheen*), which are also set in a twenty-first century where the Ottoman Empire still exists. *9tail Fox* is Grimwood's most traditional crime novel, while *End of the World Blues* is a crime-cum-Murakamiesque SF novel featuring a British sniper on the run and managing an Irish bar in Tokyo (it won the BSFA Award for best novel, as did *Felaheen*). But with a new publisher and a slightly finessed name, Grimwood has inaugurated a new chapter of his writing career with a series of thrillers featuring Tom Fox, a disgraced major from Army Intelligence. The first book, *Moskva*, is set (obviously enough) in Moscow, and mixes flashbacks to the fall of Berlin in 1945 with a hunt for the missing daughter of the British ambassador and political strife in the Politburo during the run-up to the fall of the Soviet Union.

LISA APPIGNANESI is well known for her espousal of literary freedoms throughout the world. As a novelist, in such books as *The Memory Man* her examination of human psychology has a forensic intensity, but her most astringent work is found in her dark psychological thrillers that redefine the parameters of genre fiction. In the powerfully written *The Dead of Winter*, a savage killer has murdered 14 women students in Montreal, and the actress Madeleine Blais is consumed by a fear that someone is determined to murder her too.

CHRIS HASLAM, one of the quirkiest talents in British crime writing, cites a childhood spent in rural isolation with no TV as the probable cause of his twin desires to write and to see the world. His unusual occupations included pipe laying in Africa, working as a scrap metal broker in Laos, selling bibles in Sicily, teaching weapon handling in Alabama and volunteering in El Salvador. His first novel, *Twelve Step Fandango*, was a jet-black literary crime thriller set among the drug dealers of Spain's Costa del Sol. The book introduced Haslam's comic antihero Martin Brock and was shortlisted for the Edgar Allan Poe Award.

Brock reappeared in *Alligator Strip*, Haslam's second book, a tale of grifters working the coin fairs of Florida on a 'sure-fire' plan to scam $6 million in six months. It earned Haslam the accolade of being the nearest thing Britain has to Carl Hiaasen. *El Sid*, published in 2006, marked a departure from the first-person picaresque of the Brock adventures and a return to Spain, the land Haslam clearly loves best. Seamlessly switching between the 1930s and the present day, *El Sid* chronicles a tragi-comic quixotic quest by an aged veteran of the Spanish Civil War and his two ne'er-do-well sidekicks for seven tons of Republican gold stolen and lost in 1938. *El Sid* was chosen by the *Independent* as its Crime Book of the Year for 2006.

If you hanker after strong, pungent writing, then the fierce work of **SIMON BECKETT** is for you. In *Whispers of the Dead*, forensic expert David Hunter has escaped the grim residue of his last case and has returned to the research faculty at which he learned his craft: the Body Farm in Tennessee. He accepts an invitation from his ex-mentor to visit a crime scene – a secluded cabin. The horrors that await him there take him swiftly back into the territory he knows too well: a cat-and-mouse game with a cunning and monstrous killer. Beckett's fans will know what to expect from his work – and, although the squeamish would be wise to steer clear, the rest of us will have a grimly suspenseful and edgy time. *The Chemistry of Death*, *Written in Bone* and the more recent *Stone Bruises* are equally impressive, with Beckett demonstrating a casual mastery of adroitly orchestrated tension.

The urbane **PAUL MENDELSON**'s expertise in the poker field is enshrined in several bestselling books on the subject, and he has clearly been salting away the forensic examination of human behaviour acquired in that discipline. His debut novel, *The First Rule of Survival*, bristled with a command of language and narrative that suggests someone with a slew of novels under their belt; the South African setting is also impressively realised. A decade ago in Cape Town, three white schoolboys were abducted, their disappearance a mystery that has not been solved. Colonel Vaughn de Vries finds a cold case getting hot when the corpses of two white teenagers are found. The troubled policeman becomes obsessed with bringing a vicious criminal (or criminals) to justice. Mendelson demonstrates a sense of locale to rival even such old hands as Deon Meyer (and, like Meyer, he introduces racism as a key element in the story). Some will have trouble with the utterly uncompromising directions in which Mendelson takes his narrative, but most will find this to be authoritative and unblinkered fare.

Given his thorough knowledge of Hong Kong and Thailand, it's hardly surprisingly that the writer **JOHN BURDETT** evokes his locales with maximum skill in such impressive novels as *Bangkok 8* and its sequels, from *Bangkok Tattoo* to *Vulture Peak*. At one time, Burdett was an employee of the Hong Kong government, and later worked in private legal practice, though he has claimed that he never really wanted to be a lawyer – such is the richness and energy of these novels, readers can be grateful for the fact that he abandoned his earlier career. A key novel is *The Last Six Million Seconds*, set in Hong Kong in April and May 1997, prior to the British handover of the territory to mainland China, and focusing on a gruesome murder investigation that begins with three severed heads found floating on the maritime border between Hong Kong territory and China.

Word of mouth on the pseudonymous writer **PARKER BILAL** began to circulate among critics – and subsequently the reading public – shortly after his first novel, *Navigation of a Rainmaker*, began to glean enthusiastic reviews. That book was written under his real name of Jamal Mahjoub, and over two decades passed (with several intervening novels) before 'Parker Bilal' was born. The first book under this new moniker, *The Golden Scales*, featured a Sudanese private detective living in Cairo, but it was his second, *Dogstar Rising*, that was the breakthrough. It reveals colourful, atmospheric writing, with much of the author's literary antecedents informing the elegant use of language.

It's always satisfying to be able to give oneself a pat on the back, and those readers who caught on to the solid thrillers of the protean **MICHAEL RIDPATH** right from the start have every right to be self-congratulatory. From his earliest financial thrillers to his recent entries in the Scandicrime genre, Ridpath has shown himself to be a talented stylist of real élan, and (despite the occasional misstep) his books have got better and better. *The Predator* is one of the best, engaging the reader in the lean prose of the novel's first part, and gripping even more in the considerably longer part two. This is the duplicitous world of top investment banks; at Bloomfield Weiss, the highly paid employees are rigorously instructed in the vicious art of being killer deal-makers. During a punishing training programme in New York, Ridpath's protagonists Chris and Lenka have learned their lethal skills and have established a powerful bond. But during a drunken boat trip, one of the trainees dies, and the rest conceal the truth about what happened. Ten years pass, and Chris finds himself watching Lenka's blood spill on to a snowy Prague street after a brutal attack. Struggling to keep his own company afloat, he realises that tracking down Lenka's murderer may be the only means of saving his own life. Admittedly, the canny reader will quickly work out that the tragic death in the past is the clue to the mayhem that ensues, but that hardly matters when Ridpath knows just how to keep us enthralled.

Where the Shadows Lie represented a new direction for the talented Ridpath. With considerable nerve, he has taken on the army of Nordic writers at their own game and set his kinetic thriller among the striking volcanic landscapes of Iceland, with an ancient manuscript at the centre of the labyrinthine plot. Apart from the impressive scene-setting, Ridpath makes a mark with his detective: Iceland-born, Boston-raised homicide cop Magnus Jonson. Ridpath gives his Scandinavian rivals a run for their money in this and the follow-up titles in the series, including 2016's impressive *Sea of Stone*.

London-born **MARGIE ORFORD** grew up in Namibia and South Africa and began writing while at Cape Town University. During the 1985 State of Emergency, she was detained – and did some of her writing in prison. This is a long and honourable tradition (Dostoevsky, de Sade), and Orford has transmuted her political experiences into pithy crime novels; *Blood Rose* is one of the best. She has talked about sitting in a bar in Cape Town, with the beauty of Table Mountain and the endless blue sky undercut by the feral street children lurking outside, as ready to pull a knife as to beg. For Orford, though, it is the misogynistic treatment of women – endemic in South Africa – that is one of the engines of her fiction. She noted that crime in the country is sexualised, with the highest rate of rape in the world. As an investigative journalist, she studied everything from gang initiation to the survivors of crime, struggling to find the congruence between the beauty of the country and its moral dislocation.

However, such books as *Blood Rose* are not given over to impassioned ideological arguments – Orford is canny enough to know that her principal duty is to engage the reader. This second outing in her Clare Hart series once again features her sharp and streetwise investigative journalist with a PhD in femicide and sexual murder. Clare has an on/off relationship with a good-looking captain in the South African police, Riedwaan Faizal, who uses her as a profiler on difficult cases. Admittedly, the setup here is something of a switched-gender variant on Val McDermid's DCI Carol Jordan and Dr Tony Hill, but Orford's characters enjoy a slightly more fulfilling sex life. In *Blood Rose*, Clare is looking into the gruesome killing of a homeless young boy. The evidence suggests that a serial killer is at work in the blighted township of Walvis Bay, but to track down this monster, Clare must enter the lives of these desperate, disadvantaged teenagers whose deaths are of no interest to the more privileged members of South African society. Rather like the Australian novels of Peter Temple, there is a highly satisfying marriage here between a keen desire for the betterment of society and the no-nonsense imperatives of the best crime fiction. It's an edgy union that Margie Orford presides over with great dexterity.

CHRISTOBEL KENT's intuitive Italian sleuth Sandro Cellini has proved to be one of the most distinctive coppers on the crime scene, and readers may feel that the sweltering heat of Florence offers a refreshing change from the British drizzle. In *The Dead Season*, the unrelenting August sun is beating down on the streets of Florence, leaving them deserted as the inhabitants escape to the cooler countryside and coast. Sandro Cellini, now working as a private detective (his days on the force behind him), is – to his frustration – unable to join the mass getaway to where the cool sea breezes beckon, as he has a case. He has been hired by a heavily pregnant young woman concerned about the disappearance of her fiancé. And there are other things disturbing the peace of the empty city: the distended body of a bank manager has been discovered in the grass on a roundabout, initially thought to be the victim of a hit-and-run driver. And a bank teller, Roxana Delfino, is worried by the wavering mental faculties of her elderly mother – and has also noted the disappearance of a regular client of the bank. Sandro finds that his investigations open up the proverbial can of worms, and even though he is aided by a helpful team – his assistant Giuli, his wife Luisa and his ex-partner Pietro from his police days – he soon begins to believe that he is out of his depth.

Earlier Cellini novels by Kent (notably *A Time of Mourning* and *A Fine and Private Place*) marked the series out as one of the most individual and enjoyable in the field, with the engaging Sandro, struggling to come to terms with a tragedy in his past, a truly winning protagonist. He is also the perfect conduit through this vividly realised Italian city – and Kent's evocative descriptions of Florence provide much of the pleasure here. There is never a sense that the settings and locales are simply there because they had to be – Kent makes the ancient city a major player in the narrative. *The Dead Season*, however, might best be read with a cool drink and a gentle fan playing on the reader's face. It is a book that raises the temperature.

Crime aficionados have particular cause to be grateful to the talented **PAUL JOHNSTON**: apart from the much-acclaimed Quintin Dalrymple, Scottish-set novels, Johnston has created another, equally distinctive series. The Alex Mavros books are set in Greece (where the author now lives), and this half-Greek, half-Scots private eye is a memorable creation: resourceful, quixotic and sympathetic. *Crying Blue Murder* was a powerful outing for Mavros, and *The Golden Silence* was, if anything, even better. This time, Alex is assigned to track down a missing teenager. As he conducts his search, he is aware of a host of savage deaths in Athens. Then Alex begins to notice connections, and, as he enters a dangerous criminal underworld, the remnants of the civil war begin to figure in a lethal scenario. Mavros is a more straightforward character than the eccentric Dalrymple, but this series displays some of Paul Johnston's most trenchant writing.

The loss of the dyspeptic, stylish crime novelist Michael Dibdin and his Italian-set thrillers, shoehorning that beautiful country's endemic corruption into persuasive crime narratives, was much mourned by readers. Dibdin's publisher, Faber, put their money on **TOBIAS JONES** to fill the immense gap he had left, after Jones's lacerating non-fiction exposé *The Dark Heart of Italy* set out his stall as anatomist of what was then Signor Berlusconi's compromised nation. Jones's strategy in *The Salati Case* is to drop a very Chandleresque private eye into an unnamed Italian town (though readers may pick up on the location through references to the local ham) and weave a labyrinthine plot for the detective, Castagnetti, to tackle. There's a secondary debt here to another, less heralded giant of the American private eye novel, Ross Macdonald: Castagnetti is hired by a lawyer working for a dead widow's estate to establish whether her missing son is still alive in order to settle her legacy (those who know Macdonald's *The Galton Case* may spot a certain homage here – and note the two titles). The son, Riccardo, had a host of enemies: he was a chronic gambler who owed money to unforgiving creditors – and Castagnetti's probings are further complicated by the suspicious death of Riccardo's older brother.

So... does Faber have Michael Dibdin Mark II on their books? Yes and no. As might be expected, Tobias Jones is trenchant on the detail of Italianate double-dealing, and his conjuring of the Mediterranean locales is always immensely evocative. But Dibdin's copper, Zen, was a formidably characterised protagonist, right from the first book, and Jones has opted for a more generic private eye, with all the sardonic observations we're more used to in LA-set narratives than on the sun-baked *strade* of Italy. Jones may, of course, have been husbanding his resources by keeping Castagnetti low key, with a view to broadening him out in subsequent books – which has, in fact, been the case.

It is a particular pleasure to know that the books of **DANIEL PEMBREY**'s *Harbour Master* sequence proved, beyond argument, that Amsterdam Noir is in safe hands with this capable writer. The books begin when maverick detective Henk van der Pol discovers the body of a woman in Amsterdam's harbour. But his investigation is complicated when a sadistic pimp targets the detective's family. The three books in the series – *The Harbour Master, The Maze* and *Ransom* – are all equally accomplished, sporting a vividly realised sense of locale matched by an adroit evocation of character. Holland has produced such crime writers as Charles den Tex, yet remains far less prolific in terms of noir than Britain or neighbouring Scandinavia. This is tantalising, given how well suited the country is: it is a liberal society, it has the settings, notably the great port cities of Amsterdam and Rotterdam, and there is an engaging humour and stoicism found in its people. And now British noir authors are pitching in, creating an interesting relationship between these two countries. Pembrey lived in Amsterdam's docklands for a year to create his police character van der Pol, aka the eponymous Harbour Master: a maverick, if not exactly damaged, cop, who fights authority while trying to crack cases that involve murder, drugs, fine-art theft and a high-profile kidnapping. Pembrey's violence reaches industrial levels when need be, yet *The Harbour Master* also looks penetratingly at issues including the Netherlands' colonial past and the country's trading and political position in the world. In that regard, Pembrey has found an unusual depth of vision with which to examine his British homeland, which shares the maritime history and uneasy relationship between traditions and modern-day problems (everything from immigration to anxieties over waning influence overseas). *Nooitgedacht*, as they say.

Readers' tastes for densely packed, fast-moving political thrillers remain as keen as ever, and it was good to welcome **PETER MURPHY** to the ranks of the best practitioners in the field in 2012 with the weighty *Removal*. The American president, Steve Wade, is sure that he has kept his relations with a seductive Lebanese woman clandestine, but then she is killed, and FBI operative Kelly Smith is assigned to investigate the death. What comes to light is a series of sinister connections between fanatical white supremacists and dangerous enemies abroad. Apart from the skilful mechanics of the thriller plotting, one of the pleasures here is the plausible laying out of the machinations of the American government. The writer Clem Chambers, enlisted for an endorsement, evokes the superb political thriller *Seven Days in May* as a yardstick here, and, to his credit, Murphy is able to justify that daunting comparison.

The bestseller principle that any thriller must be treated as a series of tenuously connected action set pieces with merely decorative interruptions is something that clearly doesn't appeal to **STEPHEN LEATHER**, as *The Eyewitness* comprehensively proves. He's similarly impatient with the idea that characterisation must be forced into a well-worn groove, and this book is quite as innovative in this area as it is in its plotting. As in such books as *Birthday Girl* and *The Long Shot*, the action grows organically out of the narrative, and the overriding motif here is plausibility. Toiling in the shattered country that is Yugoslavia, Jack Solomon's job is to give an identity to the victims of ethnic cleansing and to inform the grieving relatives. This ex-copper has found a way of keeping the horrors at bay, but when a truck crammed full of corpses is recovered from a lake, Jack finds his grim imperturbability shaken. The only survivor of the massacre is a young girl, and as Jack tracks her down, the killers are similarly close on her trail. And the reasons for the mass killings lie not just in this war-torn country but far away in the wealthy capital of England, with prostitution (organised via the internet) a key element in the equation.

GRAEME MACRAE BURNET's novels share a dark, fatalistic sensibility, but very different locales (at the time of writing this survey, he had published two – the second historical and set in Scotland). His debut novel, *The Disappearance of Adèle Bedeau*, takes place in the unremarkable small town of Saint-Louis in France and tells the story of the involvement of a local maladroit, Manfred Baumann, in the investigation of the disappearance of a waitress. It is steeped in the ambience of French provincial life, with strong echoes of Simenon, and, like the Belgian master, delves deep into the psychology of its characters.

'The Kyrgyz winter reminds us that the past is never dead, simply waiting to ambush us around the next corner.' **TOM CALLAGHAN**'s protagonist in *A Killing Winter*, Inspector Akyl Borubaev of the Bishkek Murder Squad, arrives at the brutal murder scene of a young woman; all evidence hints at a sadistic serial killer on the hunt for more prey. But when the young woman's father turns out to be a leading government minister, the pressure is on Borubaev to solve the case not only quickly but also quietly, by any means possible. Still in mourning after his wife's recent death, Borubaev descends into Bishkek's brutal underworld, a place where no one and nothing is as it seems, where everyone is playing for the highest stakes, and where violence is the only solution. Tom Callaghan, born in the north of England, utilises his experiences as an inveterate traveller (he divides his time between London, Prague, Dubai and Bishkek) in the atmospheric settings employed here.

The high-concept crime/thriller novel is clearly in rude health, as *The First Horseman* from the ebullient **CLEM CHAMBERS** proves. Well-heeled trader Jim Evans has only the best interests of the planet at heart, and is keen to fund research that will ameliorate people's lives. At the same time, Professor Christopher Cardini has been working on cutting-edge medical advances involving cell therapy – he will be able, he claims, to rejuvenate the dying. But if Cardini sounds like somebody who should be on Jim Evans' Christmas card list, that is most definitely not the case. *The First Horseman*, the fourth book in Chambers' series featuring the sympathetic trader Jim Evans, ends up in a titanic struggle between nothing less than good and evil. If the basic premise here might seem to owe something to the late Michael Crichton (or even Robin Cook – not the late British politician – who similarly worked in the field of high-concept medical thrillers), this is none the worse for that; the writing, while functional and lacking finesse, has the kind of energy that we expect from Chambers. The writer's ability lies not only in making a super-rich trader sympathetic (no easy task), but in marrying solid storytelling to persuasive scientific facts.

LEE CHILD has inexorably built up one of the most devoted and enthusiastic followings of any current thriller writer – and it's not hard to see why. Since his first appearances in *Killing Floor* and *Die Trying*, Jack Reacher has become one of the most enduring of contemporary heroes, and his laconic, hard-boiled appeal is easy to fathom. But perhaps it's the effortless American locales that really set the seal – particularly impressive in light of the fact that the author is English. *The Enemy* received the usual plaudits; this outing for Jack Reacher is Lee Child at his considerable best. Set before the other books, this one has Reacher finding himself in North Carolina on New Year's Day, 1990. In other parts of the world, history is being made – the Berlin Wall is being torn down. But Reacher, still a military policeman, is dealing with a baffling case: a soldier has been found lifeless in a downmarket motel, and when Jack visits the house of the soldier (a general, in fact) to break the news to the dead man's wife, he finds that she is also dead. Soon, dark happenings on another part of the globe are setting off ripples in the States, and Reacher is up against the hardest – and most dangerous – task he has yet encountered. As a picture of the early life of Jack Reacher, this has all the energy and drive of Child's best work.

How easy is it to fool Americans? Two Brits have done pretty well at pulling the wool over US readers' eyes and have enjoyed massive success in the States as (so Americans believe) home-grown crime authors, despite being from England and Ireland respectively. But both Englishman Lee Child (discussed above) and Irishman **JOHN CONNOLLY** have so thoroughly mastered the American idiom that their success was assured in a country that grows ever more resistant to all things foreign.

With John Connolly, however, it's not just the totally authentic American voice that impresses, but his jaw-dropping ambition: his novel *The Black Angel*, for instance, is not just a galvanic thriller, it's also a surprisingly sophisticated meditation on religion and the supernatural (although, it has to be said, some people are going to find the latter a little hard to take). Connolly, who was born in Dublin, made waves with his first thriller, *Every Dead Thing*, which inaugurated his risky games with the genres in which he worked. Was this a crime novel? Horror? As the modern thriller (since Thomas Harris) has become more and more gruesome, such distinctions are a little academic these days, but Connolly has virtually no match when it comes to chilling his readers. *The White Road* was a remarkable synthesis of Stephen King and Raymond Chandler, with Connolly's dogged sleuth Charlie 'Bird' Parker (named after the alto saxophonist) encountering evil that terrifyingly shaded into the supernatural.

In *The Black Angel*, somebody is collecting bodies and fashioning bizarre sculptures from the bones. Charlie Parker's associate Louis has been tracking down his missing cousin, and when her skull is found in the possession of a macabre artisan, Charlie finds himself caught up in a sinister maelstrom of which the bone sculpture is only one element. Aeons ago, fragments of a vellum map were distributed among various Cistercian monasteries, and these fragments are the key to the whereabouts of the sinister Black Angel, sealed in a silver statue. If the fragments are united, great evil will be unleashed upon the world. This is heady stuff, dispatched with all the casual brio that is John Connolly's stock in trade. In order to make us swallow the outrageous central premise, we are carefully lulled into the gritty reality of Charlie Parker's world, with its brutal pimps and bail jumpers. But while Charlie is adept at moving in this murky underworld, there are hints that there is much more to him than just a tough and resourceful catcher of thieves. Some may wish that Connolly had not plunged so deeply into the supernatural here, but those willing to take the journey will find that the rewards are considerable.

COLIN COTTERILL gleaned a slew of impressive reviews for his novel *The Coroner's Lunch*, a book that was that *rara avis*, something entirely new in the crime fiction field. His central character, the elderly coroner Dr Siri Paiboun, was something we hadn't seen before: in his seventies, but still sharp and lively, struggling with his career in the 1970s as the only coroner in Laos, a country that thrives on dishonesty and corruption. *The Coroner's Lunch* won the author many readers, with enthusiastic comparisons being made to the novels of Alexander McCall Smith – usually in Cotterill's favour, as his narratives sport a much darker hue than the less threatening world of McCall Smith. Paiboun reappeared in the equally entertaining *Disco for the Departed*, which was the third outing for this unusual crime protagonist. Siri is obliged to travel to the mountains of Huaphan Province – the region where the totalitarian communist rulers of the country hid from the authorities before their own accession to power. But as festivities begin for the 'success' of the new regime (which, of course, is beyond criticism), a human arm is discovered sticking out of a concrete walkway that has been laid from the president's cave hideout to his splendid new home under the cliffs. Siri is handed the job of uncovering the arm, and the body to which it is attached, and identifying the corpse. His autopsy reveals that the body was buried alive, but in order to track down the killer, the elderly pathologist has to call on some of his supernatural skill (admirers may have an ambiguous attitude towards this element of the books). What Cotterill's doughty hero uncovers is a complex web of mysteries, and he has to tackle both government indifference and brutal killers. It's hard to believe that even a more 'literary' book could conjure up the country of Laos – in all its beauty and corruption – as vividly as Cotterill manages here.

The choice of his *A Quiet Belief in Angels* for a TV book club selection shifted thousands of copies in the UK, and somehow **RJ ELLORY**, despite being highly prolific, has largely maintained the momentum of that book with a series of novels that almost always enjoy more than respectable sales, if not the massive success of the earlier book. What's more, these are never slim novellas, but bulky, arm-straining epics – Ellory is clearly not interested in making things easy for himself. Like Lee Child, Ellory is an Englishman who chooses to set his novels in the States; both men pride themselves on getting all the US detail correct, but there the resemblance ends. While Lee Child chronicles the bone-crushing exploits of his series hero Jack Reacher, all of Ellory's books are standalones – introducing us to a whole new set of characters and conflicts each time. And it is to his credit that he always succeeds in rigidly maintaining our attention throughout his vast, sprawling narratives.

In *A Dark and Broken Heart*, Vincent Madigan is deeply in debt to heavyweight Harlem drug dealer Sandia (whose nickname is 'The Watermelon Man') and is desperate to find a way out. An opportunity seems to arise: he will steal $400,000 from a group of thieves who, of course, will not be able to call the police. The charming, self-possessed Madigan sees this risky heist as a way of reclaiming his life – but, needless to say, things begin to go sour very quickly. Madigan is obliged to murder his co-conspirators in the theft, and he then discovers that the stolen money is marked. What's more, a child has been shot during the robbery and an extremely motivated New York police force is on his tail – not to mention the murderous Sandia. And there is another problem – Madigan's own conscience, which is proving to be as painful as any external threat. Thankfully, few of us will have tackled the problems that Madigan faces, but such is Ellory's skill that we are forced to identify with this deeply compromised antihero. As ever, the writing is pungent and lacerating – this is a book that takes no prisoners.

In **MATT HILTON**'s *Dead Men's Dust*, Joe Hunter uses his military training to take on unpleasant types – and he's not too fussy about his methods. He's on the trail of his brother John, from whom he has grown apart; John has vanished, and it's clear that something bad has happened. Little Rock, Arkansas is to be Joe's destination – but another man is on a collision course with him. The Harvestman is an implacable serial killer, with a penchant for collecting – or harvesting – gruesome souvenirs from his victims. When the two meet, it won't be pretty. Writers such as Simon Kernick lined up to acclaim this debut thriller, which inaugurated a healthy career for Hilton.

In New York, David Trevellyan comes across a corpse in an alley – and is arrested. He has been set up. But Trevellyan works for

Royal Naval Intelligence, and both he and the dead man were on a clandestine assignment in the city involving a highly dangerous woman. *Even* is the inaugural book in **ANDREW GRANT**'s series featuring Lieutenant Commander David Trevellyan, and it is a strong entry that marries high-octane action and well-delineated character. Grant's brother is top thriller writer Lee Child; so far, Grant is still very much in Child's shadow, with no sign (as yet) of that situation changing – possibly to Grant's chagrin.

How easy is it for a novelist – of the literary or the crime variety – to address religion in a provocative fashion? Salman Rushdie found to his cost that there is little room for nuance in any literary discussion of Islam, but it was unlikely that **PHILIP KERR**'s *Prayer* would raise many hackles, despite the fact that it engaged with issues involving Christian belief in a far more incendiary fashion than Rushdie ever did with Islam. Two things divided Kerr admirers: firstly, there is the fact that this was the author's first standalone novel in a decade (with his Nazi-era sleuth Bernie Gunther *hors de combat* – and not discussed in this study because of the period settings); and, secondly, for a book written by an atheist, *Prayer* has one of the most thoroughgoing discussions of religion and belief that one is likely to encounter in contemporary writing.

The protagonist is special agent Gil Martins, whose job is to investigate domestic terrorism for the Houston FBI. His once unshakeable Christian faith has been under severe strain, and he is on the point of abandoning it – principally because his job forces him to confront the bloodshed that a supposedly benign deity permits on a daily basis. His moral conflict, however, lies closer to home. He has bitter arguments with his wife Ruth, whose piety contrasts with his doubt. With his marriage disintegrating, Gil investigates a sequence of unexplained deaths that prove to have a pointed relevance to his own crisis of faith. A mentally disturbed woman informs him that the victims have all been killed by prayer. Evidence accrues that there are powerful figures on the Religious Right who may be involved with the death of prominent atheists (were Richard Dawkins American, he would surely be on the list), and Gil may have to accept that he is up against a supernatural force. It was inevitable that some would lament the author's move away from the Second World War era, but *Prayer* is a high-concept novel tackled in unabashed fashion. When Graham Greene mentioned to his co-religionist Evelyn Waugh that his faith was faltering and he was no longer comfortable being called a Catholic novelist, the more devout Waugh quickly applied a three-line whip to push him back into line. Philip Kerr, thankfully, could address issues of faith and atheism without any fear of negative influence – unless the bean counters at his publishers have persuaded him to get back to the more commercial territory of his Bernie Gunther thrillers.

In Hull resident **DAVID YOUNG**'s 1970s-set and much-acclaimed debut *Stasi Child*, we encounter East German detective Oberleutnant Karin Müller, investigating the discovery of the body of a teenage girl near the Berlin Wall. Müller is employed by the state police but believes the killing has the fingerprints of the Stasi, while the feared secret police are blaming the West. Echoes here of Tom Rob Smith and Philip Kerr, but Young, a graduate of City University's MA in crime writing, has a notably individual voice.

A considerable head of steam quickly built up for *The Samaritan* by **MASON CROSS**, a sprawling American epic delivered with panache by the Glasgow-born author. As with such writers as John Connolly, *The Samaritan* once again demonstrates that Celtic authors have the measure of crime fiction US-style and its broad canvas.

Other writers and key books
STEVE CAVANAGH: *The Defence* (USA)
TOM FOX: *Dominus* (Italy)
ARLENE HUNT: *The Chosen* (USA)
SUSANNA JONES: *The Earthquake Bird* (Japan)
TOBY VINTCENT: *Driven* (International)
TIMOTHY WILLIAMS: *Converging Parallels* (Italy)
TOM WOOD: *The Darkest Day* (USA)

Section Two:
British crime on-screen

TV and film in the new millennium

Introduction

American crime drama is in rude health, while the Scandinavian and the French are still producing work of real quality in the genre. But – perhaps in response to the high standard of material from abroad – British crime TV, and to some extent film, is similarly demonstrating a greater level of ambition and achievement. The following is a list of material from the last decade or so: the good, the bad and the indifferent. More space is given to those items that deserve it – for good or bad reasons – than to the indifferent category. Note that this section does not attempt to cover the whole range of British crime film and TV (this is a pocket guide, after all!); only the twenty-first century is included, and only film and TV with a contemporary setting. You'll have to pick up my *British Crime Film* for anything else...

ABOVE SUSPICION (TV, 2009–12)
An efficiently made quartet of police procedurals based on Lynda La Plante's novels. While popular, this quotidian series did not replicate the immense success of the writer's *Prime Suspect* franchise with Helen Mirren.

ADULTHOOD (film, 2008, directed by Noel Clarke)
After the success of the earlier *Kidulthood*, misgivings about its director Noel Clarke were prompted by the film's successor, *Adulthood*, in which earlier innovation had moved on to more well-worn lines. Clarke himself plays Sam, home from a prison sentence for murder and discovering that new young criminals have taken over

the block. It is only a matter of time before his life is on the line. Sam comes to realise that there are three things he must tackle: his enemies, those he had victimised – and his own attitude to his behaviour and his society. The picture of London presented here is even bleaker than in the earlier film, with gun and knife crime now accepted as an essential part of life for these young people, but much of the film feels warmed over, with elements adapted from such models as *Trainspotting*.

ALL THINGS TO ALL MEN (film, 2013, directed by George Isaac)

All Things to All Men focuses on a lethal game of cat and mouse between a criminal and a policeman who operates according to his own rules. With a robust cast, including Gabriel Byrne, Rufus Sewell and Toby Stephens, there are echoes here (not to this film's advantage) of James Ellroy's *LA Confidential*, but the storytelling lacks the rigour of the original inspiration. In fact, the construction of the film's narrative constantly beggars belief, but there is sufficient energy expended in its making to paper over some cracks.

BEFORE I GO TO SLEEP (film, 2014, directed by Rowan Joffe)

SJ Watson's megaselling novel – something of a publishing phenomenon – was an inevitable subject for filming, and received a perfectly creditable adaptation from Rowan Joffe (with a reliable cast of ubiquitous actors, including Nicole Kidman, Colin Firth and Mark Strong). If the viewer's pulse rate is not notably raised by the film, it may be due to the pronounced similarities with Christopher Nolan's *Memento* – another film drama in which the central character's daily battle with memory is the fulcrum of the plot, and with those around them not to be trusted. The reminiscences were more pointed up by the medium of film than in Watson's novel.

THE BILL (TV, 1984–2010)

An institution among British cop shows, with pronounced soap opera elements, *The Bill* began in the 1980s and held a diminishing place on the airwaves until 2010, with a decade's worth of episodes post-2000. Never exciting, but always reliable.

BLACK WORK (TV, 2015)

In recent years, certain actresses have acquired a quite formidable visibility on television, challenging the notion that audiences will grow tired of them because of such relentless overexposure. The most often seen in this familiar cadre is Olivia Colman, but her fellow thespian Sheridan Smith runs her a close second, appearing in a wide variety of dramas and giving a series of strikingly different performances. Matt Charman's police drama, however, suggested a faltering for the actress, who seemed unable to bring any element of individuality to her standard policewoman, Leeds copper Jo Gillespie. In addition, the narrative quickly slid into a well-worn route – though that was hardly Smith's fault. Gillespie's life is thrown into chaos when her husband Ryan (played by Kenny Doughty) is killed while he is attempting to infiltrate a gang of gunrunners. His wife had not known anything about his covert activities, which included other controversial undercover work. But Jo had secrets too, as she had had an affair with a colleague of her husband. Trust is an issue in the drama, with truth being a very tenuous thing in this murky world. The problem with *Black Work* is its sense of overfamiliarity; there is really nothing here that viewers have not encountered previously.

BLITZ (film, 2011, directed by Elliott Lester)

The prolific Jason Statham gives virtually the same performance in almost everything he does, with no variation offered in his standard broken-nosed, balding geezer character. But there is no gainsaying his box office clout, or Statham's abilities as a specific kind of actor (however circumscribed), especially when he allows himself to move slightly beyond the standard 'killing machine' persona. *Blitz* is based on the novel by the celebrated Irish novelist Ken Bruen, but most of the idiosyncratic qualities that distinguish his work are lost in the transition to film here. Nevertheless, this tale of a killer attempting to murder everyone he can in the police force uses its London locations well, and, after a slow start, exerts a hold.

BLUE MURDER (TV, 2003–09)

The creation of the talented writer Cath Staincliffe (also responsible for writing several key episodes), the unusual concept here involves a detective who is an overworked single mother of four juggling a demanding career with raising a young family. However, the capable actress Caroline Quentin was unwisely encouraged to channel her cosy popularity as a crowd-pleasing star of undemanding fare, blunting the edge of Staincliffe's original premise.

THE BODY FARM (TV, 2011)

Lasting only one brief season, this was a reasonably entertaining forensic police procedural spin-off from *Waking the Dead*. Created by Declan Croghan, this watchable series stars Tara Fitzgerald and Keith Allen (the latter playing very much to caustic type) and features scientists with less than rigorous standards and a maverick police inspector who crack a baffling crime. The characters are generally by-the-numbers, but the actors – notably Fitzgerald – manage to bring some vivacity to their underwritten parts.

BONDED BY BLOOD (film, 2010, directed by Sacha Bennett)

Sacha Bennett tackles this tale of drug dealers and career criminals under the cosh of overfamiliar, intractable material, partly redeemed by a well-cast Vincent Regan and Neil Maskell, who are impressive in the leading roles. This is yet another version of the real-life Essex boys murders, previously tackled in the films *Essex Boys* in 2000 and *Rise of the Foot Soldier* in 2007. In the final analysis, Bennett is able to do little more with this now familiar material than his predecessors – and the increasingly discredited and shop-worn mockney accoutrements drag the film down further.

BROADCHURCH (TV, 2013–)

Certain syndromes develop among crime drama viewers; there was the shamefaced apology that became necessary for not having seen *The Killing*, invariably followed by the words: 'But I've got the box set!' The British TV drama *Broadchurch* enjoyed a similar cultish devotion, with the detective protagonists Hardy and Miller – and, among others, a suspicious vicar – becoming objects of fascination. Crucial to the success of the show were the well-rounded, conflicted characters, and in particular the performances by David Tennant and the omnipresent Olivia Colman (see p181); the vivid picture of a community under siege from an undiscovered murderer was less important than the various uncomfortable personal interactions. The show was also a demonstration of the continuing influence of Nordic Noir in its measured, psychologically acute approach to the material, not to mention the desaturated visuals. The drama is full of beautifully observed brief moments that add to the texture; they even helped deal with the irritated reception that the second series prompted. David Tennant, an actor who (at the time) could do no wrong with audiences, adds to the lustre. The writer Erin Kelly fed the post-*Broadchurch* appetite with new short stories, sanctioned by the creator Chris Chibnall.

BULLET BOY (film, 2004, directed by Saul Dibb)

Bullet Boy covers familiar urban crime territory, with its cast augmented by non-acting rappers who know the world of drugs and guns personally. As in Fernando Meirelles' sprawling *City of God*, we are given an unvarnished panoply of young lives being squandered in pointless criminality and excess. The film has energy but is dispiriting in its bleak, pitiless vision.

BURNSIDE (TV, 2000)

A passable one-season spin-off from *The Bill*.

CASE HISTORIES (TV, 2011–13)

Proof (if proof were needed) that the fine art of casting is crucial to any television series is provided by the fact that Jason Isaacs, playing Kate Atkinson's wayward detective Jackson Brodie, is the reason this show has a following, rather than any faithfulness to Atkinson's quirky original. Brodie, ex-soldier and policeman turned private investigator, is incarnated perfectly by Isaacs, particularly the customary chaotic private life of the central character – always at sixes and sevens as he pursues whatever case he is working on. One thing that is less successful in the adaptation is the handling of the various interlocking plots, which seem to hang as separate integuments, unlike in the well-integrated novels. But there is an excellent use of locales, and even close attention to the use of language, which is never simply functional.

CASE SENSITIVE (TV, 2011–12)
When executive Mark Bretherick returns from a Swiss business trip, he discovers the bodies of his wife and daughter in a bath tub. While the deaths give the appearance of suicide, there is no note – nor, for that matter, any motive. Police Chief Proust, played by Peter Wight, hands the case to a transferee from London, DS Charlie Zailer (Olivia Williams). Despite a lack of confidence, she finds herself becoming ever more involved in the case. Sporting smart writing, this is a winning TV crime drama.

CHASING SHADOWS (TV, 2014)
A missing persons unit is tasked with tracking down killers who target vulnerable victims. The series is strongly cast, with Reece Shearsmith and Alex Kingston, and it builds its world steadily across the four parts of the show. The quirky Shearsmith impresses as a detective who can barely control his personal life, needing someone who organises everything from his meals to his clothes. His is a distinctive character in a drama that is not able to avoid clichés.

CODE OF A KILLER (TV, 2015)
The BBC's hegemony in creating quality crime drama was rivalled by ITV with such series as *Code of a Killer*, a taut two-parter that did not have time to accrue the audience that was its due. John Simm, an actor much utilised by ITV, plays a genetic researcher, Jeffreys, who fails to pay close attention to his duties as a husband and father. Thoroughly concerned with looking into the mysteries of the genetic code, Jeffreys is a single-minded workaholic. DCS David Baker (played by David Threlfall – always reliable) is involved in an investigation in the nearby village of Narborough – two 15-year-old girls have died over a two-year period. Inevitably, Baker enlists Jeffreys' aid in the investigation, and the clash between the socially challenged scientist and the grim copper, while all too familiar, is written and played to maximum effect. One caveat, though: the series appears to be as interested in the minutiae of Jeffreys' investigation as the scientist himself, and the extensive lab detail is simply not as interesting as the director James Strong clearly considers it to be.

COLD BLOOD (TV, 2007–09)
The familiar 'police turn to serial killer for aid' scenario gets a routine airing in this by-the-numbers ITV outing.

CONVICTION (TV, 2004)
A capable six-part BBC crime drama that was subsequently retooled as a US series.

DARK RAGE (film, 2008, directed by Lee Akehurst)
The central character in Lee Akehurst's *Dark Rage* is an ordinary man in his fifties, regarded by those around him as a solid father, amiable work colleague and non-exploitative landlord. But he has an unpleasant secret: he is a mass murderer, and beneath the placid surface lies the 'dark rage' of the title. Christopher Dunne is persuasive in the central role, and there is a canny balancing act between the crime and horror film genres, satisfyingly explored through the notion of two serial killers sharing the same house.

DON'T HANG UP (film, 2015, directed by Damien Macé and Alexis Wajsbrot)
While the basic premise here is hardly new – drunken prank calls are turned viciously against the pranksters when a stranger turns the tables in lethal fashion – it is handled reasonably capably in this 2015 film, which synthesises the crime genre with the macabre.

DOWN TERRACE (film, 2009, directed by Ben Wheatley)
In 2009, Ben Wheatley, bristling with ambition, delivered a calling-card movie with this claustrophobic study of twisted human behaviour, set largely in a cluttered house in Brighton. The film fuses the mechanics of the crime thriller with quirky character observation à la Mike Leigh; and while the result is sometimes torpedoed by the inexperience of the non-professional actors involved (the cast includes Julia Deakin, Kerry Peacock and Robin Hill), there is undoubtedly evidence here of a truly original, if unpolished, cinematic sensibility. *Down Terrace* showed that Wheatley was destined to do idiomatic work in the future – as was proved to be the case with the director's next film, *Kill List*, which was undoubtedly his breakthrough work.

Down Terrace investigates the eccentricities and betrayals within a bizarre family unit, peppering its unconventional narrative with the incendiary behaviour of its volatile characters and with some particularly savage and gruesome killings – it is a crime movie, after all. The father and son in the family that Wheatley presents are bottom-feeding, minor-league drug dealers who have managed to escape jail after a court hearing goes (surprisingly) in their favour. What follows is the pursuit of the person who sold them down the river, but these two are far from being smoothly functioning crime machines. The father has hints of leftover attitudes from his counterculture days, and he's saddled with a son who can barely hold together a succession of incandescent rages. As the cryptic and banal banter between the two (principally concerning substance abuse) is ratcheted ever higher, the audience appears to be watching a dark social comedy, but memories of Mike Leigh and company are summarily obliterated as the corpses begin to pile up bloodily. If Ben Wheatley's concatenation of different genres is only fitfully successful here, his subsequent film was to prove much more effective.

THE DRIVER (TV, 2014)

Those impressed by David Morrissey's unsmiling turn as Mark Billingham's copper Tom Thorne were hoping for further appearances by the actor in the role, but they had to content themselves with this glum but effective piece in which the eponymous driver Morrissey finds himself involved – against his better judgement – with ruthless criminals. The title may have suggested a kinship with Walter Hill's cool existential drama of the same name, but this was a much more British, and less pared-down, outing.

EASTERN PROMISES (film, 2007, directed by David Cronenberg)

David Cronenberg may have made his mark with a series of utterly uncompromising syntheses of horror and science fiction elements, but by the time of *Eastern Promises* he had demonstrated that his ambitions had spread much further. His earlier adaptation of the graphic novel *A History of Violence* had shown his authority in the realm of crime fiction, consolidated by this film's complex and textured vision of a London underworld that has become distinctly multicultural. A nurse delivers the child of a dying teenage prostitute who was working for the Russian mafia. What follows is a deceptive narrative in which Viggo Mortensen plays a soldier who works for a murderous crime syndicate. Steven Knight's screenplay is full of authentic detail, particularly regarding the Russian mob and its complex lore and codes. Cronenberg always remembers that character (customarily quirky in his case) is quite as important as the visceral excitement of the physical violence.

THE FALL (TV, 2013–)
The first series of *The Fall* was deeply controversial, with its uncompromising picture of a terrifying serial killer's invasions of the homes of his unlucky female targets. The gruesome murders and the fetishised treatment of the corpses also upset many. In the second series, which continues the hunt for the killer Paul Spector (a strong, unsettling performance by Jamie Dornan), there is evidence that the show's more controversial aspects have been toned down somewhat. Central to the narrative here is the single-minded woman on the track of the murderer, Detective Superintendent Stella Gibson (Gillian Anderson in the latest of a series of remarkable performances for British television, post-*X-Files*). British viewers were glued to their seats, although female complaints about the series continued. *The Fall*, along with such dramas as *Peaky Blinders* (not considered here due to its period setting), confirmed that British crime drama in 2013/14 was on something of a roll. Writer Allan Cubitt's evocation of the streets of Belfast has a striking verisimilitude, evoking in unequivocal terms the troubled, violent past of the city. The second series demonstrates an attempt to explore in greater depth the psychology of its two central characters.

FILTH (film, 2013, directed by Jon S. Baird)
To some degree, each new all-the-stops-out film featuring a corrupt policeman (a genre in itself) is obliged to raise the bar in terms of the truly appalling behaviour of the protagonist: in this acerbic version of Irvine Welsh's novel, an unbuttoned James McAvoy does just that, with sufficient doses of black humour to keep a shell-shocked grin

on the face of the viewer. Detective Bruce Robertson is investigating a gangland killing, but his agenda is something other than bringing unpleasant criminals to justice. He is after a promotion that will grant him real power in the department. And as he attempts to finesse his career, with a series of no-holds-barred strategies, we are shown a truly dark and phantasmagoric Scottish criminal universe in which Robertson encounters transvestite prostitutes, youthful drug addicts and punk anarchists – all of whom learn that the policeman is not a man to cross. As a vision of one man's descent into the underworld, *Filth* is initially fascinating, but the law of diminishing returns kicks in some distance before the end.

FROM DARKNESS (TV, 2015)
We've been here before – many times. Depressed female copper, fallings-out with superiors, unsolved cases, murdered prostitutes. At least a glum Anne-Marie Duff (always reliable) lends dramatic force to the overfamiliar elements.

FROM THERE TO HERE (TV, 2014)
This miniseries from 2014 focuses on the changes in the life of a man after the IRA bomb in Manchester in 1996. The cast includes such dependable actors as Philip Glenister, Steven Mackintosh and Saskia Reeves, and follows the aftermath of the Arndale bombing as the protagonist Daniel Cotton, a family man, attempts to deal with the fall-out of the atrocity. The piece is more straightforward drama than crime, but utilises elements of the crime genre.

GANGSTER NO. 1 (film, 2000, directed by Paul McGuigan)
Director Paul McGuigan's entry in the burgeoning London gangster genre is markedly different from many of the other films that began to appear around the year 2000, most notably in its commendable and refreshing lack of mockney humour. This is truly a scarifying piece of work, building its razor-sharp narrative around the picture of a British criminal of almost preternatural force, only ever identified in the film as 'Gangster'. Audaciously, *Gangster No. 1* begins with the violent protagonist, played by Malcolm McDowell (an actor with a resonance of menace stretching back to Stanley Kubrick's

A Clockwork Orange), luxuriating in the position he has so brutally achieved. But the great majority of the film deals with the gangster's younger days – and in the 1960s flashbacks he is played by the smooth-faced Paul Bettany, although the voiceover for the character is still McDowell. Bettany's character is the protégé of a criminal known as the 'Butcher of Mayfair', Freddie Mays (chillingly played by David Thewlis); he is a smoother piece of work than his violent pupil. The bloody story is told in a completely uncompromising fashion, with some striking pieces of technique, such as the image on the screen shattering then coming together again.

The story of a mobster's rise to power through a series of murderous acts is, of course, desperately overfamiliar, but McGuigan manages to give everything a sinister and unfeeling sheen, relying on some particularly striking performances – notably from Bettany, knowingly ushering in a stellar career. There is the inevitable conflict between the self-made killer and the man who was his patron (Freddie Mays has been languishing in prison, put there by his protégé), and the way this confrontation is handled is as eye-opening as anything else in the film. The visceral violence in the film is utterly unsparing and makes *Gangster No. 1* a poor choice for squeamish audiences. We are shown that unbending force of personality is required to achieve success in this pitiless world, and once again a metaphor for success in the unshown non-criminal world is stressed.

THE GOOD THIEF (film, 2002, directed by Neil Jordan)
Many felt that the director Neil Jordan's talent had deserted him when he produced such woeful, heavy-handed comedies as *High Spirits* and *We're No Angels*,, the box-office failure of both being matched by the critical opprobrium heaped upon them. But more good work lay ahead for the director, such as an arresting adaptation of Patrick McCabe's *The Butcher Boy*, a film boasting some deft insights into the influence of the media. And another ambitious and visually striking crime film was Jordan's hit-or-miss version of Jean-Pierre Melville's *Bob le Flambeur* (as *The Good Thief*), which demonstrated (if nothing else) the director's chutzpah in taking on Melville in this territory, and showcased a magnetic turn from Nick Nolte as the drug-addicted gambler protagonist, whispering every

line of dialogue but largely comprehensible. While never neglecting his Celtic origins, Neil Jordan has repeatedly shown his willingness to work on a large canvas and tackle subjects far removed from his native Ireland.

THE GRIND (film, 2012, directed by Rishi Opel)

The eponymous 'Grind' is a nightclub in Hackney, East London. It is a place where sex and drugs reign and ruthless loan sharks coexist uneasily with vulnerable punters, while the manager Vince (played by Freddie Connor) tries to hang on to the job and lifestyle he has managed to land for himself. But a friend from school, Bobby (Gordon Alexander), is released from prison, and Bobby's cocaine addiction and gambling habit destroy the friendship – particularly as he owes a massive amount of money to Vince's boss, owner of The Grind and an uncompromising loan shark. A powerful ensemble cast makes this work, and the directing (by Rishi Opel) holds things together with rigour. There are signs of compromises due to budgetary restrictions, and the female characters are underwritten, but there are good things here.

HACKNEY'S FINEST (film, 2014, directed by Chris Bouchard)

Hackney's Finest, directed in 2014 by Chris Bouchard, features characters that we've seen many times before but introduces some striking changes to the formula. A low-level drug dealer becomes involved with a bent London copper who attempts to steal a consignment destined for Welsh-Jamaican Yardies. This is a darkly comic thriller with some nice observation concerning its multi-ethnic cast of characters.

HAPPY VALLEY (TV, 2014–)

In the serried ranks of British police dramas, Sally Wainwright's six-part *Happy Valley* made a considerable impression, largely because of its faultless casting of the actress Sarah Lancashire as policewoman Catherine Cawood, dealing with a series of particularly violent crimes. The plot involved the ramifications of a kidnapping in the West Yorkshire valleys, set against the troubled personal lives of its protagonists. While such series as *The Fall* invited criticism for the graphic violence, *Happy Valley* – while often unsparing in this area – was spared such opprobrium, possibly because of the comforting presence of Lancashire, more customarily associated with softer, less demanding fare – a canny move by the producers.

HARRY BROWN (film, 2009, directed by Daniel Barber)

Much handwringing commentary followed the 2011 riots (which began in London then quickly spread throughout Britain), especially regarding the role of the police. It was initially felt that they had adopted an ill-advised 'softly softly' approach when the violence began, and had not intervened in the early stages of rioting and looting. Whatever the rights and wrongs of this particular aspect of a troubled period, there was one significant development. While the right-wing press inevitably called for Draconian treatment of the rioters (who were described by some politicians as members of a feral underclass, but who counted among their number teachers and other professionals), the expected liberal critique of such calls to action from more left-of-centre members of society was not as forthcoming as might have been expected. Was this because Britons of most classes had been able to see the smoke of burning stores, either on television or from their own windows, and had experienced a revision of the usual attempts to understand the causes of such behaviour? Daniel Barber's film *Harry Brown* (with Michael Caine) predated the looting of electronics and clothes stores, but featured in prescient fashion one much-discussed aspect of the riots: the dangers of ordinary people attempting to intervene when violence erupts.

HINTERLAND (TV, 2014–15)

Word of mouth began very quickly concerning the high quality of this mesmeric Welsh crime series, and Swansea-born playwright Ed Thomas's debut detective drama was widely perceived as being influenced by the wave of Scandinavian crime shows. The writer himself has claimed that he was familiar only with the Swedish *Wallander* and wanted to create four separate films with a powerfully evoked sense of locale and a focus on the dark psyche of his troubled detective. Set in the coastal town of Aberystwyth, the series was made in both Welsh and English, but viewers of the original showing on BBC4 were instantly persuaded by the extremely atmospheric and individual writing. The star of the show, actor Richard Harrington, has created something subtly new in the long line of alienated detectives, but it really is the writing and direction of this series that have generated an audience for the show – an audience that, in large part, would normally steer well clear of such defiantly Welsh material.

HYENA (film, 2014, directed by Gerard Johnson)

In present-day London, bent copper Michael Logan of the Met's narcotics task force is dealing with his own addiction and an arrangement with a member of a Turkish drug cartel who is subsequently murdered. Directed with some panache by Gerard Johnson (who made the similarly violent *Tony* in 2009), this pitch-black, bloody but often very funny effort showcases a grandstanding turn by Peter Ferdinando (the star of the director's earlier film) as the self-destructive, out-of-control central character. What particularly distinguishes Johnson's *Hyena* is the fact that he is clearly aware of the depressing pitfalls of the generic London gangster film, and clearly hankers for the days of such pre-mockney glories as *The Long Good Friday* and *Performance*. Apart from aiming for the texture of those films (notably missing from so much contemporary product), there are elements of both the French and American approaches to the crime genre as the director eschews the self-indulgence that has become the norm. Particularly notable is the treatment of the police protagonist: while being an efficient member of the task force, Logan is a damaged, coke-using figure who has lost any moral compass he may once have possessed in this utterly unsparing picture of corruption. There are, of course, echoes here of Abel Ferrara's *Bad Lieutenant*, but without the latter's Catholicism and sexual indulgence set against the massive self-destructiveness. The principal influence on the film, though, is clearly French crime director Jean-Pierre Melville, who continues to influence young filmmakers, particularly now that his films are gradually appearing on DVD.

ILL MANORS (film, 2012, directed by Ben Drew)

The British crime film has had a long and prestigious history, but how has it developed in the twenty-first century? Is the genre still alive and kicking? It most certainly is – and proof of that was provided by the directorial debut of Ben Drew, *Ill Manors*. The film demonstrates that the defining locale of modern British crime movies is no longer the police station or seedy Soho nightclub, but the graffiti-ridden, drug-focused urban scene, usually evoked in the most unsparing and caustic of fashions – precisely what Drew does here. The tough narrative centres on eight protagonists living in Forest Gate in East London and follows their often hopeless lives over a course of days as their various grim stories perform an awkward dance. As a picture of modern Britain, this is a film that pulls absolutely no punches but makes for utterly riveting viewing, even if its conclusions are hardly hopeful. Film aficionados will sincerely wish that Drew spends much more time making movies such as this rather than following his other career as a rapper – we have plenty of interchangeable rappers appearing on a daily basis, but few filmmakers with his obvious talents.

I'LL SLEEP WHEN I'M DEAD (film, 2003, directed by Mike Hodges)

The veteran director Mike Hodges regained in the twenty-first century some of the inventiveness and inspiration that distinguished his best work, notably *Croupier*, which starred Clive Owen as the morally compromised title character (he also plays the lead character in *I'll Sleep When I'm Dead*). Hodges aficionados, while acknowledging that later work does not match the achievement of the director's signature film, *Get Carter*, can nevertheless discern that he still has much to offer the cinema. The director also began writing quirky crime fiction, though that made less of an impression than his film work such as *I'll Sleep*.

IN BRUGES (film, 2008, directed by Martin McDonagh)

This blackly comic picture of two squabbling criminals abroad quickly achieved cult status. The two Irish hitmen Ken and Ray (wonderfully played by Brendan Gleeson and Colin Farrell as a kind of violent counterpart to Laurel and Hardy) are dispatched by their psychotic boss Harry (played by Ralph Fiennes) to escape from the heat they are feeling after the maladroit handling of a recent hit, and are languishing in the beautiful city of Bruges. And as we watch the divisive but oddly affectionate relationship between the two men (with the older Ken assuming a fatherly role), it's clear that trouble is brewing – Harry's violent intervention comes as absolutely no surprise. Farrell in particular is a delight as the none-too-bright Ray, but it's invidious to single anyone out in an ensemble cast as strong as this one.

INSIDE MEN (TV, 2012)
In this 2012 miniseries, a group of employees at a security depot make plans to bring off a multi-million-pound robbery. With Steven Mackintosh giving the assembled cast a definite heft, the impressive pacing here is the thing to note, along with a careful attention to plausible detail that makes the viewer buy pretty well everything they are witnessing.

ISLE OF DOGS (film, 2011, directed by Tammi Sutton)
London gangland boss Darius Deel is not pleased to find that his new trophy wife Nadia is having sex with another man. He hunts down the lover, Riley, and a violent series of confrontations follow. Directed by Tammi Sutton and written by the excellent Sean Hogan (who, it should be said, disowns the film), some elements here are familiar, but there are things that pass muster.

JACK TAYLOR (TV, 2010–13)
With Iain Glen in typically acerbic form as Ken Bruen's tenacious Galway private investigator, there was a guarantee of quality here before a frame of film was shot, and the use of vividly realised locales is another plus. As is the examination of Taylor's character, with both its virtues and flaws – regarding the latter, when Taylor is asked to talk about his emotions, he points out that Irish males of his generation carefully repress such things.

JOHNNY WAS (film, 2006, directed by Mark Hammond)
Attempting to escape a difficult past in Ireland, Johnny Doyle (played by Vinnie Jones) flees the country and goes to earth in London. His

former mentor, Flynn (Patrick Bergin), escapes from Brixton prison determined to derail the Irish peace process by means of a bombing campaign. The duo find themselves together in a polyglot household that is a microcosm of modern British society. While Jones is hardly stretched in his customary thuggish persona, the unusual central issue here is well handled, and some will like the insistent reggae soundtrack (though not this writer).

KILL LIST (film, 2011, directed by Ben Wheatley)

The extra command of the film medium that director Ben Wheatley had gained since the hit-and-miss but promising *Down Terrace* was immediately apparent here, although initially the spliced-together elements appear to consist of Pinteresque comedy of menace and the overfamiliar machinations of two hitmen attempting to carry out a murder in the face of a series of disasters. More than in his previous film, Wheatley establishes a verisimilitude in his detailed portrayal of contemporary Britain, with an Afghanistan war veteran, Jay (Neil Maskell) living an unsatisfying life in an unprepossessing house with his wife and son. Jay's debts are prodigious, and after a deeply uncomfortable dinner party, Jay decides to get the money he needs by taking on some contract killings with Gal (Michael Smiley) for a sinister figure played by Struan Rodger. Once again we have the odd couple relationship between two hitmen, although this is a much more sophisticated treatment of the theme than in previous films. Ultimately, Wheatley takes the viewer by the throat and the film begins a slow and terrifying journey into a true heart of darkness.

LAW & ORDER: UK (TV, 2009–14)

Against the odds, this British riff on the durable American show has now stretched to eight profitable if formulaic series.

LAYER CAKE (film, 2004, directed by Matthew Vaughn)

Among the filmmakers who Guy Ritchie may be said to have inspired is one of his ex-partners, the *Lock, Stock and Two Smoking Barrels* producer Matthew Vaughn, who directed his own striking and individual crime film in 2004. As well as being a substantial piece of work in its own right – and one of the better British crime movies appearing at a time when the great majority were already proving dispiriting and underachieving – *Layer Cake* also showcases a career-making performance by an ice-cool Daniel Craig, whose assumption of the role of James Bond was two years in the future. Craig plays a moderately successful London cocaine dealer (the film grants him no name – and makes no moral judgement on his dubious choice of career) and the narrative describes the protagonist's dizzying journey from small-time dealer to top-of-the-tree success, even as he aids in the search for a young woman, the daughter of a colleague of his boss. His other agenda while undertaking this task is to shift a large amount of stolen ecstasy. The author of the original novel, JJ Connolly, had been conscious that much fiction portrayed London criminals as none-too-bright thugs, and had personal experience of men involved in criminality who were far from stupid – and to whom violence was very much a last resort. Their reasons for being in the crime business did not involve the enhancement of their macho reputations but were directly – and simply – pecuniary. And the illegality of drugs paved the way for such enterprise. The notion that crime was being written about by observers who were naïve about professional criminals inspired Connolly to insert a new level of verisimilitude into his writing.

Matthew Vaughn's career was to take unexpected turns in the future, with such crowd-pleasing pieces as the over-the-top and parodic superhero fantasy *Kick-Ass*, but at this point he is content to deliver a piece that is much more linear and integrated than the work of his ex-colleague Guy Ritchie. *Layer Cake* boasts the strikingly authoritative Daniel Craig performance mentioned above (which trades in understatement, one of the actor's strongest suits), but it also delivers the goods when high-voltage action sequences are required. Interestingly, despite the film's attempts to retain a cool distance from its protagonist, it was clear from early showings that audience involvement was considerable, something of a testament to both Craig's performance and Vaughn's direction – and viewers were clearly ready to maintain a certain moral equivocation, whatever their view of real-life drug dealers.

LEGEND (film, 2015, directed by Brian Helgeland)
The Krays? Again? Apart from various films in which the East End gangsters appear undisguised, such as Peter Medak's violent *The Krays* in 1990, there have been films featuring villains clearly inspired by the brothers; the latter include Michael Tuchner's *Villain*, featuring Richard Burton as a gay crime boss who is essentially a composite of the twins. So any new riff on the brothers (East End celebrities visited by American stars such as Judy Garland, always nice to their beloved, ever-indulgent mother, and only killing their own kind, as their apologists routinely say) has to offer something new – as does the ambitious *Legend*, with Tom Hardy playing both twins courtesy of various cinematic tricks and cleverly differentiating the murderous duo. Hardy is value for money as ever (he seems to be in every other movie made in 2013–15), but the film finds no satisfactory equivalent for Billie Whitelaw's adored (and adoring) matriarch in the Medak film.

THE LEGEND OF BARNEY THOMSON (film, 2015, directed by Robert Carlyle)
Based on Douglas Lindsay's novel, the directorial debut of the actor Robert Carlyle aims hopefully for black comedy, with the actor himself playing (against type) the eponymous Barney, close-mouthed and insecure, who accidentally murders his boss with a pair of scissors and finds himself inexplicably linked to a busy serial killer cutting a swathe across Scotland. Carlyle's attempt to move away from his customary threatening screen persona to create a weak and vacillating character is not successful, and the director/actor encourages Ray Winstone as a vulgarian police inspector and Emma Thompson as Barney's battle-axe mother to pitch their performances far too broadly. A reminder that actors do not always make the best directors.

LINE OF DUTY (TV, 2012–)
Policeman Steve Arnott finds himself transferred to the police anti-corruption unit when a man is shot during a counterterrorist operation. Starring Martin Compston, this effort is another in the line of shows (and books) that present the internal affairs unit –

policemen investigating policemen – in a positive light, rather than the customary characterisation of these officers as weasels and rats (another example of the syndrome can be found in Ian Rankin's books featuring Malcolm Fox).

LONDON BOULEVARD (film, 2010, directed by William Monahan)
In this 2010 film, an ex-con (played by Colin Farrell) attempts to go straight by doing odd jobs for an actress living in seclusion, but criminal associates from his past have other ideas. Farrell may be a variable actor, but when at his best he is mesmerising, as in *London Boulevard*. And while this adaptation of Ken Bruen's novel was controversially received, there are many good things in it, for all its flaws.

LONDON ROAD (film, 2015, directed by Rufus Norris)
Starting life as a National Theatre production in 2011, this unusual film deals with an Ipswich community that was rocked by the serial murders of a group of sex workers in 2006. Ironically, the killings had the effect of binding the community together. Rufus Norris's film recreates the unorthodox 'musical' format of the stage show, although the various musical interludes are integrated into the dialogue in a fashion notably different from conventional musicals. A strong ensemble cast renders the transition from stage almost (but not quite) seamless.

LUTHER (TV, 2010–15)
American audiences had no idea when watching the cult David Simon show *The Wire* that two of its most magnetic stars were British actors using impeccable American accents. On their return to Britain, Dominic West found much work – as did Idris Elba. Tall, charismatic and imposing, Elba's renewed UK presence clearly called out for a showy role – which he duly received as the maverick cop Luther in a series which upped the ante for TV violence and was pitched in terms of its playing at nigh-operatic level. While the show enjoyed healthy viewing figures, it quickly became apparent that there was very little attempt at any kind of verisimilitude, and the series frequently strayed into the bizarre and the unbelievable, much

to its detriment. But, as a vehicle for Elba, it did the trick, and an even more illustrious film career for the actor followed.

MAD DOGS (TV, 2011–13)

Philip Glenister, John Simm and Marc Warren head the cast in this laddish drama, which centres on the reunion of four old sixth-form friends who take a trip to Mallorca to visit the fifth member of the group. But then events begin to take a spectacularly dangerous direction. With naturalistic acting and a wry attitude to its distinctly fallible protagonists, this is a series that largely overcomes its unpromising premise.

MIDSOMER MURDERS (TV, 1997–)

The title alone produces derisory chuckles among many hard-core crime fiction fans who regard it as the cosiest of cosy shows. Inaugurated in 1997, this coy, self-mocking series (initially based on Caroline Graham's novels) is still running, with many of its 100-plus episodes post-Millennium. The show has a contemporary setting, though it is notably twee and inoffensive, redolent of an earlier era. A massive hit, for some reason, in the Nordic Noir territory of Denmark.

THE MISSING (TV, 2014–15)

Equipped with a lustrous new crown of hair, the actor James Nesbitt proved that he was still to be taken seriously in this taut series, which quickly became required viewing for many in the UK. The opening episode established an instant grip with its plot based on the real-life disappearance of the young Madeleine McCann, a case that has furnished an endlessly replenished, deeply unilluminating series of stories in various newspapers, despite the fact that the little girl remains unfound. *The Missing* follows the increasingly desperate attempts by a troubled father (played by Nesbitt) to find out whether or not his son Oliver, who disappeared while the family were on holiday in France, is still alive. With a timeframe that alternates between past and present, the real interest here lies in Nesbitt's powerful performance as the distraught father, a performance made all the more worthwhile by the actor's refusal to seek out any easy routes to sympathy. The sense of alienation is powerfully conveyed, particularly as the parents cannot speak French, and the always beautifully photographed locales do not vitiate the anguish of the central situation.

MURDER INVESTIGATION TEAM (TV, 2003–05)

Bearing conspicuous evidence of solid research, this *CSI*-style spin-off was executive-produced by *The Bill*'s Paul Marquess and ran for two series. Heading the team for Series One is forthright DI Vivien Friend and her more intuitive second-in-command Rosie MacManus; Series Two sees old-school copper Trevor Hands taking the reins under DCI Anita Wishart. Their approaches sometimes clash, but all are polished professionals whose work demands a meticulous process of profiling, forensics and reconstruction, tracing the most intimate details of a victim's life to identify motive and murderer. *Murder Investigation Team* was the second post-watershed series spawned by *The Bill*, the UK's longest-running police procedural drama. Sharing its parent show's realism but denuded of soap-style content, this altogether darker series centres on an elite unit tackling homicide in the capital – from drive-by shootings to ritual murder.

MURDERLAND (TV, 2009)

Kept afloat by the sizeable and boisterous talent of Robbie Coltrane, this was a three-part ITV miniseries that was unfairly neglected.

NCS: MANHUNT (TV, 2002)

Underplaying rather than overplaying, David Suchet demonstrates that there is life post-Poirot in this otherwise routine crime series.

NEW TRICKS (TV, 2003–15)

Before the show visibly ran out of steam (very publicly signalled by several actors leaving the show, having critically noted that it had lost its original character and novelty), this undemanding audience-pleaser cannily rang the changes on its basic formula of three past-their-best but still intuitive coppers whipped into shape by a tough female boss. The latter was played by Amanda Redman, and it was the actress's departure from the show that led to some of the other actors – such as Dennis Waterman – publicly expressing their unhappiness with the state of the series. The notion of ageing curmudgeons who are deeply distrustful of contemporary technologies but nevertheless manage to pinch the bad guys proved to have a durable appeal – for a time, at least.

NO OFFENCE (TV, 2015–)

No Offence, a self-consciously outrageous take on the police procedural, follows a group of police officers tackling the less salubrious face of Manchester. Inspector Vivienne Deering, the station's tough and sardonic chief, is in charge of a team led by DC (and single mother) Dinah Kowalska and the repressed DS Joy Freers. Channel 4 publicity hopefully described the show as 'raucous, riotous and razor sharp' and also played up the fact that it was 'a new and completely original take on the world of the police procedural'. In the final analysis, this encomium was somewhat hopeful, but there is much that is original and entertaining here, with some energetic performances by its largely female cast keeping energy levels high.

REBUS (TV, 2000–07)

After the miscasting of the too-youthful John Hannah as Ian Rankin's tough Edinburgh copper, the TV *Rebus* found its feet with the more lived-in, acerbic presence of Ken Stott – although Rankin once told this writer: 'Even Ken Stott is not the Rebus I have in my head!' Rebus is confrontational, struggles with the bottle, ignores the rules, and, in thematic terms, carries echoes of two of the author's key influences – Robert Louis Stevenson's *Strange Case of Dr Jekyll and Mr Hyde* and James Hogg's *Confessions of a Justified Sinner*, notably in terms of the duality of Rebus and even of his stamping ground, the city of Edinburgh, which bifurcates into the New Town and the history-heavy, atmospheric Old Town (with its repressive Calvinist history). All of these elements surface – fitfully – in the TV adaptations.

THE RETURN (TV, 2003)

Julie Walters essayed her considerable skills in a worthy, if conventional, psychological thriller. Walters plays Lizzie Hunt, a woman facing a difficult freedom following ten years' incarceration for the murder of her husband during a drunken rage, an event she cannot even remember. Director Dermot Boyd is canny enough to coax one of Walters' more subtle performances, a world away from her broad comic turns. Otherwise, the direction is functional, but it's Walters' show.

REVOLVER (film, 2005, directed by Guy Ritchie)

Guy Ritchie was able to re-charm his disenchanted admirers to some degree with 2005's complex gangster movie *Revolver*, which some saw as a partial return to form – although it was the director's audacious reinvention of Sherlock Holmes as a comic action hero with Robert Downey that put him back on top. *Revolver* has some of the inventiveness of Ritchie's breakthrough film – the one that gave birth to the increasingly threadbare mockney gangster trend – *Lock, Stock and Two Smoking Barrels*.

THE RISE AND FALL OF A WHITE-COLLAR HOOLIGAN (film, 2012, directed by Paul Tanter)

When out-of-work soccer thug Mike Jacobs discovers an old friend during a violent pre-game bust-up, he finds a new solution to his impecuniousness – credit card fraud. But very shortly the good life turns very sour indeed. Standard stuff, efficiently made, but treading familiar water.

RISE OF THE FOOTSOLDIER (film, 2007, directed by Julian Gilbey)

Julian Gilbey's uncompromising 2007 film locates its criminality in the dark tale of young soccer thugs struggling for supremacy in a violent world, which is as hierarchical as the outwardly respectable business world that it sometimes grotesquely reflects. Based on the real-life tale of Carlton Leach (played by Ricci Harnett), this shows us a soccer hooligan who becomes a much-feared gang leader working for an international drug dealer. The film's truly stygian picture of organised crime in the UK links the brainless violence of soccer thugs with the more directed mayhem of the professional criminal, but suggests that the mindset of the former is a prerequisite for success in the world of the latter. The film frequently reflects the energy and grim fascination of Martin Scorsese's US-set *Goodfellas*.

RIVER (TV, 2014–15)

One presumes that the thinking here is to import Scandinavian actor Stellan Skarsgård to grant a fashionable Nordic gloss to this British cop series, and the whole thing is shot in an echt-Scandinavian style. It's something like a mirror image of the misfiring *Lilyhammer* (which inserted an American actor into a Norwegian setting), but the 'fish out of water' scenario (though not pointed up – Skarsgård's nationality is not underlined) proves to have limited mileage.

SCOTT AND BAILEY (TV, 2011–)

This derivative TV series may be heavily indebted to the American show *Cagney and Lacey* with its two contrasting female cops (one more conventional and nurturing, the other a self-destructive maverick), but Sally Wainwright manages to ring the changes very satisfactorily. In this, she is greatly aided by the casting of Suranne Jones and Lesley Sharp, who find a persuasive dynamic for the duo. Familiar stuff, yes, but with a genuine sense of reality.

SEXY BEAST (film, 2000, directed by Jonathan Glazer)

By the time he made *Sexy Beast*, the East London actor Ray Winstone had become something of a British national treasure. Making his mark as a younger man in such pieces as the borstal-set *Scum* (Alan Clarke, 1979), Winstone's career as a hard man was largely mapped out for him, and his bruised, abrasive cockney charm has tended to be the actor's stock in trade since his early days. However, by the time of *Sexy Beast*, an interesting transmogrification has occurred and Winstone's performance as top safe cracker Gal Dove functions on several levels: its own straightforward naturalistic level, as a parody of itself, and also as a wry and knowing commentary on what audiences have come to expect from such characters. Dove, after a successful London criminal career, has decided to retire and has moved with his wife to an exquisite villa in Spain. This idyllic hiatus is short-lived, after another criminal appears to throw Dove's life into disarray. This criminal is a psychopath – the monstrous, diminutive

Don Logan, a violent criminal who is unable to complete a sentence without the most colourful of epithets. His job is to persuade the retired Dove to take part in a bank robbery back in London and he is utterly determined not to take no for an answer. There is absolutely nothing that the reluctant Dove can do to dissuade his snarling criminal colleague. If Winstone's casting as the suntan-oiled and slightly laid-back Dove plays on audience expectations of earlier performances, a similar piece of double-think is evident in the casting of the psychopathic Logan, played by a terrifying Ben Kingsley.

SHAME THE DEVIL (film, 2013, directed by Paul Tanter)
In Tanter's 2013 film, a London cop on the trail of a killer finds that the murderer's 'truth or die' techniques mean that a trip to New York is essential if he is to corner his quarry. Unfortunately, any promise that the scenario might hold is quickly squandered in a film that never really catches fire.

SHERLOCK (TV, 2010–)
Sherlock belongs in this book's consideration of contemporary crime as a modern-day riff on the Great Detective. Anticipation for the third series of this latest contemporary iteration of Sherlock Holmes was at fever pitch – we knew that the detective had not died when he propelled himself from the roof of St Bartholomew's Hospital in the previous series, but whose was the body that hit the ground? This and a thousand other questions have occupied a whole new generation of Holmesians, many of whom have not read a word of Conan Doyle but love this post-modern incarnation. Old and new 221b Baker Street enthusiasts alike were pleased by the innovations in the third series, which maintains the trajectory of its much-watched predecessors, courtesy of writers and producers Steven Moffat and Mark Gatiss – although a certain over-stressed self-referentiality had crept in. The impeccable double act of the theatrical, patrician Holmes of Benedict Cumberbatch and the low-key, likeable Watson of Martin Freeman is perfect casting, and there are the clever references to the original Holmes canon, often using wordplay on Conan Doyle's original titles (for example, 'The Empty Hearse' and 'His Last Vow').

SHETLAND (TV, 2013–)

With appropriate casting – a dour Douglas Henshall – this series focuses on DI Jimmy Perez and his team winkling out criminality in a cloistered island populace, and is built around the novels by the award-winning Ann Cleeves (also responsible for *Vera*). The unforgiving environment and often-hostile, tight-knit community are counterpointed by the poetry of the landscape, making *Shetland* strikingly different from its TV stablemates.

SHIFTY (film, 2008, directed by Eran Creevy)

The eponymous 'Shifty' in Eran Creevy's film deals cocaine in London, and finds both his personal and business life torpedoed when his best friend returns home. With desperate addicts on his tail, and his alienated family about to close the door on him, his only chance is to out-manoeuvre a fellow drug dealer who has Shifty in his sights for destruction. The question the film doesn't quite answer is this: should we be concerned with this casual destroyer of lives and his murky future? Moral issues aside, there are some sharp touches here, but *Shifty* (with Riz Ahmed in the title role) is generally journeyman fare.

SIGHTSEERS (film, 2012, directed by Ben Wheatley)

By the time of his third film, *Sightseers*, each new work by Ben Wheatley had started to generate considerable interest – not least because the eccentric Englishness of his films is set against their extreme violence. This use of violence had been graphically displayed in his second feature, *Kill List* (2011), where one victim has his brains beaten out in a scene that is difficult to watch; its unemphatic presentation of hammer blows, exposed brain tissue and bloody scalp is as disturbing as a similar bludgeoning in the Gaspar Noé film *Irreversible*.

Sightseers, however, dispenses with the hitmen of *Kill List* and Wheatley's debut *Down Terrace* (2009); what it retains is the quirky, Anglocentric approach to language and performance, for which the names of fellow British directors Mike Leigh and Ken Loach are routinely invoked. The demented, 'ordinary' couple in *Sightseers* – played by Alice Lowe and Steve Oram (who also co-wrote the screenplay) – may take part in copious bloodletting and violent murder on their eventful caravan trip, but on their initial appearance in the film they closely resemble the desperately unromantic and banal duo played by Alison Steadman and Roger Sloman in Mike Leigh's *Nuts in May* (1976). While the psychopathic nature of Wheatley's protagonists is something new, the other elements – an English couple glumly determined to have a good time on their ill-fated holiday even as all occasions inform against them – are familiar to us all. In fact, the film is more about a certain, sometimes bovine, English sangfroid in the face of petty disaster as much as it is about the latent capacities for monstrous behaviour in even the most ordinary of English people. The crushing of skulls with walking sticks and rocks, or even using moving vehicles, is given a resolutely black comic treatment, some considerable distance from the comedy of embarrassment of the early scenes. And the surrealism of the writing echoes Wheatley's earlier work with such British television comedians as Vic Reeves and Bob Mortimer, who similarly take a wildly off-kilter (though not quite so gruesome) approach to their material. Wheatley is also interested in the contrast between the grotesque happenings of the film and the beauty of the Lake District settings in which they take place. Certainly, after watching *Sightseers*, such comforting British institutions as tram museums and rickety caravans will never seem the same again.

THE SINS (TV, 2000)

The late actor Pete Postlethwaite – with his distinctively misshapen features – was a considerable asset to virtually anything he appeared in, whether film or television (not to mention his stage Lear in Liverpool). His performance as the bank robber Len Green in *The Sins* is typically imposing in this consistent and well-written series that is always watchable and has many virtues, including its use of the seven deadly sins as a theme throughout. Although this miniseries enjoyed some attention, it never achieved the audience figures it deserved. Postlethwaite is admirably supported by another reliable actor, Geraldine James, as his long-suffering spouse.

SNATCH (film, 2000, directed by Guy Ritchie)

After the success of Guy Ritchie's first feature film, *Lock, Stock, etc.*, money was thrown at its successor, *Snatch*, but this time Ritchie was able to draw upon the services of such major foreign stars as Brad Pitt and Benicio del Toro – although the director encouraged both actors to disguise their physical appearance and their accents, something they were happy to do. The film had a decidedly mixed reception, although Pitt's completely impenetrable Irish traveller's accent has its aficionados – for all the wrong reasons.

In *Snatch*, crooked boxing promoters, threatening bookies, scowling gangsters and maladroit cheeky cock-er-nee thieves are on the trail of a stolen object: the McGuffin here is a stolen diamond, worth millions. The film once again sports a strongly cast and varied dramatis personae, with (for the second time) Jason Statham alongside the heavy-hitting imported names. Once again, the universe we are shown is that of organised – sometimes barely organised – crime, and the complex and confusing narrative also stirs into the brew a bounty hunter and an arms dealer with a past in the KGB.

The original response to *Snatch* was one more of mystification than disappointment, particularly as it showcases one of Brad Pitt's periodic attempts to distance himself from the pretty boy stardom that he has come to dislike – hence his brutal character's incomprehensible Oirish accent. However, subsequent viewings of the film have somewhat modified those initial responses, and it has now acquired something of a cult status. Certainly, Ritchie's kinetic directing style is fully in evidence again, as is the Quentin Tarantino-style potpourri approach to the film's music. If the wittily written screenplay by the director (recycling familiar elements) and labyrinthine narrative do not match the sheer exuberance of Ritchie's debut film – where both the eccentric character names (such as 'Brick Top') and lazy mythologising of the salt-of-the-earth cockney ethos already looked shop-worn – time is proving kinder to it than subsequent work by Ritchie or those he has inspired.

STATE OF PLAY (TV, 2003)

The 2003 series that inspired a subsequent, less accomplished movie.

STONEMOUTH (TV, 2015)

In my convivial conversations with the late Scottish writer Iain Banks, I would ask how he kept mentally separate his science fiction work from his other writing. 'It's easy,' he replied. 'I assume a different identity whatever I'm writing.' In 2012, the writer published his twenty-sixth novel, and three years later *Stonemouth* enjoyed a two-part adaptation by the BBC. Stewart Gilmour (played by Christian Cooke) is a young man who returns to the town for the funeral of a childhood friend. In fact, he was forced out of Stonemouth by an influential local criminal, the father of his friend. The crime boss is played in typically threatening fashion by Peter Mullan, a specialist in such parts (he played a similar role in the New Zealand-set *Top of the Lake*). However, despite its credentials, this is a gentler, more romantic piece than one might think, with flashbacks to memories of a new love affair. It's this factor, along with a slightly overwrought voiceover narration – not to mention its unsuitably picturesque qualities – that draws the sting from Banks's original material.

THE SWEENEY (film, 2012, directed by Nick Love)

The remake of the much-loved, oft-parodied John Thaw 1970s series about tough London cops: Thaw's famous catchphrase as the humourless Regan – though not often used – was: 'You're nicked, my son!' Good will was extended to the remake before it was seen, with a generally held view that Ray Winstone might be a solid substitute for Thaw – but a cloud of opprobrium descended quickly when the film saw the light of day, as it managed to torpedo virtually all the elements that made the original show successful, reducing it to yet another faceless, brutal cop saga.

TAGGART (TV, 1983–2010)

Not many TV shows can survive the death of their principal actor (and his character), but that is precisely what happened with this hard-edged Scottish police procedural when Mark McManus died. However, the fact that his colleagues had been solidly built up as interesting figures in their own right ensured that the series continued – and, what's more, it continued to enjoy healthy viewing figures.

THORNE (TV, 2010)

In 2009, Sky TV took up the option on the Mark Billingham Tom Thorne novels, and a considerable amount of money was spent on the first three episodes, which were also afforded top-class directing and writing talent. But the most fruitful decision concerning the adaptations was the choice of the actor David Morrissey (see *The Driver*) to play the protagonist. The fact that Morrissey was a touch too young for the role was more than compensated for by the intensity of his performance – hardly surprising given that the actor is one of the most respected and versatile in the UK, and can move from Dickens to contemporary parts such as this with dexterity. The first Thorne novel to be adapted – as three episodes – was *Sleepyhead*. It was initially shown cut together as one complete film at an event put together by the British Film Institute at the National Film Theatre in London; given that the filmmaking ethos of *Sleepyhead* (directed by Stephen Hopkins) – not to mention its expensive production values – was on a cinematic level rather than a more modest television scale, the cinema was perhaps a more natural home for this adaptation. The producers showed an intelligent regard for the source material, and a great deal of what Billingham had originally created managed to find its way on to the screen – not least Thorne's tricky, non-consensual nature, which is perfectly caught in Morrissey's edgy performance. Many of the minor characters are also given interesting lives; again, the casting here is a considerable asset, with such reliable character actors as Eddie Marsan providing solid backup for Morrissey's performance. If not quite finding a film equivalent for the idiosyncratic quality of Billingham's original – the films are often efficiently generic rather than innovative – the director Stephen Hopkins demonstrates a particular skill for the urban setting, managing to make London look simultaneously threatening, rundown and beautiful. In fact, milieu is one of the determining factors in these adaptations, with the detective's rather splendid (if unlikely) flat and its canal-side setting contrasting with the other equally well chosen (if less telegenic) locations.

The second film in the series, an adaptation of *Scaredy Cat* (directed by Benjamin Ross), takes liberties with the original material but manages to balance the caustic inter-office politics involving

Thorne and his ex-partner Tughan (played again by Eddie Marsan) with its pursuit-of-serial-killer plot. However, the series did not receive the expected attention – or viewing figures – possibly due to the sheer amount of similar product flooding the market.

THE TRIALS OF JIMMY ROSE (TV, 2015)

Does Ray Winstone – an excellent actor – ever tire of delivering his standard cockney criminal persona and feel an urge to tackle something that would extend him? That familiar characterisation is on display again in *The Trials of Jimmy Rose*, but there's no denying that he's always utterly watchable – and nobody does it better. In Alan Whiting's three-part drama, the unlucky Jimmy Rose is out of prison, having served 12 years for armed robbery – and, unsurprisingly, he finds his wife Jackie (an underwritten Amanda Redman) singularly unenthusiastic about the idea of his reintroducing himself into her life. Another family member, Ellie, has her own problems (again perhaps unsurprisingly, given her father) and has disappeared after being seen in a drug dealer's squat in Lewisham. What follows is relatively standard stuff – a justified criminal on the trail of criminals much worse than him and struggling to come to terms with the shifting modern world and its confusing technology – but Winstone's performance allows viewers to forget the clichés.

THE TUNNEL (TV, 2013–)

Honestly now – has there ever been an English-language remake of a foreign crime show that has matched the original, let alone surpassed it? The US version of Søren Sveistrup's Danish *The Killing*, say? While the American remake of that show was creditable, it didn't begin to match the memorable original. This is also the case with *The Tunnel*, an efficient enough Anglo-French remake of the Danish/Swedish cult success *The Bridge*, which attempts to transplant the culture-shock clashes of the original with ill-matched French and English coppers (Clémence Poésy and Stephen Dillane). Again, perfectly serviceable, but signally lacking the considerable distinction of the original.

24 HOURS IN LONDON (film, 2000, directed by Alexander Finbow)
In Alexander Finbow's harsh thriller, a London criminal sets about the task of permanently removing all his rivals – along with any witnesses unfortunate enough to be around at the time of the killings. Gary Olsen is the star, and is capable enough, but the film overall is ineffective on most levels.

VERA (TV, 2011–)
Ann Cleeves' memorably idiosyncratic protagonist, DCI Vera Stanhope – caustic, badly dressed and physically sloppy – is utterly single-minded about her work, and is a more talented detective than any of her peers. Her colleague is DS Joe Ashworth, who she respects – and who is one of the few people who know how to deal with her. The masterstroke in this series is the casting of the elegant Brenda Blethyn, who indelibly incarnates Cleeves' shabby, massively intuitive character.

THE VICE (TV, 1999–2003)
The Vice was a series of corrosive crime dramas, now remembered for a pre-Rebus Ken Stott as uncompromising copper DI Chappel. All the usual ingredients make an appearance: prostitution, pornography and murder are all part of the daily workload for the cynical vice team as they investigate the capital's grimmer secrets and encounter a veritable metropolitan Sodom and Gomorrah. The Vice customarily portrayed London as a city of striking social contrasts, moving swiftly from the back streets of King's Cross to the bars of Park Lane hotels. Ken Stott burnishes his credentials as a commanding actor, and Anna Chancellor shores up the authoritative acting.

WAKING THE DEAD (TV, 2000–11)
Detective Superintendent Peter Boyd (Trevor Eve) heads up a team of police detectives and scientists, the Cold Case Squad, tasked with investigating unsolved murder cases and utilising modern methods and new technologies not in use at the time of the original investigations. With the saturnine Eve attracting a solid fan base, the series proved to be a lucrative export, with American viewers avidly consuming the series. In fact, Waking the Dead rarely strays from

the well-worn parameters of such shows, but does its job (like its detectives) with efficiency.

WE STILL KILL THE OLD WAY (film, 2014, directed by Sacha Bennett)

In present-day East London, the E2 gang has the local population living in fear, particularly the older residents, who look back fondly to an earlier era of gangsters (including the unpleasant duo Ritchie and Charlie Archer – it's not hard to see which criminal brothers they are based on) who practised their own ruthless code of honour. Lizzie, memorably played by Lysette Anthony, is forced to confront the new reality when murder and rape intrude on her life. The film is not immune from the occasional hints of rose-tinted Krays nostalgia (notably in the aforementioned brothers, played by Ian Ogilvy and Steven Berkoff), and anyone familiar with similar films (such as *Legend*) will know exactly what to expect – surprises are few. But the cast of older actors introduces an unusual note and helps make Sacha Bennett's film successful.

THE WEE MAN (film, 2013, directed by Ray Burdis)

Something of a mythologising piece based on the life of Paul Ferris, played here by Martin Compston. He's on the wrong side of the law, but basically (we are told) a good guy and a family man – think Phil Collins in *Buster*, which is similarly indulgent towards its criminal hero – who deals with far more corrupt figures while a useless, bent police force refuses to intervene. Very familiar fare, and deeply unconvincing in the celebration of its antihero.

WELCOME TO THE PUNCH (film, 2013, directed by Eran Creevy)

Eran Creevy's film has ex-criminal Jacob Sternwood (played by Mark Strong) obliged to return to London from his bolthole in Iceland when his son is involved in a bungled heist, thus gifting detective Max Lewinsky a final opportunity to nail the prey who has long eluded him. Strong and James McAvoy (as Lewinsky) do well enough here, but the director's attempts to channel the techniques of Michael Mann are less successful, and viewer credulity is tested by the over-the-top final scenes.

Appendix:
Top contemporary crime novels
(In no particular order)

MALCOLM MACKAY: *The Necessary Death of Lewis Winter*
FRANCES FYFIELD: *Blood from Stone*
TANA FRENCH: *In the Woods*
ADRIAN McKINTY: *The Cold Cold Ground*
JAMES OSWALD: *Natural Causes*
VAL McDERMID: *A Place of Execution*
MARK BILLINGHAM: *Sleepyhead*
LEE CHILD: *Killing Floor*
PETER MAY: *The Blackhouse*
DENISE MINA: *The End of the Wasp Season*
JOHN CONNOLLY: *The White Road*
MO HAYDER: *Tokyo*
JOHN BURDETT: *Bangkok 8*
SOPHIE HANNAH: *Little Face*
STUART NEVILLE: *The Twelve*
ELLY GRIFFITHS: *The House at Sea's End*
GENE KERRIGAN: *Dark Times in the City*
KEN BRUEN: *The Guards*
ANN CLEEVES: *Raven Black*
CRAIG RUSSELL: *Brother Grimm*
BELINDA BAUER: *The Shut Eye*
RJ ELLORY: *A Quiet Belief in Angels*
IAN RANKIN: *Black and Blue*
MINETTE WALTERS: *Fox Evil*
MICK HERRON: *Dead Lions*
MJ McGRATH: *The Boy in the Snow*
STUART MacBRIDE: *Shatter the Bones*
KATE ATKINSON: *Started Early, Took My Dog*
TOM ROB SMITH: *The Farm*
PAUL MENDELSON: *The First Rule of Survival*
MORAG JOSS: *Half Broken Things*
JOHN HARVEY: *Flesh and Blood*
MR HALL: *The Flight*

Further reading

I've tried my damnedest to be as inclusive as I could in this volume, but I am aware that there are names that have been missed, principally for demands of space. But that's not the only reason I would recommend the reader to buy two further books, which complement this study perfectly: *Tartan Noir* by Len Wanner (Freight Books) and *Crime Scene: Britain and Ireland* by John Martin (Five Leaves Publications). Apart from being authoritative and comprehensive resources, both are written in accessible style, covering many of the same writers I've included, but also others.

Acknowledgements

I'm immensely grateful (in various ways) to Craig Sisterson, Russell James, Mike Ripley, Ayo Onatade, Kim Newman, Katherine Armstrong, Bill Massey, Trisha Jackson, Alison Hennessey, Angus Cargill, David Shelley and Judith Forshaw. I've also kept the synapses in my brain firing through lively discussions with my fellow newspaper crime critics Jake Kerridge, Marcel Berlins, Laura Wilson and John Dugdale.

Index

Index

Index